# Pra'
## *The Satisf*

`CW00693581`

2022 Global ~~Doo~~
## Motivational Self-Help
The Satisfied Introvert
Silver Medal

## WINNER
2022 Reader's Favorite Silver Medal
## Non-Fiction – Inspirational

## EDITORIAL REVIEWS

"...an undeniably remarkable life..." —**Kirkus Reviews**

"...a revelation...wildly honest...humorous, heartfelt, and deeply human..." —**Self-Publishing Review**

"...revealing, and refreshing read...RECOMMENDED" —**US Review of Books**

"...a page-turner which one moment would have me smiling and the next brushing away a tear...highly addictive...may well go down in the literary canon as the introvert's manifesto..." —**Reader's Favorite**

"A liberating book...a useful tool for both introverts and extroverts alike." —**Book Viral**

"...an immense resource for helping professionals, teachers, and parents..." —**Reader Views**

"Great for fans of: Holley Gerth's *The Powerful Purpose of Introverts*, Jenn Granneman's *The Secret Lives of Introverts*." —**Booklife/Publisher's Weekly**

"...read like a novel at times..." —*Reedsy Discovery*

"People who identify as introverts will find this an excellent read...a clear insight to a personality trait that is often misunderstood and little discussed." —*Chanticleer Book Reviews*

## CUSTOMER REVIEWS

### 5-Star Ratings from Amazon Verified Purchasers

"...a heartfelt and genuine memoir that is impossible to put down..." —Alex

"...this book speaks to me from the first page." —Jessica Evans

"...profound and beautifully written book full of feeling and full of insights." —Marina Lujan

"An unusual book with a new vision." —A. Romano

"Reading this book was like seeing myself in a mirror..." —Russ Ann

"...an exciting read...Anyone who is an introvert will gain insight into themselves..." —Coffee Drinker in Florida

"Fun read with great insights..." —Alex

"Inspirational...extremely captivating..." —Tatiana

"...a wildly exciting life...stunningly written and deeply engaging..." —Sai Chauhan

"A must read!!...I highly recommend this book to introverts..." —Ray Rowan

"There is new, valuable information for introverts in this book." —J Jimenez

"I could not put this down!...reads fluidly with amazing stories." —J. Cosentino

## 5-Star Ratings from Goodreads

"Love it! ...written in a soft, well-spoken way and it is a joy to read..." —Saya Jacaranda

"...compelling...life-changing..." —CaritasFox

"This story was made with love, I was able to feel that through the whole book..." —Agustina Sureda

## 5-Star Ratings from Amazon Top Reviewers

"Eye Opening Read" —V.E., Amazon Vine Voice

"...a beautifully crafted book..." —Karrie, Amazon Vine Voice

"...it really sucks you in...the experiences and theories the author introduces are fascinating." —Sanjin, Amazon Top Contributor

"Understanding the concept of introversion vs. extroversion has rarely been made so accessible..." —Grady Harp, Amazon Hall of Fame Top 100 Reviewer

# The Satisfied Introvert

## A Memoir About Finding Safety In An Extroverted World

Benjamin Plumb

Published in the United States of America by The Satisfied Introvert LLC, Odessa, FL.

www.thesatisfiedintrovert.com

This book does not contain medical, psychological, or health advice. It provides information for general and educational purposes only.

Paperback ISBN 979-8-9854941-0-5
eBook ISBN 979-8-9854941-1-2
Hardcover ISBN 979-8-9854941-2-9

Cover and interior design by Sandy Kreps

Most names have been changed.

# Contents

*For my wife, Sandy*

"Once you have mastered a technique, you hardly need to look at a recipe again and can take off on your own."

~Julia Child

# Prologue

WHEN I WAS four years old, I ran away from home. I had to get away from my mother, who was so vivacious and talkative that I felt overstimulated just by being around her.

My destination was the house next door where an elderly couple who always doted on me lived. Not only was their house much quieter than ours, but also they had a plywood scale model of a building complex under their bed. It was beautifully crafted, although unpainted, and I never tired of them bringing it out for me to see. The man was an architect and for years that was what I wanted to be too.

I had some serious parent exchanging to do so I planned well for the journey. I found a large brown bag from Von's grocery store and threw in all the essentials: a pair of underwear, a t-shirt, two bright copper pennies that I had been saving for an emergency such as this, a stuffed dog named Woofie, and some canned goods (although I could not read the labels and had no clue how to get them open–that was what new parents were for).

Thus prepared, I left the house. Dad was out and

Mom was cleaning, so my daring escape was fairly easy. The bag, however, was too heavy to carry, so I dragged it across the rough pavement of the driveway. By the time I got to the curb, a hole had appeared; halfway to the neighbors' house, the bottom fell out and everything spilled into the street. Devastated that I was never going to make it, I sat down on the curb to figure out what to do. I can still see the sun glinting off the golden pennies, their image becoming blurred and then washed away by the tears in my eyes.

I sat there and cried, feeling discouraged, unappreciated, and unloved by both sets of parents. I was sliding deeply into the despair of having no one to love me when I felt my mother's arms picking me up and holding me to her breast, soothing me and telling me she loved me more than anything in the world. Ever alert, she had noticed my absence within sixty seconds and, by her warmth and sweet words, made all the hurt and fear go away.

She carried me back into the house and sat with me for the longest time, stroking my back and holding my head against her chest, making me feel like the most special and wanted little boy who ever lived. Dad soon came home carrying my precious belongings from the street and joined us where we sat. He put his arms around me and said beautiful things too.

Never again did I question their love, nor did I entertain the thought of leaving them for a quiet space and pieces of plywood.

Even today, I look back on that moment as the time when I learned what love was, and commitment, and the willingness to drop everything to make a difference in the life of a child.

o

DURING MY ESCAPE, I discovered that I am an introvert. I did not know the word then, but I did know that I did not like being around other people all that much. The noise was too emotionally stimulating. I much preferred to live inside my head, looking at books and thinking.

As I grew older, this personality trait became a problem; society had designed the world for extroverts. As Susan Cain points out in her bestselling book, *Quiet: The Power of Introverts in a World That Can't Stop Talking*, "Many of the most important institutions of contemporary life are designed for those who enjoy group projects and high levels of stimulation."[1] In contrast, most introverts prefer less external stimulation and more silence.

In reading her book, I saw other traits that described me with uncanny accuracy:

- listening more than talking, and thinking before speaking

- expressing myself better in writing than in discussions

- detesting conflict

- hating small talk, preferring deep conversations

- concentrating on one thing at a time, working slowly, and being able to focus deeply on the task at hand[2]

1. Cain, Susan. *Quiet: The Power of Introverts in a World That Can't Stop Talking.* New York (Random House, 2013), p6.
2. Cain, p11.

Introvert children are encouraged from a young age to develop strategies to make themselves appear more extroverted. Relatives admonish shyness. Strangers bend over backwards to coax a smile or a giggle. Educators urge quiet children to be more expressive.

My first recollection of developing and implementing a plan to overcome what I perceived to be a weakness and appear more extroverted, happened one Friday afternoon in 1953 when I was ten. My teacher told our Los Angeles public school class that each of us would have to pick a current event and report on it that Monday, without notes, standing in front of the room.

I was terrified. But that afternoon, I calmed down enough to come up with an approach. I looked in the newspaper and found an article about our new president that interested me. I cut it out along with Eisenhower's picture and underlined the main points. I then walked into our garage and, amid the scent of engine oil, rehearsed the points out loud twenty-five times. Over the three chilly fall evenings that remained before Monday, I memorized my script.

The results astounded me. On Monday, I stood at the front of my classroom panning my vision from the floor to the walls to the ceiling, anywhere but the faces of my audience. My memorization diluted my fear, engaged the class, and at the end, put a beaming smile on my teacher's face. The strategy shifted my focus from the external world, where I was nervous, to the internal one, where I was confident.

In junior high, a similar process helped me to do particularly well in Spanish. Grammar and pronunciation had rules, and sometimes, even the exceptions had rules. For two years, I listed and rehearsed the rules, and soon I found myself speaking the language. My teachers—Ms. Romero and Mr. Mendoza—shook their heads at what this gringo kid was able to do.

Skinny and bespectacled, I became a process fanatic. In high school, I created a process for every class: to learn the valences of chemical atoms, reconstruct the history of the United States, and solve quadratic equations. I broke each task down, put it back together as a series of steps, and then completed those steps in order.

This allowed me to interact with the world and get predictable outcomes without having to focus too much on people. I only had to complete the steps I had identified, and results would appear at the end. People came to me with praise, which was not as emotionally disruptive as having to interact with them to get outcomes.

All this compensated nicely for something that, at age four, I had decided was *wrong* with me—that as an introvert I did not have what it took to "win" in life on my own. Without a process in hand, I had had to improvise, failing often, and that was scary. But with a procedure of some kind I could get results, and that made me feel safe.

The more processes I created, the more my grades soared. I became co-valedictorian of my high school class, went on to graduate magna cum laude from Stanford, and was accepted to the Harvard Business School.

I concluded that using processes was a terrific way for me to "win." Never mind that I had almost no friends, was socially inept, and got nowhere with girls. I had my lists of steps and believed those were all I needed to navigate the minefields of a world that constantly pushed me to be more extroverted. I was convinced that my lists would bring me security and ultimate success in life.

o

MY THEORY IS that as a quiet child you, too, decided early on to cover up what you believed was wrong with you: that you were not outgoing enough to succeed in an extroverted world. You likely created a "winning recipe" of some kind that allowed you to feel secure by projecting more sociability than you really felt, and thereby to act in a more acceptable way than if you allowed your authentic self to come out.

Thousands of winning recipes exist for introverts. We embrace things like: be diplomatic, be thorough, be likable, be relentless, be dependable. The list is as extensive and varied as the entire introvert population. That Friday afternoon in 1953, I discovered my own winning recipe: be methodical.

I believe that all people, not just introverts, have a winning recipe of some sort. Extroverts tend to use theirs to compensate for any defect detected in childhood that they believed would prevent them from "winning" in life. Introverts, on the other hand, tend to compensate for something much narrower: simply not being outgoing enough to succeed in the world.

An introvert's winning recipe is ultimately about safety. It parades as a safe way for you to be more successful in the world. That is a large part of the hold it has over you. In situations where the recipe is inappropriate, or otherwise does not work, you will likely feel defenseless. When you are in that state, despite how often the recipe has failed you in the past, it will still make a loud claim to be your safest strategy for success. You'll see how this has played out many times throughout my life in the pages of this book.

A recipe may work for a while when used in a narrow domain, as mine did in school. But when used as a general guide to living, a recipe eventually causes self-harm. It creates distant relationships, generates drama from unintended social missteps, and prevents you from feeling fulfilled. It is an attempt to cover up who you really are, so it ultimately does not make you feel any safer. Because of this, *the recipe itself is a major barrier to attaining a feeling of safety in your life.*

If you are a dissatisfied introvert, your recipe may be the main reason why. In order to recognize this, it helps to expose a contradiction:

- *You built the recipe* to help you create a safe path through a scary, extroverted world.

- *Yet, the recipe is a tool for hiding your introversion* so you can appear to be something you are not.

- *As a result,* engaging in the recipe is unnatural, uncomfortable, and locks in the very anxiety you have designed it to overcome, leaving you feeling dissatisfied. You cannot be a satisfied introvert until you feel secure as an introvert.

o

THE PURPOSE OF this book is to help you find safety as an introvert in an extroverted world and gain more satisfaction in life. The best way to do that is to detach from your recipe as much as possible.

The recipe is a coping mechanism that works in

some situations, but you can't stay dependent on it. To feel truly safe, you must move beyond your winning recipe and take off on your own.

## "You cannot be a <u>satisfied</u> introvert until you feel <u>secure</u> as an introvert."

By accompanying me on my journey, I hope you will be able to see that engaging in the false security of your winning recipe can distort your life—especially if you apply it too closely for too long—and that it is never too late to put yourself back on track by detaching from the recipe.

That is a challenge, because every recipe has three striking features:

- *It is static.* It never changes, always operating with whatever key element you designed into it as a child.

- *It is relentless.* It brings early successes, becomes entrenched, and despite repeated failures later in life, it keeps insisting that it is your best bet for dealing with any situation.

- *It is indelible.* It is so deeply rooted that you can never fully get rid of it. That does not automatically make you its victim; you always have the choice to not listen to it. But the overwhelming temptation is to do as I did: listen so closely that you end up hurting yourself.

Fortunately, my story shows that the recipe is also *escapable.* Escape starts with exposure, since most introverts are asleep to the nature and toxicity of their recipes. For coaching on how to identify your own recipe, please visit www.thesatisfiedintrovert.com.

Once your recipe is out in the open, you will become more aware of the kinds of safety-related problems which it fails to solve. In this story, I illustrate four categories of events in which the recipe consistently kept safety out of my reach: solitude, fear, danger, and vulnerability.

Seeing my recipe in action may help you to avoid blindly applying your own. In the end, yours will still be there. But the more you recognize it and detach from it, the more you will be able to render it harmless.

o

MY WORKING DEFINITION of an introvert is someone who prefers settings that are calm and have minimal external stimulation.

This preference is probably caused by a genetic disposition to be highly sensitive to dopamine, a neurotransmitter in the brain. We introverts get satisfaction from very small amounts of it. In large groups and other loud situations, our brains generate more of it than we can handle, and we feel overwhelmed. We then withdraw into ourselves, seeking quiet.

Extroverts, in contrast, prefer just the opposite: stimulating environments that usually involve being physically present with lots of other people. This appears to result from a genetic inclination to be relatively *insensitive* to dopamine. To feel satisfied, extroverts need a lot of it. And to produce it, they tend to seek the company of others in loud environments.

Because both introversion and extroversion occur along a spectrum, there is no clear point at which one tendency switches to the other. And since both tendencies are genetic, they are hard-wired into us. The whole purpose of a winning recipe for introverts is to make us more outgoing. But eventually, it bumps up against our genetics, so it cannot deliver sustained results over a lifetime.

Introversion is a significant piece of several theories of personality that you may have heard of:

- *Enneagram.* Three of the nine Enneagram types (4, 5, 6) are most likely to be introverts, while two others have partial introvert tendencies (1, 9).
- *Myers-Briggs Type Indicator (MBTI).* Eight of the sixteen personality types involve introversion in some way.
- *Highly Sensitive Persons (HSPs).* About 70% of HSPs are thought to be introverts.

o

WHEN I FIRST succeeded with my recipe at age ten, I chose to become dependent and even fixated on it. This brought triumphs that helped me avoid some of the pain of being an introvert, so I used the recipe to overcome every major challenge I faced—first in academics, then in love and war, and finally in business.

The cost of doing so was high. The recipe did not make me feel protected when I faced almost every one of the events I describe in this book. In fact, it often made things worse. My obsession with it impaired what had been a promising life until it was almost too late to turn things around. Only by accident did I discover the tools that finally defused the recipe and allowed me to feel secure in my authentic, introverted self.

The story spans sixty years, takes place in more than a dozen locations across Latin America, Asia, and the United States, and plays out in the extrovert-dominated, high-performance environments of Stanford and Harvard, the US Army, and the competitive world of American business.

This book chronicles one particular winning recipe: being methodical. But it is a case study in what can happen when any introvert's recipe is carried too far. And it shows the extent to which the hunger for the safety promised by a recipe can warp a life. Only after I distanced myself from the passion to live by it, did I find the security, satisfaction, and peace I always wanted.

For introverts and those who love them, this story is both a warning and a ray of hope.

# Part 1
# Solitude

# Chapter 1
# Anabela

SEPTEMBER 1960. LOS ANGELES, CALIFORNIA. To attract a girl in a suburban LA high school in 1960, a guy needed one of three things: a hulk of a body honed through years of athletic competition; a group of cool and good-looking friends, rich, if possible; or a hot car, preferably a 1932 Ford Little Deuce Coupe.

The correct look was mandatory. Even on the hottest days, if you were an athlete, you wore a heavy cardigan sweater with a big school letter on the side and walked around so serenely that you never broke a sweat. If you were a cool guy, you wore an oversized black leather jacket with a menacing name like "The Retaliators" arched across the back above a drawing that in some way featured dripping blood. And if you had a car that looked even remotely like a

Fig. 1 High school picture, age 17. Van Nuys, CA, 1960.

Deuce Coupe convertible, you roared up to school with a grin on your face and the skin peeling off your nose.

As for myself, I had flat feet and was in a remedial gym class. My few friends were the ugliest, most socially inept guys in the school, people who carried tiny plastic chess sets in their shirt pockets and blew their noses on handkerchiefs that they stuffed back into their jeans. My car was the family sedan, a 1946 Plymouth four-door that looked like a blue balloon turned on its side.

Thus, it was with great hopelessness that in October of 1960, I observed the arrival of a mysterious, olive-skinned sixteen-year-old girl at our school. She had short hair, wore no makeup, and dressed in a plain white blouse and black skirt. Stunningly beautiful, she carried herself with the assurance and piercing gaze of a runway model.

Nobody could talk to her. It was not that the surfers and jocks didn't try. It was that she spoke no English, and nobody could figure out what language she did speak.

At seventeen, I was desperate for a girlfriend, but all girls intimidated me. Approaching one required being bold, confident, and entertaining. This girl's silence, her bearing, and my lack of the attributes needed to approach any girl—let alone one as gorgeous as this—kept me away.

Several weeks passed. Word circulated that her name was Anabela, and that she had just arrived from Portugal. That tidbit sent my mind racing. One attribute I did have was that after three years of Spanish, I was a whiz and knew it to be a close cousin of Portuguese. Spanish was excessively uncool, and much too hard for the athletes, the social climbers, and the hot-rodders on campus to bother with. Those who spoke Spanish as a first language did not approach Anabela because they had a nearly impervious social clique.

I was too scared to seek the new girl out. But one crisp fall day, I bumped into her in the outdoor lunch pavilion and before I knew it, amid the aroma of hamburgers and grilled cheese sandwiches, I found the courage to introduce myself to her in Spanish. Her eyes narrowed because she thought that language was crap, and at once began correcting me on the right words to use if I was going to speak to her. She particularly detested *usted* (oo-*sted*), the Spanish word for "you," and insisted that I use the more mellifluous Portuguese *você* (voh-*say*) from that instant forward.

I complied and we were soon talking in a jumble of all three languages while I struggled to understand the Portuguese words she was using. We both thrashed around at a two-year-old level until we ended up laughing at the whole mess. I was the first person she had said much of anything to at school, and she was the first beautiful girl I had ever approached in my life.

It is impossible to overstate the thrilling effect that Anabela had on me. I had never had a girlfriend, never kissed a girl, and here I was gradually getting closer to this lovely, exotic young lady. She had full lips, a bust that challenged every blouse, a tiny waist, and a soft voice that spoke a tropical language. The great irony was that a consummate dork such as me should be the one hanging out with her, sharing laughs over things that nobody else could understand.

o

ONE COOL AFTERNOON several weeks later, I found myself walking up the front steps of Anabela's house. It was a three-bedroom bungalow in Northridge near our high school in the San Fernando Valley. I had offered to teach her English and help her with her other courses but doing so during school hours had been difficult to arrange. One day she stunned me with an invitation to meet her parents and study at her house.

I rang the bell. My heart was pounding. I had no idea what I would find. Luana, a slender, attractive woman in her mid-thirties, with black hair, a kind face, and the same olive skin as Anabela, appeared and thanked me in Spanish for coming to help her daughter. Before she could finish, however, a giant German shepherd raced from inside to the doorway and buried her nose in my crotch.

Embarrassed, Luana yelled a tumble of Portuguese back into the house, after which I heard, "*Gerta, hop yer plotz!*" The dog understood whatever language *that* was and skulked around the corner.

We walked into the living room, where I saw Anabela's stepfather, Lars, sitting in a recliner, the big dog settling down at his feet. Lars was quite young—only about thirty—a lanky, affable Dutchman with blond, curly hair on top and a close shave on the sides. In good English, he apologized for the dog and gave me a grin that revealed a set of blackened, crooked teeth; I later learned they were a legacy of the Nazi occupation of Holland during his childhood when no dental care was available.

Anabela came in all giggly and gay, showing none of the regal stance she kept at school, and shook my hand. We sat on the couch with Luana and began to talk as best we could. Lars translated, since the women spoke no English, my Portuguese was a joke, and he did well in both languages. It was an odd group, but they were warm and kind.

That was the first of many such visits to Anabela's house. I was there to help her learn but I quickly discovered that she had little interest in studying. She was bright, picking up English from TV and the girls at school, and refused all lessons. The rest of the subjects were nonsense to her, and she declined even to discuss them.

Our visits became purely social. The three family members accepted me as one of their own, each for their own reason. Luana saw me as a Lars-in-training, a person who might take care of Anabela one day in the way she herself had found a man to rescue her from a dead-end life in Algarve Province, Portugal, the poorest part of one of the poorest countries in Europe at the time. In me, she saw none of the rapaciousness of the stereotypical Latin male, a type from whom she had probably fled in her past.

Lars saw me as a safe bet. He would not have to police me to keep my hands off his stepdaughter; I was doing just fine in that department and, if anything, I needed to be encouraged to get a little closer to her. He often tried to get the two of us to pose for a photo, only to find me turning red with embarrassment and Anabela saying, in broken English, "Oh Pa, you so *silly!*" and prancing away.

For Anabela, I was a toy. No doubt she saw how besotted I was with her and enjoyed driving me crazy with flirtations in front of her parents. One of her favorite tricks was to climb into the easy chair beside Lars, all tits and arms and legs, put her hand behind his head, and mess up his hair while looking at me as if to say, "See, if you weren't such a wimp you could be getting some of this too." Lars was a stand-up guy who had massive quantities of ice in his veins. As soon as he had had enough, he told her to get off him and she did so without a peep, but always with a sideways glance at me.

If English lessons for Anabela were off the table, Portuguese lessons for me were a passion. I had gone into overtime building a process for learning the language, thinking it could help me win her over. And I thought it might help to handle Anabela's controlling behavior. She told me where to sit on the couch, slapped my shoulder when I tried to offer a different opinion on just about any idea she held, and angrily corrected me on any of my accidental lapses into Spanish. She was sometimes downright unfriendly, and I was constantly anxious around her. But I persevered.

Luana was thrilled that I was trying so hard to learn their language. She showed me her two-volume Portuguese-English dictionary set and helped me order my own copy from Lisbon. Anabela was annoyed that I was not learning faster, curtly correcting me when I did not get a verb ending right, especially if I had used the Spanish version.

She gave me three or four teenage romance novels to read in Portuguese, which I took home and devoured, looking up anything I could not understand in my wonderful new dictionary. I got up early before school every day and read about cardboard characters acting out puerile plots as if it was the grandest literature ever written.

As part of my plan, I devised a set of rules for translating Spanish to Portuguese and wrote them on 3x5 index cards for easy review. Only once did I get a compliment from Anabela for my progress. I got better and better at the language, but still received scorn and laughter from her when I inevitably misspoke, which left me feeling like an idiot. Nevertheless, I kept plugging away with a slow and steady approach, convinced that if I could learn her language, I could attract her to me. When I spoke it, even haltingly, it somehow made me more outgoing. For the first time, I was extending my step-by-step approach from academics to getting a girl, and I was sure it would work.

As the months rolled by, the visits degenerated into watching *Make Room for Daddy* and *Leave it to Beaver* on the couch with Anabela and Luana. Lars was working part-time and studying engineering at California State University at Northridge, so I saw less and less of him.

The shows bored me, but I kept busy by translating the fragments they did not understand. This provoked great howls of laughter from Anabela when I did not quite get the words right, and admonitions from Luana to treat me a little better, which Anabela ignored.

The first time I ever touched Anabela was over the Christmas holidays. One chilly night, the four of us piled into Lars's car and drove around the Valley looking at holiday lights—parents in front, kids in back. The magic of the setting somehow gave me the courage to take her hand, and as soon as I did, I felt an electric shock that went all the way down to my toes. We drove around for hours and the feeling of her soft skin and whiffs of her light perfume were unbearable. She toyed with me, taking her hand away for a while, and then groping for my fingers again to produce another bolt of electricity that nearly made me jump out of my seat.

That night I got home with a pain in my groin that I

had never felt before. It was excruciating. My mother was still up.

"Mom, I have hard rocks."

"Well, go in the shower and take care of it."

Mom was like that. Practical. I could say anything to her. She was a petite, round Oklahoman. She smoked and drank too much, which I hated, but she was sweet, and she was tough, and she loved me to bits. And I loved her deeply for all those things. Three years earlier, my father, a musician, had contracted Bell's palsy and could no longer get his lips to make a seal around the mouthpiece of his saxophone. Mom kept food on the table for Dad, my sister Carla, and me by going to work for a dollar an hour in the book department of Bullock's Department Store in Sherman Oaks. She was a real character. Her favorite advice: "Want to get flies out of the kitchen? Put a bucket of shit in the living room."

Her shower solution worked. It got me through the holidays.

o

AFTER CHRISTMAS, I was on two tracks. The first was shining and exhilarating: my assembly-line processes had made me co-valedictorian of my high school class.

I wrote a speech and rehearsed it in the chill of the garage with one hand on the fender of the blue balloon Plymouth for security. During that time, I got the joyous news that I had been accepted to Stanford for the class entering in September 1961 and had been awarded some financial aid from the state of California. It was only an $800 stipend, but it felt like a million dollars.

The second track was dismal. I continued to go over to Anabela's house, even though it was always the same.

The visits began with Gerta's intrusive crotch sniffings, followed by a cowed retreat when Lars told her to go to her *plotz*. Gerta did add some variety by falling asleep in her spot, twitching her feet during doggie dreams (no doubt about the delicious but forbidden crotches she had sniffed that day), and lifting her tail to pass gas. I could always tell one was incoming by watching her tail. From the earliest days I was able to label the event in Portuguese as a "bufo," along with its verb, "bufar."

Anabela would only flirt with me when Luana or Lars was in the room, then abruptly flip a switch when we were alone, reverting to the lofty indifference that she adopted at school. I was constantly off balance.

I felt powerless, hypnotized. Her every movement, word, facial expression, and playful shoulder-slap bound me more tightly to her in a way I could not explain. Maybe I was so drawn to her because she was my near opposite. While I was reserved, stiff, stuck in my head, she was free, sensual, and dominant. She knew what she wanted, and I found that to be irresistible—and a little frightening.

It did not produce a sense of security, and that was what I longed for in a relationship. Despite that, I futilely continued looking for safety in Anabela. I now understand she was just a sixteen-year-old girl trying to make sense of an entirely new world in America, exercising control in the only way she knew how.

At times I thought, "Do I really want this?" I did not know what I wanted in a girl but was coming to think that maybe this was not it. Beauty alone was not turning out to be enough for me to build love on.

Then I would say to myself, "She is gorgeous. I just have to figure out how to attract her." I did not have muscles, cool friends, or a nifty car and had no idea what would appeal to a girl like her. I kept persevering with the language, but clearly the process was not working.

I graduated from high school in February of 1961 because LA County had split its huge number of students into winter and summer cohorts. Six months remained before I would leave for Stanford, and I could not bear the thought of keeping up the mindless routine with Anabela for that long. But neither could I face letting go of her.

I wanted to get away for a while and fill the coming months with something interesting to do. So, I came up with a plan that solved everything.

It involved getting on a plane and going to Mexico City.

o

WHEN IT CAME time for the flight, I was overjoyed to head to the LA airport with my father.

He had made the trip possible. He was an immensely loving man with a broad face and wavy black hair whose own father had died when he was three. He wanted to be the father he himself never had. A source of deep kindness and wisdom, he was a role model, a good man who was humble, proud, and thankful for the happiness he possessed and was able to pass on.

A talented saxophone and clarinet player with the unforgettable name of Neely Plumb, my father had perfect pitch and often wrote the score for an entire orchestra on huge pages of yellow sheet music, automatically transposing the notes in his head for whatever key a given instrument was played in. He honed that skill on the road in the 1930s with Ray Noble, Artie Shaw, Tommy Dorsey, and other big bands of the era, as well as in the pit orchestra of RKO pictures in the 1940s, recording the musical scores for motion pictures. By the late 1950s, after largely recovering from Bell's palsy, he had parlayed himself into a job as Director of Artists and Repertoire with RCA Victor Records in Hollywood. A dapper dresser, Dad often walked around town sporting a skinny white tie, a red vest, and a blue sports coat.

One of his recording artists was Juan Garcia Esquivel, a hugely popular Mexican bandleader who also had a following in the US and was quite close to Dad. I hatched a plan for Dad to ask Esquivel to help me find a job in Mexico that would keep me busy until I started at Stanford. Esquivel was enthusiastic, and shortly afterwards, at age eighteen and with an arm sore from inoculations, I was on a Western Airlines flight to Mexico City.

While there, I never found a job, but did meet Eduardo, the dark, thin, and intimidating attendant at the Angel of Independence, one of the biggest monuments in the city. We talked and my initial fear of him quickly passed. I found him to be warm and compassionate. He was twenty-two, had a wife and a baby girl, lived in a two-room apartment, worked two jobs to earn fourteen dollars a week, and read Tolstoy.

The Angel was just a block from my boarding house. I visited Eduardo at the monument every day, and we became fast friends.

It may seem unusual that I, as a young introvert, was so comfortable in reaching out to a stranger, particularly one who initially intimidated me. The difference was, all

*Fig. 2 Neely Plumb producing a live recording session at the top of the Mark Hopkins Hotel. San Francisco, CA, 1961.*

the encounters occurred in Spanish. Speaking this second language somehow took me out of my normal self, and put me into the personality of someone more outgoing. The same thing occurred when I spoke Portuguese with Anabela. I was playing a role, and that partially insulated me from the overstimulation I normally felt from close contact with people.

I had come to Mexico to get away from a girl and be alone for a while. Yet Eduardo's friendship had helped me see the deep value of being connected to another person. I had felt safe with him after just one hour, something I could not say about Anabela after knowing her for five months. He truly was a friend.

In May, after I had been in Mexico for seven weeks, Eduardo and I said a poignant good-bye. We would write regularly for only two years, and then, sadly, would lose touch with one another.

I went to the airport and boarded the mid-morning flight to LA but one of the aircraft engines would not start. I did not arrive home until well after midnight, giving me a lot of time to reflect on the situation that awaited me in California.

# Chapter 2
# Hell Hath
# No Fury

MAY 1961. LOS ANGELES, CALIFORNIA. I visited Anabela the day after my arrival. She, Luana, and Lars were happy to see me and restored the old routine in every detail. Gerta went into my crotch, was told to go to her plotz, and Anabela and I sat on the couch with Luana to the unfolding of sitcoms and shoulder slaps.

Quickly disillusioned, I saw Anabela less frequently, and when one of my few friends invited me to go to his grandmother's house on Balboa Island, south of LA, I went. After two weeks I received word there that a car had struck Anabela and broken her pelvis. She was in a hospital in the Valley and was asking for me.

o

IT TOOK ME three days to get to her. That was the soonest I could arrange transport off the island and back to LA, but the delay allowed me time to ask my father to get something for me that I knew she would want.

Through business dealings at RCA, Dad knew Colonel Parker, the talent agent who had masterminded the career of Elvis Presley. Dad relayed the story of

Anabela's accident to the Colonel with a request for an autographed photo of the King, and it arrived just in time for me to take it to the hospital.

When I got there, I saw Anabela sitting up in bed, looking shaken but beautiful as always. A vase of bright yellow flowers was on the table next to her. Luana was there and gave me a hug; I leaned over and gave Anabela an awkward embrace over the bed, careful to avoid the vase. I could not get a straight answer from either of them about what happened. It sounded like Anabela had stepped off the curb into the street in front of her house without looking, but neither she nor Luana wanted to get into it, seemingly embarrassed by the story.

I handed Anabela the large manila envelope I had brought with me and she slowly withdrew the picture, letting out a shriek as soon as she saw what it was. I had never seen her so ecstatic. The inscription was not personalized, but it looked like Elvis had signed it with something like, "To a big fan – Elvis." The glossy black and white photo showed him in a classic pose, legs apart and a sneer on his face as he held a guitar and looked seductively into the camera.

"Ma, look at his *peesha*," said Anabela in Portuguese. Luana instantly doubled over, her face turning red as she tried to stifle a scream of laughter.

Peesha? What was a peesha? In all my vast studies of the language I had never run across that word and had no idea what it meant. Surely it referred to a part of the body I was not familiar with, such as the elbow. Alternatively, perhaps it referred to some aspect of his demeanor, such as the smirk on his face, or the flow of his hair, which of course was provocatively out of place.

I should have known something more consequential

was involved from the snorts, the hoots, and the tears coming from them both every time, in my best Portuguese, I said, "Peesha? What is a peesha?" I grabbed the photo, looked at the bulge in it, then looked at Anabela and Luana with the dawning realization that yes, this peesha (spelled p-i-x-a, I later learned after much coaxing) was indeed worth commenting on.

Armed with her photo of Elvis, Anabela was joyous. From all the noise we continued to make, I was surprised the hospital staff did not throw the three of us out.

o

THE *PEESHA* INCIDENT in the summer of 1961 was the high point of my relationship with Anabela. My hopes after that grand gesture were quickly dashed, however, when Anabela returned home and promptly forgot about my Elvis offering.

A few weeks after the hospital visit, I got so dissatisfied with the boredom and the insecurity of the on-again, off-again flirtations at her house that I stopped seeing her altogether. One night during *Gilligan's Island*, I could not take it anymore. I simply got up, said nothing, and walked out the door, riding my bike home in the smoggy LA air with tears streaming down my cheeks at the futility of it all. Today, I am embarrassed at how rude and childish that was but also appreciate how desperately I wanted to avoid any potential conflict with her.

Two years passed. During that time, I moved three hundred and fifty miles north to Stanford University without making any effort to explain myself to Anabela or otherwise contact her. My studies captivated me, and after a rocky start to adapt my high school study process to college-level courses, my winning recipe once again began producing one success after another.

The only course I did not enjoy was ROTC, which I had signed up for on registration day to avoid getting drafted right after graduation. Given the ructions in Southeast Asia, the future did not look bright for any conscript. Anti-war sentiment at Stanford would grow steadily during my years in the program, but being an officer might someday save my life, so I held my nose and stuck with military studies.

At the end of my sophomore year, I spent six months at Stanford's campus in Tours, France, located about one hundred and fifty miles southwest of Paris. After a year and a half of study I spoke French fairly well. However, I did not pursue any of the local French girls because, for the first time in my life, I was now constantly around American women. The dorm was marginally co-ed, with men and women on alternate floors. Women were everywhere—in the elevator, at meals, and on long field trips. I loved being around them in such informal settings and gradually changed my philosophy of love.

Before France, women were mysterious. I viewed them with awe. But now I learned to see them as people. Some even became confidantes, partners in laughter, buddies in intellectual discussions, and good friends. They no longer intimidated me. I shifted from seeing love as an experience of reverence for someone above me, to more of a mental and emotional intimacy between equals.

Before and after Europe, I had disastrous relationships with girls in LA whom I saw during breaks. One was an alcoholic named Nikki; the other was a girl named Fiona who was obsessed with a suicidal ex-boyfriend. I was faring no better with girls at Stanford, where I was now a junior. In all these cases, there was only petting and none of the security and sense of closeness that I sought.

I had found no way to build a process that had anywhere near the power of the Portuguese language to help me relate to American women. With Anabela, the second language had given me competition-free access to a beautiful girl. But despite being more confident and relaxed around English-speakers, I was still not finding the quiet understanding I wanted.

o

IN THE FALL of 1963, I was back at Stanford. At 10:00 a.m. one November morning, I was dozing over a report in the overly warm government documents room of the Stanford library. A tall boy came in and started whispering loudly to the two women at the front desk about the rumor of a shooting. In my sleepy state, I tried to keep reading, but soon had to put the work down and ride my bike back to the dorm out of curiosity.

Nobody was around downstairs, so I turned our new stereo record player and radio complex to the first news broadcast I could find. It was true; a would-be assassin had shot the president in Dallas. Kennedy was on his way to a hospital, presumably still alive.

Bits of information kept rolling in about the murder attempt, of who was hit, who was safe, who had been told what. Juan Carlos, a friend from Colombia, came in, sat with me at the lounge table I was leaning my elbow on, and I explained each piece of new news to him in Spanish as it came over the radio. We wondered together how this could be possible. For twenty minutes we waited, dumbly patient, to hear any official word from the hospital.

At length, the announcer said, "Ladies and gentlemen, the president is dead."

It was a collection of words that defied belief. When we heard them, Juan Carlos and I looked into each other's eyes and then turned slowly towards the radio, open-mouthed.

I put my glasses on the table and brought my hands to my face, pinching the bridge of my nose. I bent my head forward and wept.

It rained that afternoon. People disappeared from sidewalks and dining halls, and those that showed themselves in the libraries or the Student Union were quiet, subdued, listening to the repetitive newscasts on radios and portable TVs. The mental and physical heaviness of the atmosphere fed on itself and would continue to do so for days until they buried the President. Something of the worst in life had triumphed over something of the best.

o

STILL REELING FROM the assassination, I was back in LA for Thanksgiving when Anabela called to invite me to her house. Against my better judgment, and to my later embarrassment, I went.

I was soon sitting on that familiar old couch, speaking to the same giggling Anabela, except that it was all in English, which she now spoke fluently. I could not help but notice the contrast between her coarseness and the sophistication of the college girls I had met. Eighteen months of moneymaking as a model and the cultivation of her own beauty, which was drop-dead stunning and now included a subtle and tasteful wardrobe, had not helped Anabela to mature much. She still did not possess the elegance and poise I was looking for in a partner.

She owned a Chevrolet Corvair, which a few years later Ralph Nader would expose as "unsafe at any speed,"—a fitting metaphor for my whole relationship with Anabela. Now older, she seemed pliable and willing, less inhibited when we were alone than before.

She did not come on to me, but her sexuality was so flagrant that I recoiled as if she were a scorpion. I saw that there was nowhere to go in this relationship. By even sitting there, I was violating the philosophy I had adopted in France to seek a close intellectual and emotional partnership. Disgusted with myself, I left early.

When I was home for Christmas, she called again to invite me to go to a holiday party with her parents in bone-dry Riverside County. The insights I had gained in France were now more distant, and after yet another month of no results with women at Stanford, I was lonely and horny.

"What the hell," I said to myself, and accepted.

During the festivities, she suggested that we take a walk out to the edge of the Mojave Desert. The landscape was starkly beautiful in its freedom from the LA smog, and in the boulders and earth that piled in waves up to the sky, the terribly blue sky. The panorama before us was breathtaking.

My buttocks were cool in the little patch of grass that we had found to sit on, and were it not for the voluptuous, flashy-eyed, eager young beauty next to me, I could have spent the entire day in that very spot.

When Anabela's desire boiled over, she pulled us

flat on the ground. She kissed and held me, providing me with depths of physical and emotional gratification I never knew existed. After the petting, she showed me an embarrassing tenderness for the rest of the afternoon and evening.

I had not expected any of that. All I could do was laugh at the thundering irony of it all, thinking I had at last fallen into the achievement of what I had wanted for so long. But I did not love Anabela and did not worry that I ever would. My introversion and reticence had probably driven her crazy. And it was likely that all along I had been as exotic to her as she was to me.

My now-compromised philosophy of love allowed me to continue seeing Anabela without any self-recrimination. I needed experience, an ego-massage and a little fun, and I refused to deny myself such things since they had fallen into my lap. But I was too honest and sensitive to let it go far; I knew I needed to be careful not to hurt her.

A few nights later in my parked car, Anabela came on to me as we sat in the front seat. I responded with passion, holding and kissing her as if it were my last moment on earth. She pulled me in close to her, pressing her firm, abundant breasts into my side and chest, causing me to gasp. I don't know how we avoided having sex right there in the car. But once the petting was over, she started to question the propriety of what we were doing.

She was particularly concerned that I only wanted physical pleasure with her; she was shocked at how I had "changed." Long and patient explanations of the ethic of mutual enjoyment I was trying to live by seemed lost on her. She was upset that I should *want* to hold and kiss her and not just fall into it spontaneously. At the time that made no sense to me, because in every case she had been the aggressor and I was merely responding. But in hindsight, I now see that her attitude was probably a coverup for her frustration that every time *she* had to be the one to initiate contact, not me.

The talk was quiet but got colder and colder, and by 2:00 a.m., when we drove up to her house, we had lost what patience we'd had and were sitting firmly entrenched in our own ideas of the other sex.

I was beginning to feel that by seeing her, I would only prolong the hurt feelings that were pricking her insides. We had nothing in common. I did not love her, could not even consider her to be a friend, and saw no sense in our continuing to be uncomfortable with each other. I turned off the engine.

"Anabela, I'm wondering if we should ever see each other again."

She sat still for a long time. "I guess I have your answer," I said.

We got ready to go inside. She looked at me and smiled.

"You sure are in a damn hurry," she whispered, then raised herself up, slipping down on me and into my arms with such a fury that I jumped. Her eyes were wet, and she kissed me with such passion that the top of my head nearly blew off.

o

ONE AFTERNOON A few days later, Lars and Luana drove us to a holiday party at the home of some friends of theirs. Anabela and I were in the back seat with the windows rolled down to let in the warm California air.

She showed off her latest-style high heels and shapely legs by scooting down in the seat and pointing her feet towards the ceiling of the car. Her skirt fell back over her thighs so that I could see luscious olive skin all the way up to where her legs met, giving me a budding case of hard rocks. She was giggly and squirmy, moving her legs around so much that Luana had to turn around and tell her to be careful not to hit Lars and herself in the head. It reminded me of the display she used to put on when she would climb into Lars's recliner and wiggle beside him to get my attention.

For all of her outrageous flirtation, Anabela had a concept of morality that was as quaint as the small town in Portugal where she grew up. She believed that a man should get as much experience as possible, but not with nice girls, and that a decent girl could give herself to only one man in her lifetime. It repulsed her to think I just wanted her for fun and learning without fully appreciating how special she was to me. Only our years of knowing each other, and the hope that I would change because she was so sexy, were able to keep her from erupting emotionally.

To me, the thought of a pseudo-platonic relationship where no basis for one existed was equally repulsive. In the car several nights earlier, I had tried to pull our views together by explaining that physical attraction was not a sin, and that we would not rot in hell for a little enjoyment. The poignant way she then turned and slipped down on top of me might have shown how well I succeeded, but it was more likely that I accomplished nothing, and she was just obeying an impulse. She seemed just as unpredictable as ever.

My scruples were screaming at me to stop seeing her.

I knew much enjoyment remained for her and for me, but I was leading her where we had no business going. I searched for a process I could build to get me out of this impasse, but none in the world would have worked.

When we got to the party, Lars parked in the driveway. The smell of fresh grass clippings came in the open windows from down the street. He and Luana got out. I started to open my door, but Anabela asked me to stay for a minute. We watched her parents walk across the driveway and onto the path to the front door. As soon as they were out of sight, she brought her legs down and rolled over on top of me, covering my mouth with hers with such violence I could hardly breathe. I tried to kiss her back but quickly began to feel suffocated. It hit me that I had to be free of her and now had the integrity to act. I put my hands on her shoulders and pushed her back, looking into her eyes.

"Anabela, I can't do this anymore."

I had always thought the saying, "Hell hath no fury like a woman scorned" only applied in Victorian novels. But in the last days of 1963, it exploded in my face.

"What, you think I *love* you?"

She got off me, glowering in a rage unlike any I had ever seen in her.

"Whatever the *hell* gave you the idea I was in love with you? Who needs you?"

I replied that it was best we did not see each other again. Instead of the smallest sign that she understood, she only went deeper into indignation and wrath. Masking tears, she let loose a string of words that impressed me with her command of English obscenities. Once satisfied that she had blasted me with everything she had to say, Anabela got out of the car, slammed the door, and went to join the party.

The next four hours were awful. Luana could see from our faces that something had gone terribly wrong and avoided me so she would not further upset Anabela. Lars was oblivious, so I could at least talk to him, but I knew no one else at the party, and the time ticked by very slowly. On the way back to their house Anabela was silent, sitting as far away from me as possible, looking out the window with her arms folded. When we arrived and I started towards my car, I said good-bye to Lars and Luana, but Anabela rushed into the house without speaking to me.

I never saw nor heard from Anabela again.

o

MY PROCESS HAD taught me Portuguese and had given me access to a gorgeous, passionate girl.

But the approach had a serious unintended outcome: it led to the wrong kind of partner for me. We never once had a serious discussion about anything. Even back then, I saw that her sexual mores were old world, and she had a controlling behavioral style I could not tolerate. Plus, her unpredictability made it hazardous to be around her.

In the early days, my methodical focus on the language played nicely into her desire for control because she was always more fluent than I was. Two years later, she switched to English, and tried to use her beauty and sexuality to capture me.

My desire and youthful hormones had blinded me, making me think my recipe would give me the same success in love that it had given me in school. I was too young to discern that I was using the recipe in the wrong way, at the wrong time, and consequently had attracted the wrong type of person. But at this point, I had achieved near-fluency in another tongue beyond Spanish, and now that the tactic had sort of worked with one girl, I was eager to overcome my solitude by trying it once more.

I did not know it, but an opportunity to meet two more Portuguese-speaking belles was about to come my way.

# Chapter 3
# Two Girls in Rio

AUGUST 1964. OVER RIO DE JANEIRO, BRAZIL. As our plane descended into Rio, I relaxed in the morning sunshine, panning my sleepy eyes along the sweeping arc of Copacabana Beach below us.

My head was shaved, and I was exhausted. I had just come from ROTC summer camp in Fort Lewis, Washington, about forty miles south of Seattle. The purpose of the camp was to help prepare us cadets for commissioning as second lieutenants when we graduated from college in a year's time. I was sore, recovering from the nonstop fear and harassment that the Army had put us through. It was all I could do to stay awake.

The white sand below the plane reminded me of Zuma Beach, the prosaic little LA County seashore where I had swum many times since childhood. I slipped into a daydream about California. *Mary Poppins* had had its world premiere two days earlier in Los Angeles, catapulting Julie Andrews into the international spotlight. My Dad was a big fan of hers.

We could not have imagined it, but the following

year he would sign her with RCA Victor Records and go on to produce *The Sound of Music,* one of the most popular soundtrack albums of all time selling twenty million copies. Despite all that success, we would still live in the same small, three-bedroom stucco-clad bungalow in a classic, 1950s-style middle-class neighborhood in the San Fernando Valley. Except for a second-hand Cadillac that he bought, we had none of the trappings of the artists and executives he worked with.

The growl of the engines brought me back. I was on this plane because, at the end of my junior year at Stanford, my fluency in Portuguese had gotten me and five other young men selected to be part of a State Department seven-week cultural exchange program with a university in Brazil. The country was huge—bigger than the lower forty-eight states. The six of us had spent weeks touring from north to south, meeting with college students along the way. Our last stop was in Rio.

Over the roar of the jet, I kept hearing our student sponsors using a Portuguese phrase: *a filha do reitor,* meaning "the rector's (president's) daughter." In Rio, we were the guests of a university, and our hosts kept talking among themselves about the girl whose father was the president of the institution.

I could understand them well because while they were visiting Stanford, I had used their help to shed my European Portuguese accent and adopt the Brazilian one.

"Who are we going to put in with the rector's daughter?" said one.

"I don't know. Why do you keep asking me?" replied the other.

"Because we're about to land in Rio, and we need to get this right or we're screwed."

I was not sure why the topic kept coming up, figuring she must be seven years old and a real brat or they would not keep referring to her. Yet they were debating a serious question: which one of us would they place in the rector's home? Just before we arrived, they announced that her name was Ana Maria, and that the person they had selected to move in next to her bedroom was me.

After we landed, Rio overwhelmed me with its dream-like atmosphere. Egg-shaped mountains jutted high into the clouds, brightly colored shops lined the streets, and the smell of sweet coffee wafted out from curbside stalls. Being in Brazil was so wholesome and enjoyable that it was hard to believe it was happening to me.

The fantasy doubled every time I returned to my room in the Botafogo section of town, where the university president and his family lived, because on top of the unbelievable world outside, I had an astonishing situation going for me in the home. Not only had they accepted me as one of the family, but they had also introduced me to their stunning daughter. She was not seven years old but seventeen, and played bossa nova on the guitar as if she had invented it and the instrument as well.

Three days after our arrival, I knew why our student hosts had chosen me instead of anyone else in our group. Ana Maria was a steamy, headstrong, young Brazilian woman who represented a potential disaster for the exchange program. If the student they placed in the home did not control himself, or made it impossible for her to control herself, because of the same outmoded values Anabela possessed about "nice" girls, the whole project could blow up in the faces of the sponsors. The simplest solution would have been to insert no one into the president's house, but that would have been a monumental personal affront to him. They had no choice but to send one of us there.

Our group included a consummate ass, so my guess was that they did not even consider him. Another guy was too impulsive and unpredictable. My friend Jake was too good-looking and smooth. The fourth had a surfer body that would be too appealing. The fifth guy might have worked—he would keep his hands to himself—yet at thirty-one he was too old, too married, and too fatherly to be a good fit. No, the only logical choice was me. Introverted, predictable, a bit geeky, and a good scholar, I would appeal to the president and amuse the daughter without either boring or seducing her. That was the plan.

Ana Maria's face was plain and clean. At times it seemed harsh, because she never let her eyes wander. She stared at the person she was talking or listening to, or at some undefinable point in space with intensity. She had beautiful, long, dark-blonde hair and an extremely attractive figure, yet she always appeared to be either deceptively good-looking or deceptively homely. When she left for school every morning in her uniform, she looked like a hundred other Brazilian girls, but every afternoon in sunglasses and a bathing suit she turned heads, including mine.

She was decisive, ambitious, able, and frank. She fixed all her attention on whatever she was doing and admitted freely of likes and dislikes. She had no truck whatsoever with Brazil's dominant religion of Catholicism, exuding a sense of independence and self-control that I admired. She was feminine, radiating sex appeal with a husky voice, self-assured movements, and not a trace of fear. She could be delighted with little jokes from me, seeming to have a different laugh or snicker for every situation. She enjoyed life to the fullest and was highly engaging to watch.

After two more days, I concluded that she was pretty. She had started putting on makeup and flattering clothes to wear around the house, making me even more aware of her good looks. She knew how to wear her hair to good effect, and every time I saw her, I was more impressed with the tasteful, subdued beauty she knew how to produce.

For the first few days, her behavior towards me was cold and determined. I later figured she was only playing a role to satisfy the antiquated social obligations of a young girl in this country. I was a stranger and all she could do was present herself to me in the most formal way possible. But the façade of distance was now starting to fall away; she was breaking the rules by allowing people to see her in public with one of the other guys in our group and me, and I was curious to see how far she would let herself go.

o

ONE DAY, SHORTLY after I moved into Ana Maria's house, we six Americans stood on the lawn in the back yard of a luxurious private home where our student hosts had arranged a party.

Looming above our heads, close enough to touch, it seemed, were rounded mountain peaks, lush with vegetation.

When invited, we all turned and went inside, glad to get out of the late afternoon heat. In a large recreation room, we found six chic Brazilian girls waiting to dance with us. To approach one of them, I would need to be more outgoing than I was comfortable with. But I knew my Portuguese was good and quickly found my confidence. I approached a petite, pretty girl who smiled up at me and accepted my invitation to dance.

As we moved to the rhythm of the hit song "*Chega de Saudade*" ("I've Had Enough Sadness"), I learned that the girl's name was Sofia. Refined in manner and appearance, she was the daughter of a German-Brazilian family in Rio. I took her to be about nineteen, which would make her two years younger than me. She later stunned me with the news that she was only sixteen.

I loved her smile and her laugh and asked her to dinner. Her older sister Aliza was there, so we double-dated with her and Jake, my friend and fellow exchange member. We were amazed that the girls would even go with us, a sign of their highly un-Brazilian behavior.

Quiet and judicious, Sofia was fascinated with people and spent long moments watching them. Her mother was a practicing psychologist, so it was no doubt an inherited trait. Sofia kept a journal—an outgrowth of her analytical approach to life—and had frighteningly adult opinions of herself and of the people she saw. In her maturity, she seemed more outward-focused than Ana Maria, who was a year older but had her eye more on herself.

"I have a troupe of *bandeirantes*," she said, referring to the Portuguese word for "pioneers."

"Do they have machetes?" I asked, half-serious. She laughed.

"No, silly. They are little girls. Seven to ten. We go on hikes, visit museums, and talk about life." I later learned that they were the Brazilian counterparts of the Girl Scouts in the US.

We had dinner and strolled along magnificent Copacabana beach for two hours. Beautifully lit apartment towers paralleled the shoreline as far as we could see in either direction.

Afterwards, we went back to the girls' apartment in Ipanema. Their parents were gone for the night, so we came inside to dance. Sofia impressed me far more than I wanted to admit; she was so gentle that I wanted to hold her in thanks for such a rewarding evening. An animalistic desire for her body came over me.

Jake began to hustle Sofia's sister Aliza with great success, in spite of the bright lights in the room, but I felt paralyzed. I wanted Sofia, yet made no move towards or away from her, staying on an awkward neutral ground amid the parlor love scene to the right. Jake was good-looking, rich, and smooth; I was none of that and feared this high-status young Brazilian woman might be out of my league. I could easily blow it. The night that had been so beautiful began to go sour, and I was lucky to leave before it became completely ruined. As we left, Sofia was sweet and polite, seeming not to judge me for my lack of initiative with her.

Afterwards, I was glad of my good sense. I would rather have her see me for the introvert I was than for her to be disgusted at a typically Latino advance on her body. Time remained to pursue her, and my conscience was clear that I had done the right thing.

Apparently, I had. The next night we sat in the back seat of a taxi that was taking us from her parents' apartment to Copacabana Beach for another walk. It was dark and we snuggled close, holding hands. Her touch was so incredibly soft. I turned her hand over and playfully scratched her palm.

"In Brazil, you should not do that," she said in Portuguese. She did not remove her hand; it was just a clinical observation about local etiquette.

"Why? Does it mean something?"

"Yes. That right now you want to have sex."

We laughed. I assured her I did not know (later I found out it meant the same thing the US).

When we arrived at the beach, a warm, salty breeze blew in from the sea. The tall apartment buildings that lined the shore got more breathtaking every time I saw them. A neon Coca-Cola sign outside a bar in the distance added even more to the charm.

As we walked, I noticed how much Sofia intrigued me.

*"Quiet and judicious, Sofia was fascinated with people and spent long moments watching them."*

She was adorable, dainty in body and face, bearing a strong resemblance to a young Audrey Hepburn. She was gentle and graceful, soft and warm. Every time her normally serious face morphed into a quiet smile, she seemed to light up everything around her.

She ably defended her thinking but was not blind to innovative ideas. She laughed easily out of a well-developed sense of humor, one fed by her highly observant mind. Intelligent and critical, but not overbearing, she made me open my eyes and wonder if she were real.

ONE NIGHT, ANA Maria and I were talking on the couch in her living room before dinner. A tall vase of tropical flowers sat on a nearby table filling the room with a soft perfume. She began revealing secrets to me, first about her relationship with her boyfriend, then her thoughts about my budding romance with Sofia (whom she had met but did not know well). We talked about my friend Jake's relationship with Sofia's sister, Aliza, and had a ball analyzing the different situations and sharing stories about them.

Close contact with Ana Maria had uncovered a few things about her and me. She put her independence out in the open where no one could miss it. Because of the confidence she had in her own abilities and intelligence, she did not listen to differing views well. She knew how sound her own judgment was. She was open to reason but not to the assertion she could have been wrong all along. Spending time with Ana Maria made me realize, as an introvert, I was more comfortable with people who were not so dominant in their views.

She wanted to know me. But in the custom of her social class, she could not bring herself to ask about me in a direct way. American girls would do so after a far shorter time than I had known Ana Maria. For her to understand me, she would have to get more basic data than she could compile just by looking at me.

More days passed and all the logic in the world could tell me the person I spent every day with had a personality that was simply incompatible with mine, but I could not help myself from slipping into a warm, comfortable attraction to her. The distance between us got smaller every time we looked at each other.

I was interested in Sofia, but I could not help being

drawn to Ana Maria. Oddly, my daily contact with these two fascinating girls produced little conflict within me. I considered Ana Maria to be forbidden, and that was that. But like a kid in front a candy store, I couldn't stop looking.

At first, I studied Ana Maria to watch for indications of what made her tick. I caught clues and chewed on them until I drained them of all possible meaning. Her personality fascinated me, and I struggled to understand everything I could about her.

Soon I began to watch her for a different reason: to see how she reacted to *me*. I looked for signs that she knew I was alive and that she, too, felt the tickling of something about to begin. She looked at me and smiled on a crowded bus and I was happy for an hour; she leaned over to whisper a secret to me on the couch at home and I was weak with excitement; she shook my hand to say good night and I had enough to dream about until morning. It was crazy. It was unreal. But it produced a special kind of happiness that had me on a warm emotional cloud. The Portuguese language-learning process I had built four years earlier was paying off handsomely.

A relationship was so prohibited that my desire for her was likely far sharper than it would have been otherwise. Her father was the president of the university that had received the six of us; she had a reasonably steady boyfriend; I was in a foreign country where I could unwittingly blow everything up at any moment. Being around her was risky. Yet I could not stop the feelings that were growing inside me.

AFTER SEVERAL LENGTHIER walks and intimate talks along Copacabana beach, I came to know Sofia better. But more contact was dampening my desire and enthusiasm for her.

I felt like I had nothing in reserve. In no time, she found me out intellectually and emotionally. When her beautiful eyes set upon me and looked gently from top to bottom, I knew she saw straight through. She detected that my confidence with women was shaky, that I was sensitive to every word or glance that came from her, that I was confused and evolving politically and religiously, and that I had seen over half the world but remained a kid looking for warmth and security. I had revealed so much of myself to Sofia, she could almost read my mind, giving me pause about making advances towards her and making me feel insecure in her presence.

"We must only remain *colegas* (friends)," she said, reinforcing my hesitation.

In Sofia, as in Ana Maria, I had met my mental match. The girl was sixteen years old but could run circles around me in psychology or philosophy—not because of any extensive education, but rather out of her acute common sense and reasoning powers. Critical and clear-sighted, Sofia analyzed people and ideas with ease and precision. Everything she said was simple and unpretentious, and I often wondered if my mind could stand all the exercise that she put it through.

"Remember that we must always remain friends," she said again.

I agreed. I loved every minute of contact with her, but I knew inside she deserved a lot more than I could offer.

Two nights after reaching that conclusion, I sat on a couch with Sofia kissing and holding her for one of the most overwhelmingly enjoyable hours in my life. Not since Anabela had I felt anything remotely approaching that level of passion.

The following day should have been just as rewarding. But despite interlaced fingers and encircled waists, our day at Copacabana turned into one of frustration and resentment. A little conversation with her was enough to make me furious. The endless expanse of sand and sea before us was a painful contrast to Sofia's reserve.

In the US, I believed two people could get physical and psychological satisfaction out of each other, and go their own ways the next day without too much of a problem, at least in university circles. I knew this was true about Sofia, and believed she knew it about me.

"We must only remain friends, Ben." This third time I blew my stack.

She was killing a growing hope in me that buoyed our little game—the possibility that one or the other of us might really be getting interested. It had added spice and mystery that quickly disappeared when she was so outspoken. If commitment was off the table, how could I ever be emotionally intimate with her? How could she ever be the rewarding partner I wanted?

Worse, I took her frankness to be an open attack on my ego. I was not yet big enough to keep from feeling chagrined when a girl gave me a handshake rather than a kiss. With her oft-repeated line about friendship, Sofia had given me a handshake.

Oddly, once I realized all that, I was able to go back to enjoying her. Now that I could see *why* I was angry, I let it pass before I ruined our time together. We told each other that we regretted none of our pleasure. The proof was a repeat performance, this time petting in the stairwell of her apartment building, thoroughly enjoying one another with no questions asked.

o

ONE DAY, THE entire group and three of our student hosts decamped to the president's rustic beach house at Cabo Frio, about eighty miles due east of Rio de Janeiro. I drove out there with Ana Maria and two other people, plus Wilson, the president's personal driver, in a new Brazilian-made Toyota jeep. Good-natured and obviously used to being badgered, Wilson happily put up with Ana Maria's driving instructions, the most frequently repeated of which was *Fé em deus e pé na tábua!* ("Have faith in God and step on the gas!")

Over the next few days, Ana Maria laughed with me and told me secrets, came to me with problems and earnest questions, and called me to go places with her in the salty air. Earlier, all that had excited me, making me think something was brewing between us, and I was blissful from morning to night. But I now started to see that her interest was merely a harmless expression of happiness at having someone to pay attention to her.

One night in Cabo Frio, we got all dressed up to go to a party in town, but everyone left before Ana Maria and I had a chance to hitch a ride with them; we had to wait for the car to return. In the meantime, we sat on rough-hewn furniture in the dining room, glad to be alone. The elegance of her clingy but tasteful dress contrasted sharply with the furniture we sat on.

She began to talk without restraint, giving me a

picture of what the world looked like to her. Problems with her boyfriend Bruno, with her parents, with the phony people she met every day because of her father's position; it was thorough and animated. This view into her mindset helped me see that her reaction to me was merely one of interest and diversion, but no more. When I looked through her eyes, I saw the multitude of issues that preoccupied her and found myself to be low on her list of priorities.

Ana Maria had never had a broken heart. She attracted boys wherever she went; she had never loved someone and not had him reciprocate. She knew she was lucky in this respect and could not help but lack humility in her approach to love. Today I surmise that her attractiveness and self-confidence pushed her to overestimate her own powers.

She told me her relationships with her parents were superficial, and that she had only received the most general kind of guidance from them. What she knew about life, its problems, and its tentative solutions, she learned from her two older brothers or on her own. Her parents had not warned her of things, nor been accessible for discussing sorrows or joys, and she held it against them. In private and in public, she tried to dominate them, contradicting their words to force her own point of view, and using no moderation in putting across a suggestion or a criticism.

o

AFTER SPENDING MORE time with Sofia, I did not know what I thought of her. She was mature and conscientious, tender and affectionate. She was a beautiful companion for many happy and instructive hours, and I was willing for her to get a grip on my heart. But the intellectual bantering had been too relentless and emotionally draining for me. I took comfort in thinking that because it had not taken place in English, I still had a tiny corner of myself into which she did not penetrate. Yet if all she wanted was friendship, then she could not be the intimate life partner I longed for.

The process I was following with Sofia was not about learning Portuguese, as it had been with Anabela. It was about *using* the language, seemingly to stimulate my brain into new neural pathways that would allow me to be outgoing enough to engage in mental games with her. I was much like the character Colin Firth would play almost half a century later in *The King's Speech*. When the king sang, his stutter disappeared. In an extroverted world, what I considered to be my equivalent "stutter" at the time (introversion) temporarily disappeared when I spoke Portuguese, just as it had in Mexico when I spoke Spanish with Eduardo. Like the music that King George sang to, the beauty and passion of those tropical languages took me out of myself whenever I spoke them.

Consequently, I had not been authentic with Sofia. I responded to her wordplay by acting as if I loved it when I truly did not. She was so perceptive that I do think she saw through my talkative façade to the quiet person inside. But amid so much give and take, all in a foreign language no less, I was not able to project that person. I came off as much less of an introvert than I really was, attracting her as if I were an eager debater.

o

THE MORE I watched Ana Maria, the more I concluded that probably every seventeen-year-old displayed a condescending side occasionally. Moreover, the kindnesses she extended to me far outweighed any of the negative behavior I saw. The most thoughtful thing she did was offer to teach me how to play bossa nova, the quintessential Brazilian music that in the mid-1960s was sweeping the world.

Suddenly, I was thankful both of us would be focusing on music. My Portuguese ability and introversion had made Anabela nuts with desire, and I most certainly did not want to have the same thing happen here. Music would be an outlet for Ana Maria's extroversion and reorient my growing desire for her, hopefully preventing both of us from getting too involved. I had been exploring music on the piano since childhood and on the guitar for the past two years. I saw it could be another formula for transmuting whatever might be going on between us into something harmless and beautiful to listen to. It would be safe.

I was drawn to music as a system with its own processes for chord fingering, rhythm, melody, and lyrics. But I foolishly hoped it could work to *avoid* attraction rather than encourage it and ignored whether I could even keep at it, since playing guitar and singing in front of an attractive girl were exercises in extroversion. I simply leaned into music as a way to lessen the risk I felt being in such close physical proximity to Ana Maria every day.

The living room couch, which began as the site of our sharing many mutual secrets, was now the classroom. The first lesson took place one day in the late afternoon when she got back from school. Outside it was hot and humid, but inside, thanks to the thick stone walls of the house, it was cool despite the lack of air conditioning. We sat together, guitars in hand (I had brought mine from home) as the sounds and smells of dinner preparations floated in from the kitchen.

Ana Maria had a deep, resonant singing voice that matched the sonorous sounds that came from her guitar. Brazil was famous for its hardwoods, and they gave the guitar (in Portuguese called the *violão*) a rich sound, the likes of which I had never heard. I imagined hers had been made from wood harvested deep in the Amazon, and that the dark mysteries of that jungle had somehow been ported to this instrument to give it the unparalleled bass notes and crystal-clear high notes I heard every time she played.

My guitar, hauled all the way from California and probably made from a pine tree in New Jersey, simply did not cut it and we both knew it. After our first lesson, she kindly offered to help me buy a locally made instrument, and I jumped at the chance. She took me on the bus to several shops and tested instruments until the word *ótimo* (*ahh*-chi-mo), meaning top-notch, came easily out of her smiling mouth.

During that first lesson, we had done some playing together with my American guitar, but she had also brought out a Brazilian one for me to try. It felt like a completely different instrument. As I held it, I could feel the deep bass notes surge from the box of the guitar into my chest, filling me with even more sound than was emitted into the atmosphere when I plucked the strings. It was intoxicating, even more so when I looked over at Ana Maria with her head tilted, her long blonde hair hanging to one side, her husky voice complemented by the chords from her own instrument. Seeing and hearing her like that was incredibly alluring.

We had agreed to teach each other some songs we knew, but in the ensuing days, the instruction was lopsided in her favor. My repertoire was very 60s, with folk songs such as "Where Have All the Flowers Gone?" that had mindlessly simple chord progressions and sweet, haunting melodies. They were so utterly different from the music Ana Maria played that often she would sit open-mouthed and sometimes have tears in her eyes when I played and sang. For someone as skillful a musician as she was, this was not a sign of awe at my talent, but at hearing beautiful sounds that seemed to come from another planet.

Her music, in contrast, was complex in the extreme. She played the songs of João Gilberto, who audiences in the US were just coming to know. "The Girl from Ipanema," sung by his wife Astrud, was a huge hit and demanded great skill from a performer. The melody had an enormous range and was anything but simple. The guitar accompaniment required changing musical keys, had dissonant chords—nothing like the simple C's and G's of American folk music, and progressed to a complicated rhythm that was very hard for a gringo like myself to even pat my foot to. She saw that.

"Okay, now we need to work on the bossa nova beat," she said in Portuguese. "Here, use your thumb, forefinger, and middle finger to tap it out on the box of the guitar."

"I hear you do it, Ana Maria, but my brain doesn't get it," I confessed.

"Nonsense. You will get it." She tapped it and watched while I tried and failed a dozen times. Not once did she make fun of me.

"That's close—but here—put in an extra beat...*yes!*

You got it!"

Once the syncopated rhythm snapped into place in my mind, I could then focus on the next step in the process: the finger positions of the strange-sounding chords on the fret of the guitar. Again, she patiently walked me through it until the positioning became second nature. She was a fabulous teacher, and my only regret was that I did not have more to offer her in return.

She took enormous pride in my progress, singing in Portuguese with me by the hour, correcting a little here, showing me a little flourish there, and beaming when, after struggling for a bit, I was able to replicate her sounds. Moreover, I took pride in her work, especially when she sang an American song in English. Her exotic Portuguese accent made the songs sound truly remarkable, sung in a deep and mellow voice that injected the sound of the tropics into the Anglo folk songs she was gradually mastering. The American music was rural, born of the plains and mountains of the West; the Brazilian sounds were urban, born in the small apartments that lined Copacabana, and never before nor since have I heard the two executed so well as when Ana Maria sang and played them.

o

ANA MARIA WAS only the fourth girl I had ever gotten close to. Her social position made her far too dangerous for me to approach, so I channeled my desire for her into music. The approach of not pursuing Ana Maria was a compromise and turned out well. The musical results were exquisite and extremely satisfying, reducing the risk of being near her. And by not getting involved with her, I avoided blowing up the foreign exchange experience for us both.

But I paid such close attention to the music that I did not see how acutely lonely she was. The night before I left Rio, I was in my room packing when she came in. She embraced me and held me close. She said she feared we would never see each other again, then put her head on my shoulder, and wept.

Shortly afterwards, I left the house and took a cab to Ipanema to the apartment tower where Sofia lived. She led me into the stairwell, sat us down at the top of the flight, and embraced me with such fervent kissing and touching that it left me dizzy.

I could not explain why she wanted to do that after she had pushed the concept of friendship so often. I guessed she was starving for affection, or she wanted me to have a good last night in Rio, or she wanted some experience now that she had it at hand.

The next morning, when my plane pulled away from the gate at Rio's Galeão airport, I saw Sofia waving to me. When we took off, I cried, and did not stop until I could no longer see Copacabana Beach below me.

# Chapter 4
# Blood on Ice

SEPTEMBER 1964. BELÉM, BRAZIL. On my way back to LA via New York, I first stopped for a few days in Belém, a Brazilian metropolis near the Equator where the massive Amazon emptied into the Atlantic. The river and the surrounding jungle had fascinated me since childhood, and I figured this might be my last chance to see either one of them up close. Thoughts of my goodbyes with Ana Maria and Sofia were with me the whole way.

Every time I walked out of my hotel to sightsee, the heat and jungle of Belém hit me in the face, making me wish I were still in Rio. Exotic plants invaded every square foot that was not occupied by concrete. Lizards and huge spiders turned up everywhere, themselves terrified at this bustling settlement on a river that many creatures had found inhospitable even before the arrival of humanity. Sweaty clothes stuck to my armpits. I fervently wanted to be back with those two stunning girls.

On my last day in Belém, I returned to the hotel looking forward to a cold shower and a quiet meal. At the reception desk, my glasses began to steam, and I hardly noticed the note a messenger handed to me; only upstairs did I look at it. It was in English—a curious request from a British medical student to be downstairs in a few minutes to discuss something of great importance. I laughed, expecting to be hit up for some money, but decided to cut my shower short to go see what he wanted.

Downstairs I ordered dinner, and shortly two young English gentlemen joined me. Both were ruddy and brisk. One was a chubby and bearded fellow who looked like a young Sebastian Cabot, the actor who played Santa in the 1974 version of *The Miracle on 34*th *Street*. The other was a hollow-eyed and lanky imitation of a young Peter O'Toole in *Lawrence of Arabia*. Wearing shirtsleeves and boots, they had just come in from the jungle, where they had been working at a Brazilian government outpost doing research on a drug-resistant form of malaria. They were going to leave Brazil themselves, but could not do so for a few days and consequently came to me with an urgent request.

After weeks of searching the Amazon forest, they had finally found a Native Brazilian who would not only admit to having the disease but would also let them take a blood sample for research. As yet, no cure existed for this particular malaria strain. Although the sickness was becoming serious among Brazil's Indigenous people, it was hard for researchers to locate and gain cooperation from enough of them to run a viable study.

The researchers' success in finding a willing participant was only partial. The obstinate refusal of the Brazilian authorities to let the blood out of the country without the proper papers meant the valuable malaria sample would soon be worthless. The red tape would have taken days.

"Only London has the facilities for proper analysis," said the thin one.

"And it has to be done within seventy-two hours or the blood won't be useful," said the stocky one. "Either the blood has to get out right away, or five weeks of effort will be lost."

I looked from one to the other across the table. "So why are you telling me this?"

To make their lengthy, tactful, and well-constructed reply short, they wanted me to take the sample in a thermos bottle to New York, and during my layover there, get it on a London-bound plane as soon as possible. We talked for a solid hour, and in the end, I agreed to do it.

o

TO ACT IN a way that was so thoroughly against my nature, and do so without reservation, was unprecedented for a cautious introvert like me.

These were two strangers, asking me to add another item to my huge hand-load, a large thermos bottle with a handle. I had two guitars and a stack of records to carry on the plane as it was.

More important was the consideration of risk. Who the hell were they, and how could I be sure I wasn't carrying narcotics, jewels, or a bomb aboard? And how did they know I was leaving for New York in the morning anyway? In retrospect, given the almost total lack of airline security in those days, it was not hard to imagine them tipping somebody to find out who would be on a given flight. But when I look back now, it seems I should have shied away from agreeing to become a "mule."

Yet I know why I was willing to do it.

After only an hour's conversation, I respected and trusted these two. They answered my every question humbly and frankly, no matter how suspicious and pointed it may have seemed. I could see they understood my desire to know everything. Their story was internally consistent and after a while quite believable, enabling a wave of idealistic trust to come over me.

I accepted also because I identified with them. Their story was so forthright and straightforward that I could put myself in their place. I felt as if I had experienced their frustrating trip into the jungle, and the infuriating encounter with the civil functionaries who were destroying all their work. I loved hearing about the meticulous process they had followed to obtain the sample, and totally understood their desire to bring everything to completion.

I stepped back and looked at what was happening here. Two English scientists were appealing to another English-speaker in a faraway jungle city where such contact was rare and were asking him to take an action that could benefit humanity. How cool was that?

But there was more. After I left Rio, I had thought a great deal about my relationships with the three Portuguese-speaking girls I had met. What stood out was my reluctance to take the initiative with any of them. In a sense it was positive, because in time it had provoked all three of them, even Ana Maria, to reach out to me. That felt good. But it was a terribly lengthy and passive way to seek a lifetime partner. If I was serious about finding one, I needed to change my approach.

In the back of my mind, just below the level of consciousness, the blood project attracted me, because, of all things, it would get me more comfortable with risk. That would make it easier for me to hazard approaches to more women than in the past, which in turn would increase the chances that I would meet someone who was right for me. I never articulated that stupidly naïve sequence in so many words. But it operated subconsciously and helped to explain why I did not run the other way when the Englishmen came to see me.

To me, the risk involved seemed small. I was an experienced international traveler and prided myself on thoroughly understanding the step-by-step process of bringing goods into one country from another. On the plane, I would fill out a form declaring the nature and value of the things I was bringing in, usually limiting them to the categories shown. Incredible as it seems today, back then I could not remember ever seeing medical specimens as an item to declare. Once I landed, I would arrange all my stuff on a table for the customs inspector to see. In an age before terrorism, these staffers were overworked and underpaid and gave only the most cursory look at the items before them. I would then collect my things and walk out the door. That was it. I had done it so many times that the risk seemed to be trivial.

As I climbed the stairs back up to my room, I realized they had called my cargo not a "thermos bottle" but a "vacuum flask." The exotic name portended that this could indeed be a memorable adventure.

o

THE NEXT MORNING, the two earnest Englishmen met me at the Belém airport and stood by in case I could not take the blood on board. The sky was clear except for the beginnings of a few puffy clouds that would surely billow into blackness by noon. But for now, the weather was perfect for flying.

As I walked to the boarding gate with the handle in my fist, I could feel the weight of the vacuum flask. A letter of explanation was in my pocket in case of trouble, along with an important-looking label to put on it if, in New York, I felt that would help me get it to London. With typical British calm and thoroughness, they even gave me a roll of Scotch tape for affixing the label. In an era when the authorities inspected nothing before a passenger went on board, I was on the jet before I even had time to reflect on the success of the first step.

I had checked the inside of the thermos bottle before attempting to board and checked it again before we took off: it contained a small test tube with 10 cc of dark red liquid wrapped in moist cotton, surrounded by ice cubes. Satisfied that I could at least get it safely to New York, I put the flask on the seat next to me and started to plan what I would do when I got there. New York customs might be a challenge, but I knew the real issue was finding a way to transfer the goods to a London-bound plane.

Between Belém and New York, the plane was to make four stops. My hope was that more Americans would board and that they could give me a hand. Reaching out to them would not be something an introvert would normally do. But neither was reaching out to women, and I needed the practice.

At Paramaribo, Dutch Guiana, only a handful of people got on, all of them speaking Dutch. But at Georgetown, British Guiana, a flood of English-speakers joined the flight and I started to look for likely help.

Just after we took off for Trinidad, I heard a young man behind me speaking to a girl in English. I looked between the seats and was floored to see that he had a ticket for London laid out on his lap. I could not believe such luck, and inside of five minutes I was explaining my problem to him. Stylish and debonaire with a goatee and tinted glasses, he was a British Guiana resident in his early twenties like me, on his way to study art in London. After only the scantiest bit of picture painting he agreed to take the flask to England. Jubilant, I went back to my seat and began to relax, aware of the great concern I had developed for the welfare of that thermos bottle. I thought of the two Englishmen and was glad I was going to be able to deliver on my promise.

I slept through the stops in Trinidad and Barbados and tried to think of other things on the way to New York. But about an hour before landing, it occurred to me that Howard, my cooperative friend, would likewise have to pass through US customs even though he was merely in transit to a London plane two hours later. I decided to take the thing through customs myself, since I could explain more than he could, and we agreed that after we touched down at JFK airport and the flask was safely through, we would meet.

Despite my bravado the night before, I began to get worried as I put my suitcase, duffel bag, and two guitars on the display table for inspection. I placed the thermos bottle innocently in the middle of the whole pile, knowing well that my best hope for success was in keeping the contents unknown to the inspecting officer. I was going to have enough trouble with the collection of curious biological souvenirs in my duffel bag—a coiled, stuffed rattlesnake and the hairy skin of a wild

Amazonian boar—and began to fear the discovery of a test tube of blood containing virulent malaria parasites would be enough to try the officer's patience.

Unexpectedly, the inspector became the least of my problems. Howard was in line directly behind me, and just as I was opening my suitcase he was informed that as a transient he did not have to go through inspection after all. So much for my expertise about the procedures at a point of entry. Quickly, silently, Howard was gone before I could turn my head to agree on a meeting place.

That was strike one.

The officer gently pawed through some of my belongings. I was nervous, searching for Howard in the crowd across the vast room, then watching the officer's hands glide back and forth past the thermos bottle between my suitcase and duffel bag. My forehead was cool with sweat.

Evidently the duffel bag served as a decoy, for the officer never touched my precious flask. He ended the search suddenly and cheerfully, moving on to another passenger before I was fully aware that I was free to go. Hastily, I pulled my things together and called a redcap. I ran into the main lobby of the Pan Am arrival terminal and searched frantically for Howard.

My heart pounded in my ears. All I had to do was find him, but he was nowhere. Pan Am told me his flight was to leave in one hour, and that it was the last flight to London until the following morning. I had him paged, then when nothing came of it, I put my baggage on a pushcart and searched the lobby for fifteen minutes.

Another talk with Pan Am had me struggling with the pushcart outside, in the dark, making my way to the departure terminal two blocks away; he had to be there.

Nervous and frustrated, I entered a new crush of people after a slapstick trip of falling guitars and suitcases and was in no mood for face-searching. I parked the cart in a corner, and recklessly abandoned it to run to the departure gate with the flask. After a minute, I spotted a woman that I recognized as Howard's mother. Surprisingly young-looking despite a dowdy flower-pattern dress, she seemed intelligent and capable of reason.

My nerves were so frayed by this time that I changed from depression to over-exuberance. I nearly trampled the woman in asking for Howard. I had done it. I had succeeded after so many heart-pulling worries, and I began to feel weak throughout my body.

"Howard is about," she said with a clipped British accent. She looked at me from top to bottom. "What do you want with him?"

Distraught, looking over her shoulder and around the room, I mumbled something unfortunate about "blood" and "malaria" and "your son," not even seeing the look of horror that came over her face. I stopped myself for a moment and fixed my eyes on hers, then closed mine tight as I gritted my teeth at my own stupidity.

That was strike two.

I spent half an hour with her, pleading, explaining, even begging, but it did no good. Pan Am told her it was legal, even though an employee could be fired for taking the flask. I told her it was legal, recounting my own trip four times and showing her the letter twice. Howard reappeared just then and told her it was legal, reminding her that he had been through London customs many times with many strange things. She reminded him that she was a worrier and had never been happy with that behavior of his. Time came for their departure, and they left without the blood. In subdued fury—more at myself than at Howard and his mother—I turned my back and returned to my luggage cart to pout.

I sat down in a corner and cradled the flask in one arm. Sweat dribbled down my face. I felt protective of the little bottle nobody wanted. Tenderly, I opened it to see how it was doing, and found the test tube surrounded by a pitiful slush of melted ice. Not even considering that I had absolutely no way to get the thing to London, I slowly picked myself up and with my cart took an elevator up to a coffee shop on the second floor to get some fresh ice. The waitress looked at me with frightened curiosity, but I hardly noticed, gently packing individual cubes around the red test tube.

On my way back downstairs, I had a flash of an idea. I ran outside with my luggage cart to hail a cab. There was a chance, just a chance, that another airline, British Overseas Airways Corporation, would have a flight that evening. Already twenty-six hours were gone, and unless the thermos bottle got out that night, the doctor in London would have very little time to examine the sample. I was sick of explaining and wheedling, and decided to try the air freight office of the airline for help. My thought processes were so clouded that this had not even occurred to me before. If they could ship the thing out right away, I would gladly pay for it. If they could not, that would be strike three and my foray into risk would be a failure.

Typical of the day's ups and downs, as soon as I arrived at BOAC I hit the jackpot. Not only did the airline have a flight in three hours, but they could also reverse the charges to the hospital and have the flask shipped as life-and-death cargo. It would arrive in London the next morning, and word would be rushed to the hospital immediately with the same British thoroughness and calm that had gotten me into this mess in the first place.

Tremendously relieved that the blood would get there in time, I patted my little thermos bottle good-bye, hailed a cab out in the street, slapped the driver on the back, and collapsed in his taxi for a ride out to my cousin Angie's brownstone in Brooklyn.

I'll never know if the flask got there in time, or if it helped the doctors come up with a cure for the drug-resistant mutation of malaria that the blood contained. But I had done my part, and had overcome all the odds. I took subconscious comfort in knowing that if I ever needed to take a big risk again, I was qualified to do so.

At the same time, I had the uncomfortable feeling that next time my risk-taking might not have such a happy ending. I had succeeded here only because somebody else's process, the BOAC's, had taken over when I floundered.

# Chapter 5
# Tropical Legacies

SEPTEMBER 1964. LOS ANGELES, CALIFORNIA. A few days later, I flew from New York to LA. Dad was there to greet me at the airport as he always was, without fail, whenever I returned from a trip.

Dressed in a cashmere sports jacket and fruit boots—which in the mid-sixties did not refer to rollerblades but to soft leather shoes that came up around the ankle—he looked casual and elegant. We took my luggage to the curb, and I waited for him while he went to get the car.

It was late afternoon. Even though the terminal was less than a mile from the Pacific, I could smell the city smog. I looked along the vast expanse of curb in front of me and saw a parade of people being picked up and dropped off.

As I stood there, it occurred to me that for someone who lived in his head so much of the time, prone to analyzing everything down to the last detail, I also had a deeply emotional side. It drove me to seek love and affection from girls in hopes of finding a lasting relationship. But too often it also drove me to think of the past with pangs of sadness.

That was happening now. I plunged into sorrow that would last for weeks. The Brazilians had a poignant word for it: *saudade* (sow-*da*-gee), a melancholy longing for what had been in the past and now was no more. The song that Sofia and I first danced to was about *saudade*, and now it had me in its grip.

I spent the first five days at home in the Van Nuys suburb where my parents lived. What little I had to do, namely

*Fig. 3 Experiencing saudade. Los Angeles International Airport, 1964.*

unpacking, was precisely the thing that brought my mind to Sofia's doorstep time after time. I kept finding little things that she had given me: a rock we kicked along Copacabana Beach for half a mile late one night; a toothpick she broke in half to make peace with me after an unkind remark.

I talked to my parents about the trip. Doing so caused the difficulties I had with Sofia to move into the background and the good times to stand out much more than they had when I was in Rio. Sofia started to appear in my dreams at night. When she was right at hand in Rio, I did not once have those dreams.

In longing for her, I gathered all the beauty and warmth that I found in Rio and put it into her face. She was now the incarnation of the seven happiest weeks of my life, and my feelings for her grew stronger every time I thought about her.

That September, I returned to Stanford to begin my

senior year. I had hoped to break free of my melancholy, but once I smelled the eucalyptus and asphalt that filled the air with a distinctively Stanford aroma, I felt even more remorse at what I had left behind.

o

SOFIA'S FIRST LETTER reached me at Stanford a few days later on October 1, 1964. Hoping for some joy to lift my spirits, I instead found five pages of heartbreak. Her words were quiet, so quiet that I could barely hear her voice as I read the Portuguese, but so touching that they exposed the depth of my feeling for her.

To her I was not cold and aloof, nor mentally and emotionally stunted, nor a bungling and inexperienced foreigner who failed to communicate, but the man she now realized she was in love with. This made me put aside my previous hesitations and brought me great happiness, but also a sense of devastation that she recognized her feelings only now. She could well have been an intimate partner. And maybe after she got to know me better, she would not be so intrusive in her probing and thereby allow me to feel more secure around her.

Sofia's letter drove me out of my mind. Each time I read it I was in Rio, seeing her close to me and hearing her voice. Then I would look up and find my dorm room staring at me. This could be the kind of relationship I had always wanted, but now I would never be able to experience it. I wondered if there was a Portuguese word that described the top of the scale of *saudade*, because that was where I was.

Why did I rush off from Rio when even one more day with Sofia might have allowed the love she expressed now to blossom between us? It could have changed everything. But that universe had closed itself to us now. Given my commitment to graduating from Stanford with honors—driven by my obsession with a whole suite of study processes—reopening my relationship with Sofia was unthinkable.

Or so I thought. When I was the saddest, I went up to San Francisco to have dinner with Mom and Dad, who were in town for one of Dad's recording sessions. Both wore their city-by-the-bay finest, Dad in a coat and tie and Mom in a dark dress with a sparkling pin on the front. I expected to hear them say they were proud of me for enduring this as well as I was and give me advice on how to hold on until things passed.

"You know," Dad said, "years ago before Mom and I met, we both went through the same kind of thing you are going through now."

Mom nodded. "It was excruciating. It's so hard for us to see you like this."

"What we want to say is to stop thinking that the situation is hopeless." Dad said. "Rio is only twelve hours away, and you could be there any time you wanted."

If I truly chose her, then she and I would end up together, they said. If she were the girl for me, then they would make sacrifices to help eliminate the distance between us.

My head spun. Over the years, they had given me valuable advice about my girl problems but nothing as specific nor as well-timed as this. In retrospect, I marvel at how deeply and consistently they always supported me, given that they often did not understand me. I was utterly different, the only introvert and scholar in the family. The other four were or had been performers: Dad a big band musician, Mom a dancer, and my two sisters, actors. Yet whenever their loner son needed help, they were right there to provide it.

Their support, and especially their coaching to change the way I was thinking about the situation, gradually made life more tolerable for me. Sofia was still in the forefront of my mind and emotions. Now when I thought of her, I no longer shrouded myself in blackness.

Still, I took no action on their offer. I was committed to finishing Stanford, graduating from ROTC, and accepting a commission as a second lieutenant in the Army. Right after college, I was likely to be drafted as an enlisted man, and getting a commission was the safest option. I could be sent to Southeast Asia, and it would be far less risky to serve there as an officer.

o

IN LATE OCTOBER, I received a letter from Ana Maria.

She was alone in a big house among people with whom she had little communication. I saw her missing the joy of having me as a trusted companion in word and song for so many days, picturing her pass by my vacant room with the knot in her throat and the tears in her eyes that she so vividly described in her letter. My heart went out to her as I read through each line of her sad and labored text.

I was overjoyed that she thought so highly of me, that I made such a deeply positive impression on her, and that her daily routine had centered on me far more than I had known at the time. I was flattered that such an attractive and intelligent young woman would write such a touching letter so many days after I had left Rio. She said she and her family planned to come to the US in six months and hoped to see me then.

o

I DID NOT hear from Sofia again until December, more than two months after her previous letter. I was beginning to wonder if the present had captivated her, but when her next letter arrived, I learned that, if anything, her feelings for me had intensified.

She felt overwhelmed at the card and flowers I sent for her birthday; until they reached her, she had been sad and alone, surrounded by unsatisfying and insipid people. In that, she was like Ana Maria, who had made a similar comment about her own life. In retrospect, this helps me to see why both girls might have been so interested in me. My impression of most men back then was that they rarely listened to women or showed them much respect, and here this gringo was, consistently doing both.

Sofia felt this year was particularly significant for her development and had accorded me a place in her pantheon that was at least as high as the one I accorded her in mine. She loved me sweetly and gently and was sorry for the terrible heartbreak I had gone through over our separation. Even though I could not hold her close to me, I was happy at the thought that such a girl even existed, and that I meant so much to her. Our full and open self-expression had drawn us closer than ever before.

One morning in January 1965, I bounded up the flights of stairs to my dorm room with another letter from Sofia in my hand, its familiar scent filling me with anticipation. The sun outside was bright and LBJ had just proclaimed the hugely optimistic Great Society in his State of the Union address. Something new called Medicare would be available for seniors. There would be money for a Teacher Corps, a Head Start program for children, new housing, mass transit, and a slew of other initiatives that made me proud to be an American.

I hoped Sofia's letter would bring good news about the upcoming trip to California that she mentioned in her last letter, but as I eagerly scanned, I realized she was not coming. She had planned to travel with Ana Maria and her family, but they had postponed their trip from the spring to the fall. She knew that by that time I would be in the Army and stationed at a base who knew where. Her parents would not let her travel alone, so she could not come sooner. It was a hard blow.

In the months afterwards, life intruded on us both and we wrote less and less often.

o

ANA MARIA did not come in six months as planned, but for the next year we exchanged letters, cards, and little gifts. Each time I heard from her, she was warmer and more tender than the time before.

When she finally did travel, it was September 1965 and I was already in Army officer boot camp at Fort Benning, Georgia. She and her parents were in California and managed to get a call through to me at the base.

Over the phone, all three of them sent me an outpouring of emotion that I did not expect after the passing of a year since I left Rio. In came in a flood of love and kindness that I hardly knew how to integrate into the Spartan military atmosphere I was living in.

The sincerity, the genuineness and wholeness of the emotions that the entire family expressed, moved me. All, and especially Ana Maria, were unequivocal in their praise and expressions of love, uncritical and approving of all that I was and had done. They gave of themselves in a way and at a time that meant more to me than they could have known. It was as if the cultural differences between us were a filter, a screen shutting out any impurities of feeling. Only the most constructive, the most joyful and warm emotions passed through in either direction.

"Ben, I miss you!" said Ana Maria. "I am so sorry we are near your home, and you are so far away!"

"I am too, Ana Maria. I'd give anything to be able to give you a hug right now!"

It was ironic that Ana Maria was now free of the constraints that had kept me away from her in Brazil. The cultural exchange program was long over, so there was no longer any risk of ruining it. Her parents were far more welcoming and accepting of me than they had been when I was staying in their home. I did not know if Bruno was still in the picture, but she herself was reaching out with emotions stronger than anything she had allowed herself to express in Rio except on that last night. All of this affected my heart, and in the quiet of the night at Fort Benning, I saw her smiling face and long, dark blonde hair. I asked myself whether I should reconsider and seek to find with her the love I had been looking for with others.

I did not realize it at the time, but the flaw in my winning recipe—its automatic shift in my focus from the character of the girl I was with to a step-by-step process— had appeared again. My winning recipe had attracted another girl who had a controlling behavioral style and would not have been right for me. She tried to dominate her parents. She was haughty with servants like the rector's driver, Wilson. She laced into our Brazilian student hosts when they played a prank on me at the Cabo Frio beach house even though they were in their twenties, and she was only seventeen. Plus, due to her class position in Brazil, she was used to a lifestyle with servants, something I would never want.

The music process did work to redirect the energy between Ana Maria and me, so in that sense it was a success. But in the end, we were attracted to each other anyway. I was so caught up in learning the steps to play Brazilian music, I naively missed seeing that spending so much time with her might lead to complications.

With Ana Maria, I learned that no amount of distraction provided by a winning recipe, the music process in this case, could prevent an inappropriate attraction from developing. Back then, I was too young to see that this had happened because I was trying to use the recipe in the wrong area of life. More than ever, I was committed to finding someone I could experience satisfaction and safety with by sharing intimate feelings and thoughts. But I still had not learned that trying to use a process to do so would be a problem.

After the phone call, the emotional disruptions I faced in the Army became unprecedented. Those nighttime thoughts about Ana Maria quickly vanished, and I never had contact with her again.

o

IN NOVEMBER 1965, two months after I got the phone call from Ana Maria and her family, I received another letter from Sofia. Her brief note exposed a misunderstanding that had characterized a good part of our relations. It was not until that letter that I fully understood what her choice of words meant when she had described our tie as one of "friendship."

"I wonder if perhaps the language got in the way when we were together in Rio," she wrote in Portuguese. "I used the word *colegas* to describe us."

She was right. She had studiously avoided the word *amigos*, the usual word for "friends," and instead used *colegas*.

"*Coleguismo*," she continued, "means camaraderie and spiritual rapport. That is what we have. I meant it to be used in opposition to simple friendship, but in Rio I think maybe you took me to mean the reverse, namely friendship in the normal sense."

She was right. Given my growing feelings for her, I had been upset at being just a "friend." But I now saw she had elevated my tie to her as *coleguismo*, a much higher place. In all those walks on Copacabana Beach, I had totally misread her intent.

Writing this now, over half a century later, two additional insights have struck me. First, for years I held *her* to be the one largely responsible for the relationship going nowhere at the start—I wanted it, but in Rio she held back by wanting to be just "friends." Now I see my responsibility was huge. At the time, I was too immature to just accept what she was saying. Instead I resisted, and it made things much worse than they would have been otherwise. I could have laughed off the "friendship" conversations and let them go away on their own.

Which brings up the second realization, an even deeper one: when she kept insisting on being *colegas*, she was probably directing those words at *herself*. In her very first letter after I left Brazil, she said with great eloquence that she loved me. To me, that suggests in Rio she was fighting the growing love she felt by insisting on friendship, then caved in after I was gone when she first sat down to write.

By the time I got that latest letter, I had finished with the required infantry training for intelligence officers at Fort Benning and was now at the Army Intelligence School in Baltimore. Sofia simply was not an available choice. I had to complete my two years of military service and after that intended to go on to graduate business school. So, for reasons of mental and emotional health, I pushed her into the realm of fantasy. There was no happiness to gain by deeper feelings now. I could not have her, so I began to tell myself that I did not want her.

Like Ana Maria, Sofia was used to an upper-class lifestyle that I would never want to adopt. More importantly, my youthful infatuation with her after I left Rio made me forget how unsafe I had felt around her when I was there. Her scrutiny of me was so penetrating it made me uncomfortable. Being around that kind of energy for years would not have been particularly healthy or much fun.

Sofia was still delightful to contemplate, and I expected I would think about her whenever great periods of happiness were triggered in my memory. But until I could do something about her, she would have to stay where she was, floating in a pleasant daydream.

I had fallen harder for Sofia than for anyone before, but time had proven that a Portuguese-speaking woman, for me, did not work. This third time, the language had helped me to be less introverted and brought me love, far more than I had ever hoped for. But it had again produced only delayed success and now revealed a new flaw: a problem in the approach itself. The mechanics of the language had killed a promising relationship because I had misunderstood Sofia's meaning.

I have no record that after November 1965 she ever wrote me again.

o

DECADES LATER, I was glad to learn that Ana Maria had become a published author and prize-winning professor of philosophy at a university in Brazil. By the time she was in her early seventies, she had three children and nine grandchildren.

Sofia became a clinical psychologist, married a civil engineer, and by her seventies had two sons and two grandchildren. Someday in the far, far distant future there would indeed be a slender, sweet, and insightful woman for me to share my life with. But her name would not be Sofia.

o

IN RETROSPECT, PORTUGUESE had served me well. It compensated for my quiet nature and lack of boldness when approaching women.

But Portuguese as an approach, was clunky. It could be used only with women who spoke little or no English. The results it produced were always delayed—two and a half years in the case of Anabela, thirteen months for Ana Maria, and eight weeks for Sofia. And it had the flaw of always creating unintended consequences that produced little safety or satisfaction. All three times it had attracted girls who were not right for me in some way, and in the last case it had killed off the most promising of the three.

Processes were about achieving things, not about building relationships. Had I thought about it, I would have seen how obvious that was. As a ten-year-old, I had formulated my first series of steps precisely to get a result *without* having to focus on people too much.

Two months after returning to California from Brazil, I was so lonely that I could not think clearly. My long-distance contacts with Ana Maria and Sofia were still alive, but when I saw the chance to be involved with another girl, this time an American at Stanford, I jumped at it.

# Chapter 6
# A Bipolar Connection

NOVEMBER 1964. STANFORD, CALIFORNIA. The wonderful summer days in Rio were receding into the background. One night as the cold rain tapped against my window, I sat in my room at Stern Hall and noticed my emotions for Sofia had settled into a dull ache.

I was lonely and still so inexperienced in love that as soon as a new girl appeared, I leapt into pursuing her. I had left Brazil just eight weeks before and felt strangely confident in taking the risk of approaching her.

She was a prize—a blonde freshman, which loner seniors like me valued greatly because we could be manly and mature with them, even when inside we were withdrawn and hopelessly captivated by their freshness, their charm, and their lack of cynicism.

Her name was Roberta Jones and she was from Ohio. Five feet five inches tall, she was a little withdrawn herself, sweet, kind, serious, and intense in conversation. I was attracted to her because I thought she might be a fellow introvert. She appeared to be mature, conscientious, sweet, and fun, everything I was looking for. Plus, she was luscious and affectionate, just the thing to assuage my loneliness, I thought. After several dates, her warm lips and engaging talk made me hope I had found another Sofia, especially now that I was not willing to upend my life to go back to Brazil for the real one.

Yet I could not have been more wrong. Roberta was a volcano of hidden emotions that quickly surfaced.

The first indication of trouble came ten days after I met her. She had disappeared, so I called her dorm.

"She went to San Rafael," said Wendy, her roommate. "She put herself on a bus."

"What? Why?" San Rafael was in Marin County, an affluent area across the Golden Gate Bridge just north of San Francisco.

"She has relatives up there. She was confused and couldn't stand being on campus for another second."

That did not sound good. Neither was the news that Roberta was not going home to her parents, but to her aunt and uncle. She had told me she had not seen her parents in five months, and that she was not close to her mother's Bay Area sister and husband either. I pictured her crying on the bus and then receiving a less than warm reception from people who might offer her food and shelter but little else.

A few days later she was back, seemingly better. I took her to a party at the Lake Lagunita boathouse where my former roommate Jeff Henderson lived. He asked me to bring my guitar, so I did and sang "Meditation," a popular bossa nova tune by Antonio Carlos Jobim that Ana Maria had taught me. Roberta loved it. Afterwards she rewarded me with lots of kisses and hugs, and a warm, subdued tenderness when I pressed her to me.

Later that week, I flew home for Thanksgiving where I took long walks around the neighborhood in the warm evenings. As I watched the twinkling lights on the mountains above the San Fernando Valley, I took stock of what I knew about Roberta. She had been educated in England and traveled all over Europe and America with her aunt and uncle before arriving at Stanford. They gave her many material things, but during those years she had suffered from uncertainty and unhappiness. Starving for companionship and guidance, she turned to the Mormon Church, of which her relatives were members. She rejected most of the dogma but got some comfort from the sense of community it offered her.

When I got back to Stanford after Thanksgiving, I learned that Roberta had attempted suicide. After she failed and an ambulance had taken her to a hospital, she descended into a catatonic state, withdrawn so far into herself that she neither spoke, recognized speech, nor moved. Her eyes were in a wide, dilated stare that symbolized her total rejection of the world. I rushed to the hospital with her roommate, but because Roberta's condition was so critical, they would allow no one to see her for an indefinite time.

Attempted suicide and nervous collapse were blatant signs that she was dangerously ill. Still, I did not walk away—just the opposite. I took it upon myself to save her, to "fix" her. I had lost Sofia because I left Rio too soon. I was not going to lose Roberta by giving up now and making the same mistake.

However, I failed to understand just how severe Roberta's mental illness was. My hubris had me believing that I had the ability to use a process of loving attention to simply encourage her to be okay, when in reality, Roberta needed professional help and still might never have been "okay" by my standards.

Heavily influencing my passion to hang on to her was the powerful lesson I had learned just two months before with the Brazilian blood sample. It showed me that I could succeed at a difficult task if I were willing to take a risk and keep going no matter what.

The memory of that triumph in the face of every obstacle was still so vivid that I felt almost omnipotent. I would be damned if I was going to just let Roberta go without a fight, especially now that I knew I had it in me to bull my way through.

Despite this resolve, my distress over Roberta caused my back to break out in a rash. Each morning, I woke up with such heart-pounding anxiety that I had to force myself to face the day. When I was by myself for too long, tears welled up in my eyes.

I made no plans to go home for Christmas. Surely Roberta would be treated somewhere in the Bay Area, and I wanted to be there when she woke up. On the fourth day of her catatonia, she did wake up, but her mother arrived from Ohio and whisked her away to Toledo before I or anyone else could get into the hospital. She was gone, probably never to return.

The sensible thing for me to do at that point would have been to let go of her, but I could not. Instead, I became angry that the very people who were probably the most responsible for Roberta's mental and emotional condition, namely her mother and stepfather, were now in charge of caring for her. I did not know for sure, but hypothesized that if she was this messed up, something traumatic must have happened to her as a child at home.

Her having been away from her parents for five months indicated to me that she was probably trying to distance herself from them. Now they were likely compounding the damage by taking her back to a small apartment in Toledo where they would only make things worse.

At age twenty-one, I had a dangerously inflated opinion of my own ability to help her. I had no idea that she was mentally ill, suffering from what today we would call bipolar disorder. That condition did not appear in the *Diagnostic and Statistical Manual of Mental Disorders* of the American Psychiatric Association until 1980, some sixteen years later. People with the disorder cycle through bouts of lows and highs, depression and mania of various intensities, with the cycles lasting anywhere from hours or days to weeks or even many months. Roberta tried to kill herself most likely during a prolonged period of severe depression and breakdown. It ended up lasting two months, from November through December 1964.

I knew none of this at the time, only that she was sweet and I thought all she needed was the kind of love I could provide. This made me forget everything I knew about how processes could cause problems in relationships. Instead, I was ready to launch a new one designed to rescue her. I would coach her, give her love and attention, and through the example of my positive outlook, would help her to get well. This conveniently allowed me to avoid taking an honest look at her illness and thereby avoid realizing she needed help only a trained psychiatrist could provide.

In retrospect, I marvel at how much my impulse to intervene conflicted with the normal, risk-averse behavior introverts are often known for. I was loyal to her and optimistic about a future with her. But the successful outcome of my risky adventure with the Brazilian blood left me naïve and over-confident, and through my recipe, I sought to help in the only way I knew how. It made me supremely certain that by caring for her in a patient, methodical way I could overcome any obstacle. This guileless approach drew me to her at the very moment when I could have walked away. Instead, I resolved that if she were only to reach out to me I would rush to save her.

She did so in January, saying in a call from Ohio that she had recovered. It would have been more accurate to say she had cycled from depression into the beginnings of a manic phase, but at the time I did not know such distinctions existed. She said I was the first person she thought of when she came to and was the first one she had written to, although I had not received the letter yet. The best news was that she planned to be back at Stanford in a few months. Her warmth and tenderness opened my heart, making me want to see her as soon as possible.

Yet just as with Sofia, a girl was becoming attracted not to me but to the shell of a winning recipe I had presented to her. When she first snapped out of catatonia, she immediately thought of me, not her parents or her aunt and uncle, and I took that to mean that she saw me as being just who she needed—someone who could rescue her. But in that role, I was not authentic. Rescuing her required not only medical expertise that I did not have, but also a high degree of extroversion to cope with the manic phase she soon would be cycling into. On both counts, the introvert inside that shell was totally unequipped.

o

I WENT INTO overtime figuring out how I could get myself to Toledo to see her over the upcoming spring break. One afternoon, I came in out of the rain and closeted myself in a dormitory phone booth to work out my options. I left the door open because the space stank from the previous occupant.

> "Yet just as with Sofia, a girl
> was becoming attracted not to me
> but to the shell of a winning recipe
> I had presented to her."

After a few calls, I found that the cheapest way to Ohio was by bus, but I could not face it. The train, however, sounded glamorous even though I would be sitting up all night. I bought a ticket from Oakland to Chicago and booked the bus from there to Toledo. I did not mind that it would take me fifty-five hours to get to Roberta. It would prolong the delicious sense of anticipation that had taken hold of me.

Three days before leaving for the East, I was acutely eager to go. With tickets and money in my pocket and arrangements made with my professors for a late start after spring vacation, I had traveling fever and wanted to get out of Stanford right away. In Roberta's latest letter, she told me how excited she was to see me, and that she had things ready for my arrival. If going were purely a matter of will, I would have found myself on the train at that very moment.

On the morning of March 18, I went into the

Student Union for some breakfast. The newspapers for sale at the door had headlines about a huge civil rights march from Selma to Montgomery, Alabama, but I was too excited about my trip to read about it.

o

WHEN I ARRIVED in Toledo, a bit dazed and depleted from the long trip, I found that Roberta was rebuilding her life in possibly one of the bleakest environments possible: a crowded apartment in a cold, industrial city. She had created her own world of happiness at the University of Toledo by using her persuasive talents to open doors.

Each day she took us through a full round of activities in math, literature, and music. We went to seminars and lectures on everything from religion to education. The prestige of Stanford went a long way in Toledo, and she showed great skill at saying she had spent time there and at my being a senior there. Bright, optimistic, and analytical, Roberta had cheerful and animated expressions on her face that, by contrast, made the people around her seem colorless.

Even though Roberta and I looked at each other as strangely new people, she gave me all her attention. She was warm and friendly, open and frank, expansive and intimate. She took me on as a travel agent might, with her one-willed purposefulness providing me with rich, full days of fun and learning.

I had never seen her like this. Years later, I learned about type II bipolar disorder and realized that was likely what Roberta had been suffering from. Type II was more common in women than in men and did not consist of full-on mania. Instead, it entailed "hypomania"—a high energy level, impulsiveness, and an extremely excited state, exactly what I was observing without seeing it for what it was.

Her mind was constantly active, so much so that she overwhelmed me at times with her understanding and desire to learn. She saw life, love, and joy everywhere around her, and was able to extract meaning from events that, to me, seemed insignificant. She had a deep, heartfelt commitment to all we did, and my positive feelings were strong enough to make me forgive another side of her that was starting to appear.

I began getting uncomfortable with the negative gestures, facial expressions, and words that sometimes tumbled out of her. In the heat of argument, her eyes blazed with hatred, but I rationalized that they only reflected her passion. When I mentioned this, she encouraged me to grow up and learn to deal with her intensity. She convinced me that I needed to become more of an adult.

o

THE MORNING AFTER I got back to Stanford, I stood in the lobby of my dorm house and used my mailbox key to raise the thin, squeaky plate that covered the slot under my name. The brilliant sun outside was such a contrast to Toledo that it filled me with joy, but that was nothing compared with my elation over what I found in the box.

Starting that day, Roberta sent me a steady barrage of letters, phone calls, cards, tapes, and pictures. She said she loved me and found so many ways to communicate it that she overwhelmed my heart. Rather than seeing her excessive behavior as a sign of instability,

I used it to wipe away the memory of the petty conflicts and worries I had endured with her in Toledo.

In one of her letters, she reported that she planned to arrive in late June and needed a cheap place to stay; so I began working on it. I asked if she would be willing to come earlier in the month, since I would be going into the Army in July. I was overjoyed when she said yes, she could come in early June.

I succeeded brilliantly in finding Roberta a place to stay, the same house where I would be living in the few weeks between graduation and my induction into the service. It was at the thirty-room mansion on Jackson Street in San Francisco that belonged to the family of Drew Faulkner, a former Stanford roommate. Drew and I were still friends, and when he learned a few weeks earlier that I needed a place to live before going into the Army, he kindly offered up the roomy basement apartment in the building. When Roberta's need for lodging came up, I went back to him to see if there could be a room for her as well, and, after talking to his mother, he said they would be happy to help.

Drew's father had made a fortune in the mining business in Peru. While he was rarely around, his wife was a leading community organizer in the city and kept a constant parade of fascinating people coming through the house for dinners and parties. I knew the stimulating environment would be to Roberta's liking, so I was happy to tell her about the arrangement.

However, so many unexpected twists occurred in our relationship between securing lodging for her and her arrival that by the time her train pulled into Oakland on June 5, 1965, I was tentative. Despite the initial torrent of letters, I saw that the time apart since Toledo had caused some backsliding in our relationship. But I was not prepared for what happened next.

Two days after her return, we met on campus and stood next to the dry bed of Lake Lagunita, not far from the boathouse where months earlier I had sung "Meditation" for her. I looked out to where there should have been water and saw only weeds.

"You know," she said, "in Toledo I had virtually no choice. You were the only desirable guy in my life at that point. Something very rapid occurred within both of us."

I did not like where this was going.

"But time has diluted the feelings on both sides, and I'm now in a wonderful world which offers me opportunities at every turn, even in love."

"So what are you saying?"

"Well, you can expect neither rapid developments nor single-minded attention from me." In retrospect it is hard to believe that she spoke in such stilted language, but that was exactly what she said. She meant our relationship was not going to get any better, and the reason would be her focus on other things, presumably other men. In her voice there was no apology and quite a bit of condescension.

To me, it seemed that she was feeling all-powerful, and now that she was back in California, she saw me only as a limitation she could brush aside. Especially since she would soon be living in a prime location in a prestigious, politically active home in the center of San Francisco—a situation I had naively arranged for her.

If I needed any further proof that I could not trust her judgment or stability, that was it. Once again, incredibly, I ignored it. I had invested in her for so many months that I could not turn and walk away. Instead, I regrouped and told myself part of the rescue process had to include her freedom. It made sense not to pollute the relationship with a sense of obligation. Even though I was dying inside, I felt magnanimous in dispelling her concerns. I thought that with her cooled feelings out in the open, we could get beyond the exasperation of the moment and begin rebuilding.

o

ON A BRISK, sunny morning, predictably cool and breezy for early June in San Francisco, Roberta moved into a room on one of the upper floors of the mansion on Jackson Street. The house was perched on a hill, with some of its windows looking out on snippets of the blue waters of the bay.

For the moment, I was still at Stern Hall. "I Can't Get No Satisfaction" by the Rolling Stones had just been released and was in the air everywhere. It was perhaps one of the greatest rock-and-roll songs of all time and perfectly encapsulated how I felt about my frustrating relationship with Roberta.

After her long convalescence and isolation in Ohio, Roberta seemed determined to embrace her life in California again with a frightening vengeance. She talked about herself quite a bit, was supremely confident in her views or at least sounded like it, and proved herself to be a poor listener. I knew and understood these traits in her, but others did not. People around her saw them as cover-ups for a case of anxious insecurity.

Communication between us became awkward and difficult. I wanted to talk things out with her but found myself inhibited for fear that I would forget something she had told me, and she would call me out on it.

I would ask, "Roberta, for Christ's sake, can we just sit down and talk?"

Her eyes would narrow as she shot me a stare of exasperation. "Don't ask me that. I already told you not to. Don't you remember that? Why do I have to keep reminding you?"

I was not used to having anyone talk to me like that, but I let it pass.

I was also forever tiptoeing through the minefield of potentially saying something that, to her, was so obvious that she needed to remind me of it with a loud and disparaging remark. When I suggested something (a worry, a thought, a point of view) she confronted me with a whole array of aggressive arguments designed to slam me to the floor. I felt as if she was trying to break me of a vicious habit by pruning my conversation of nonessentials, forcing me to be accurate and succinct, and obliging me to throw up a defense behind every statement. I was starting to lose interest in this whole thing.

On June 15, ten days after Roberta's return, my Stanford graduation took place, and thanks to ROTC, I was now a second lieutenant in the US Army. Soon after my family went back to LA, I stood in my dorm room, dazed. I looked through the window from tree to tree, realizing that for the first time in days, I was just a guy rather than a celebrated institution.

And I was not the vaunted rescuer I thought I would be by now, just someone coping with his own naivete. This whole situation was a sequel to the risk I had taken with the two Englishmen in Belém, and this time it was not ending well.

I soon moved into the basement at Jackson Street and was now sure of several things about Roberta. Her constant talking about herself was not something borne of re-establishing herself in California but a sign of a desperately unsure self. What I took for a genuine expression of the fullness of life was simply a constant, feverish need for attention. Every person in the house I talked to about her had come to the same conclusion. My parents even saw the red flags when they came to town for my graduation and refused to let Roberta and me babysit for my young sister, Nan.

Roberta and I finally did talk. We admitted that we were not compatible.

"Roberta, I can't keep up with you. I am bored with trying and exhausted from it all."

She gave me a cynical smile under eyes that blazed at me with condescension. "I see that, Ben. You're...lethargic and pretty complacent." Her mind ran free and wild, and she wanted a man who would revel in its hyperactivity.

"Fine. I am tired of trying to make this work."

I had taken on too much and was finally glad to admit it. That was my first healthy realization about her, and it put some long-needed distance between us.

I saw the deterioration of our relationship not as a result of her mental illness, but rather as a result of my exhaustion and failure to make it work. Had I been more mature, I might have been able to view the situation with more perspective. I had a deep, quiet confidence based on years of loving care from my parents and years of real achievement in the academic world. I wish I had sooner seen that there was no possibility of her providing the sense of safety I wanted in a relationship.

o

BY NOW, MY friend Drew had moved into the house. He and Roberta soon became attracted to each other. I kept to myself, staying in the basement as much as possible.

It was oddly light and airy down there, since half-windows peeked above ground, and through them, I could see small parts of the bay below. The large room had the clutter of old furniture and a washer and dryer in it, but I had a comfortable twin bed in one corner and access to my own bathroom. I found a small space heater in a closet and used it to offset the cold that crept in even in June.

Late one night, soon after I moved in, I looked up from my bed through a half-window and saw the stars. Ed White was up there. He had just made the first-ever spacewalk, and his *Gemini 4* spacecraft was still circling the earth.

While I was trying to keep warm under the covers, I thought about how excruciating it was to watch the growing magnetism between Roberta and Drew at close range. I did not blame either of them; I just did not want to know anything about it. Yet soon it was obvious to me and everyone else in the house that the two of them were sleeping together, something Roberta and I had never done.

I thought of what might have been with Ana Maria, and especially with Sofia. They were so healthy, so stable, and in comparison, had been so kind to me.

Eager to escape, I jumped at a chance to spend a few days up in the Sierras with friends. The peace of the mountains and the tall pines were infectious, allowing me to calm my mind and reflect on all that had happened. I based my self-respect on competence, so it was devastating to admit I did not have the ability to build a relationship with Roberta. Thoughts of Drew gave me an even more severe shake-up because I realized that he *did* have the capacity to draw her in. Plus, he was outgoing, rich, and well connected. He could offer her a lot more than I could.

In the end, I faced up to the tremendous extent of my self-delusion. I had created an entire world based on false premises and did not even know it until the whole structure collapsed.

When I returned to Jackson Street from the mountains, Mrs. Faulkner, Drew's mother, brought me out of my gloom in an act of pure kindness and compassion. She had a solid grasp of the situation and cared about me enough to spend time talking through my problems. Her experience, warmth, and realistic approach helped me to get over Roberta.

A handsome and impeccably dressed woman in her late forties, Mrs. Faulkner was politically energetic, had a commanding presence, and spoke in a husky voice from years of smoking. She saw how much I had been hurt by Roberta's switch of affections from me to Drew, and she made not the slightest suggestion that I should be taking the whole thing more nobly. More importantly for my ego, she showed me the attraction between her son and Roberta would probably turn out to be one-sided. As soon as she said that, it helped me to remember Drew, who was known around Stern Hall as "The Snake," was not satisfied with any one girl for long. He was just too busy. It was not about if but *when* Drew would dump her.

Mrs. Faulkner sat in an easy chair with a magnificent view of San Francisco Bay behind her and studied my face.

"Oh, come here," she said, opening her arms.

When I went to her and leaned over, she gave me a hug and several pats on the back, remaining seated.

"You're going to be fine, Ben. This will pass. I will help you."

I was wide open to more of Mrs. Faulkner's views. She pointed out that Roberta's mental illness was apparent. She was dangerously insecure and not being able to "handle" her or keep up with her mind were not shortcomings on my part. A quiet sense of contentment came over me as I realized how much I had respected my limits and maintained my integrity when I had refused to operate at Roberta's manic speed.

After that talk, I began to enjoy contact with Drew, feeling myself strangely removed from the whole tired mess. We laughed about it, talked about it frankly, and used it to bring ourselves closer together. Our conversations were so intense and carefree that I almost forgot he was the man who was taking Roberta to bed.

Mrs. Faulkner continued to be my greatest source of strength. Every day she watched out for me, making sure I was never alone in the house for long, offering me the car, taking me to parties, and keeping me occupied while Drew and Roberta were together. Despite all that we did not have another sit-down session, and I slowly became depressed again. When Mrs. Faulkner noticed that she called me in for another talk, and I left feeling revitalized. I saw how much she cared for me, actively worked for my best welfare, and loved me as her own son.

By mid-July, Roberta was deteriorating before

everyone's eyes. At dinner with the family and the other residents, I looked across the table at her and saw a complexion blotched with dark areas of skin placed forebodingly at the corners of her mouth, under her eyes and below her nostrils. She said she had not been able to sleep well for days, so maybe that was the cause. She kept her face locked in a hard, cold stare; eyes wide open as if attacking an unseen object. She gobbled every meal as if she feared someone would steal it from her.

She began to slide inexorably from her long months of frantic activity back into a new cycle of depression. She was irritable, withdrew for long periods into her room, and had headaches. She followed people around and talked incessantly about her depressed feelings and sense of anxiety.

I had given her more of myself than I cared to remember, and now Drew was doing the same. For Drew or myself I could not get too upset, but when she started latching onto Mrs. Faulkner, or Drew's sister, or another boy who was boarding downstairs, I got angry. In the house, she had become a grasping, consuming problem.

On July 16, I was ecstatic to leave Jackson Street for Fort Benning, Georgia to begin active duty in the Army. I was still corresponding with Ana Maria and Sofia, and after what I had just gone through with Roberta, I missed them both.

Six months later, I learned from Jake Mayer, my good friend and traveling companion in Brazil, that Roberta had returned to Stanford in September, but by December had dropped out again and was back in Toledo. That news was the last thing I ever heard about her. I hoped she was getting the psychiatric care that she needed.

Recently, I was sad to learn that thirty-two years later, in 1997, Mrs. Faulkner died a long and painful death in a Bay Area hospital due to emphysema. Only seventy-six years old when she passed away, she was one of the finest people I ever knew.

o

MY WINNING RECIPE had now failed to bring me romantic success four times in a row.

Captivated by my early triumphs with the recipe as a child, I kept coming back to the same strategy even when it stopped working. Twice I allowed it to seduce me into paying far more attention to processes—learning Portuguese with Anabela and learning Brazilian music with Ana Maria—than I did to the girl herself. And twice I fell into being inauthentic, projecting an outer shell that attracted Sofia as if I were a willing debater, and as a capable rescuer to Roberta. Except for when playing music with Ana Maria, I never felt safe with any of them. I was still alone.

At the time, I was not yet self-aware enough to realize it, but I must have felt that having someone else could help shield me from an extroverted world. If she were an intimate companion whom I trusted, we could face life's noise and commotion together. This might explain why I searched so devotedly in one relationship after another to have that person in my life.

As a child, I had created my winning recipe to help me feel safe in the world. My formula, being methodical by executing some kind of a process, had worked brilliantly in high school and college academics. But with women, it had ended up being a counterfeit and unsatisfying solution. Instead of bringing me the safety of a lasting relationship, it had turned out to be perhaps the greatest obstacle to finding one.

After four attempts, I was thoroughly disillusioned with my ability to find a life partner. I was ready to turn the page, and the Army was the perfect place to do it.

Or so I thought. In reality, I was about to endure far more fear than I had ever faced. I would not be dealing with girls and hoped that the recipe would be an ally. But events would soon prove otherwise.

# Part 2

# Fear

# Chapter 7
# Evasion and Escape

AUGUST 1965. FORT BENNING, GEORGIA. At dusk on a steamy evening, I sat on a bench in the back of a two-and-a-half-ton truck with eleven other young men. We bumped along a dirt road in a convoy of eighteen trucks near a forest that harbored scores of angry German Shepherd dogs and their handlers.

The two hundred and twelve of us, all newly commissioned second lieutenants in the US Army, were about to jump out of the backs of the trucks in groups of threes and fours as soon as the vehicles came to a stop. We were to scurry across an open field and into the forest beyond without getting caught.

Faces and hands darkened with shoe polish, shirts reversed to hide labels, all shines dulled and clinks muffled, we had only a compass as our guide across nearly five kilometers of treacherous, rattlesnake-infested terrain through the woods that night. The air was thick with humidity, and there was no moon. Hidden holes, briar patches, creek beds, sharp sticks, and above all, two hundred hardened soldiers with dogs, clubs, and flashlights were between us and a designated rendezvous point to the north. If these privates—who were eager to see how much a second lieutenant could endure—caught us, they would beat, harass, and torture us beyond the breaking point.

This was the dreaded evasion and escape exercise, the high point of the Infantry Officer's Basic Course at Fort Benning that I, as an intelligence officer, had to complete. This was half a decade before the Army became involved with today's Survival, Evasion, Resistance and Escape (SERE) training, although the Air Force, Navy, and Marines had been conducting it for years.

The exercise took place in a patch of wilderness among the Georgia pines. Just three months earlier, every one of my classmates and I had been celebrated at our college graduation ceremonies and had looked forward, some with excitement and some with fear, to the prospect of our Army induction after completing four years of Reserve Officers Training Corps classes. The Vietnam War was raging, and ROTC provided an honorable way to beat the draft, but now as the drop-off point approached, I would have bet not one man was convinced that joining the service voluntarily had been a good idea.

Sitting in the truck, I recalled that my normal response to the exercise would have been to think it through, nail down the alternatives and probabilities, and create a process to increase my safety. Despite my failure in relationships, I knew my recipe worked in academics, and I assumed it would not fail me in the Army. As an introvert, I had achieved fabulous, repeated success by doing just that: becoming dependent on rigid, highly evolved plans and their sequential steps to manage the world for me.

But the Army had designed the exercise in a way that rewarded the extroverts among us. To succeed, we had to be bold, take risks, and, more than anything, not *think* too much. As we bounced along, I realized I had spent my entire twenty-two years doing the opposite: foreseeing problems, avoiding risks, and designing elaborate schemes to control my environment.

Fear had pried me loose from my normal world. Rather than examine the details of what was going to happen, I fell prey to unfounded rumors, fantastic dreams, and unlimited speculation on the horror of being alone in the woods at night, chased by savage German shepherds and enlisted men who thought nothing of beating a young officer senseless.

Fear overtook me because I did not have the comfortable safety net of a process. I now wanted one badly. As the truck moved deeper into the forest, I tried to build something on the fly by asking myself things I should have thought about days ago.

How did a person chased by dogs at night in a dark forest avoid detection? Of the five senses, touch and taste were not likely to give me away. The pursuers would touch me only if some other trigger had gotten them close enough to do so. And while taste might apply to a dog that sank its teeth into my leg, it would happen only if the animal found me by some other means.

The most obvious giveaway would be sight. I was well protected in that sense, having rubbed half a can of black Kiwi shoe polish on the back of my neck, forehead, nose, cheeks, and hands. I had turned my green Army fatigue shirt inside out so no insignia or labels would stand out in the dark; my soft baseball cap had nothing on it. Yet no matter how diligently I smeared black wax on my skin, there were still lily-white streaks showing through because of how much I was sweating. All it would take for the privates to see me would be the quick scan of a flashlight through the woods.

Another obvious betrayal would be by sound. As a guy who grew up in suburban Los Angeles, I knew a lot about how to maintain a swimming pool on a sunny day. But I knew absolutely nothing about how to pick my way through dense growth in silence on a slate-black night and uneven ground. It was best that I did not think this part through, because it was hopeless. Far from tiptoeing to avoid snapping twigs, I was going to be running full out, crashing through anything smaller than a tree that stood in my way, evoking all the night goblins in the forest.

If fear had not so overtaken me, I might have realized that mine would not be the only show on display for the eager young privates and their dogs. There would be hundreds of other guys running for their lives in a line stretching to my left and right. There would be a hundred dogs barking their brains out. There would be two hundred soldiers shouting commands to the animals, swearing, and calling to each other. It would be absolute bedlam, which meant my potential captors might not hear me if they were even a few yards away.

The way they would catch me, I was sure, was by smell. That was why the dogs were out. They were aggressive, carefully trained military animals that received prompts day after day to follow the scent of a human. As far as the designers of the exercise were concerned, the spectacle of dogs snarling and straining at their neck chains added a nice touch of horror. However, that was just a side benefit. The real advantage of the dozens of canines was that their brains could penetrate through the darkness and the cacophony of sound to sniff out a trembling man, especially since he would be sweating. Against those beasts there was simply no defense; they would lock onto me and bring a club-wielding soldier right into my face.

Yet would they? In the depths of my anxiety, I neglected to recall two things that might confuse and disorient the dogs. First was the sheer number of bodies they would have to detect. For all I knew, the air would be thick with the smell of humans; there was little wind, and having so many of them clustered in confined spaces between bushes and trees might well have the dogs going in circles.

Then there was the mosquito repellent. The woods were teeming with hungry insects. The instructors cautioned us to slather the chemical on thickly, and even put it on our fatigues so the bugs would not bite us through the cloth. The mosquito goo and shoe polish on a hot, fetid Georgia night were disgusting beyond words to apply, but I did so diligently: perhaps too much so, since the repellent caused some of the white streaks that still showed through the shoe polish on my skin. Here was an unexamined question: Were the dogs trained to home in on repellent, or in the infinite wisdom of Army planning would the designers of the exercise have overlooked that detail?

In the days leading up to the exercise, none of this fact-finding entered my brain. Even if it had, I knew that analysis was necessary but not sufficient. I had to convert the thinking into a series of practical steps, and in this situation, that was impossible.

Terror dried my mouth and filled my bladder.

I went over it all again: The trucks would drop us off at the edge of an open field. Our would-be captors lurked just inside a tree line several hundred meters away. There seemed to be no possibility of escape—they would catch me, beat me for an hour, and toss me outside the prison compound to crawl my way through the rest of the night.

o

THE CONVOY SLOWED and lurched to a stop. The drivers did not kill the headlights, so as men jumped out of the backsides of the trucks they were in full view of the captors in the woods, lit brilliantly as if to whet the appetite of the privates and their dogs. When I hit the ground, I made the mistake of looking directly into the lights of the truck behind me, causing my night vision to vanish as I stared blindly towards the distant forest.

At the pre-launch briefing an hour earlier, the trainers had impressed on us to honor Article V of the Armed Forces Code of Conduct: if captured, all we could reveal were our name, rank, service number, and date of birth despite what the privates might do to get more out of us. But at this moment, when I strained to see anything at all in the darkness, the admonition seemed to be a perfect setup for some aggressive guy my age to whack the daylights out of me until I betrayed a friend or begged the kid to stop hitting me. In a world long before smartphones, there was no way to document what the captors might do to us.

There was no starting gun; the stopping of the convoy signaled the beginning of the exercise. With several others, I turned and ran out of the headlights and soon felt bumpy soil beneath my combat boots. I struggled to keep my balance and not twist an ankle as I ran as fast as I could across what felt like a plowed field. My night eyes gradually returned as I ran, allowing me to see the shadowy outlines of the long line of men to the right and left of me lurching towards the forest. Dogs were barking in the distance along our entire advancing front.

The more we ran toward the dark tree line in the distance, the more it seemed to recede. Then suddenly, it was upon us, just ahead but blocked by unexpected clumps of tall grass we had to part with our arms to get through. This slowed us down and confused us. Stupidly, four of us clustered together against all warnings not to do so, and now all we could think to do was hunker down to get our bearings.

As soon as we crouched down, a dog handler spotted us from the right, and two soldiers came at us from the left. They charged us with lit flashlights, screams and snarls, the highly trained dog straining against its neck chain and pleading for freedom so it could tear into whatever was hiding in the grass.

We scattered. We could not go back; the only way was directly ahead. So we all broke into a run, driving straight into the forest. I was in the lead, with two of my classmates behind me to the left and one behind me to the right.

Our pursuers were behind us. I was outrunning them, but, in the darkness, I slammed into a tree and busted my lips. The escapees to my left passed me by. Now behind the others, I fell on the ground near the base of the tree that had stopped me. My mouth filled with the taste of blood. A pile of dead sticks and branches stabbed me from ten different directions, but I lay in as much silence as I could muster, my lungs bursting for air and my vocal cords straining to cry out from pain and fear.

The other lieutenants had kept running, and in the noise and confusion of scents, the dog handler and two soldiers passed right by me in pursuit. They captured two of the men not six meters from me, then beat the bushes and shone lights to flush me and the other one out of hiding.

I lay motionless as they crisscrossed my position, moving out as far as fifty meters only to come right back.

"There's too many of 'em; the dogs can't smell nothin'," said the dog handler.

"Try over there," said the other soldier, his voice carrying away from where I lay.

"Naw, I was just there. Clipper is onto something over here."

"Come on, Gary, I heard something over *there*!" He turned away from my direction.

"Dammit, Chuck, I'm the dog handler, and he's gonna go where I say."

The handler then turned the dog in my direction. It went a few steps and stopped, sniffing and pawing the underbrush. Right at that spot there must have been a strong scent because the animal fixed on something and came no closer to me.

The longer I lay there, the more I understood what football players meant when they said it was the first hit of the game that knocked the fear out of them. Although the hit had affected me in a comparable way via the pain of the bruises and cuts all over my body and the sweat and blood running into my mouth, it was still low on the pain scale in comparison to what I would suffer if caught. The danger from the unbearably close dog and soldiers was so critical my mind could not handle it. Before long, I noticed I had stopped fearing capture. A supreme confidence rolled over me in waves, making me foolishly indifferent to what might happen next.

Eventually my stalkers withdrew, chatting and laughing on into the night as if this was all such great fun. When their voices became fainter, my ears became hypersensitive to every noise around me. For a long while, there was no sound other than a gentle whistling through the pines as a slow wind came up. The air movement was delicious beyond words, but potentially hid any rustling that just a few moments earlier I might have heard.

I considered my next move. If I only had a process to rely on, I would know what to do.

I could not stay where I was. I was too exposed, and next time I might not be so lucky if soldiers and a dog came by. Yet this spot had saved me so far, and I was not keen on letting it go, especially since I had no idea whether there might be a better place to hide up ahead.

Out came my compass. The dial was barely visible, but it did have some of the light left in it from when I shone a flashlight on it during the pre-launch briefing. I could see which way was north. The goal was to go in that direction and rendezvous with partisans who would take us in. Reaching them meant completing the exercise successfully; any other outcome—capture, or staying hidden in the forest—meant failure, at least as far as the course scoring went.

Some deep breathing helped me to ratchet my fear level down to a tolerable level. My slow, analytical approach started to kick back in. I saw again that there was no way to build a process to reduce the danger of this situation. To find a way to get through the night without detection I had to improvise, and that thought scared the daylights out of me.

I was convinced the whole premise of this event was an exercise in fighting the last war. The Army based it on Army Field Manual 21-77, *Evasion and Escape*, which I had read a few days earlier.

Last updated in 1958, the manual baldly stated that it derived from the experiences of World War II and Korea, which meant it contained nothing of the knowledge now emerging from Vietnam. Those earlier conflicts had quaint relics such as front lines and partisans, neither of which existed in the maelstrom of guerrilla warfare sweeping across Southeast Asia. This night would have been great training if I were behind German lines in 1944, striving to reach the French Resistance a few kilometers ahead across wooded European terrain. But this exercise did absolutely nothing to further my chances of survival in the tropical hell of a fluid war where neither side held ground for long, and the only safe way out was straight up on a rescue line from a helicopter.

As I lay in the dark, contemplating, it occurred to me that I had bought into the instructors' definition of what the exercise meant. They had said that escape was the only option, meaning we not only had to evade capture as we wound our ways north, but also had to escape by reaching the free zone. But what if that was not true? What if there was another possibility, such as only doing half the exercise by just evading, staying hidden and not even trying to reach the safe area? Failing the exercise would be far less painful than getting captured.

Given where I started, as a city boy who had never been in a fight, never participated in sports, and certainly never spent a night in the woods alone, success for me would be evasion—making it through the night without any of the scores of dogs and soldiers who were prowling the forest finding me.

Giving the exercise a new interpretation in that way buoyed me with a rush of adrenalin. Just evading was so far beyond anything I could ever have thought possible that it gave me an enthusiastic goal to strive for. Some of my classmates might call me a coward for not even trying to reach the partisans in the free zone. But they would have had no idea how much courage it took for me just to press on and survive this night of horrors without a dog or a soldier catching me.

o

I CLOSED THE compass and put it back in my pocket. I waited until the wind subsided, slowly raised myself from the leaves and brambles I was lying in and stood erect, facing north.

My assessment that this exercise was doing nothing to help me survive in Vietnam was too harsh. As I stood there and brushed myself off, I now recalled that the 1958 manual did have some words of wisdom.

"During World War II and in Korea, a vast majority of those taken prisoner were captured while in groups. The larger the group, the greater the chance of detection and eventual capture. In most cases, Americans were not taken prisoner while alone."

So far so good.

"If alone at the time of isolation and confronted by

a superior force, leave the immediate area rapidly for a hiding spot out of the path of the enemy advance. If possible, remain there until you collect your thoughts and make plans."

Been there, done that.

"When you lose contact with your squad or platoon, it is normal to experience a feeling of helplessness...If you are well briefed on evasion tactics, you will tend to react automatically to the situation, knowing you must quickly decide upon and execute a plan of action."[3]

I was not feeling helpless, simply scared. My briefing on evasion tactics had been precisely zero. And it was no shit that I needed to figure out what to do.

Hearing shouts and dog growls in the distance but nothing nearby, I took a few cautious steps, keeping my arms in front of me so I would not do any more damage to my face. I discovered that walking at night in a dark forest played enormous tricks on the mind. I would take a few steps and then freeze, certain the object looming up to my right or left was a man. Once I had stopped, I would see that the object was a tree and had only seemed to be moving because I was moving.

In the dark, I could not see any detail below the level of my knees. Periodically, I would snap a twig loudly and expect ten flashlights to come alive and swing in my direction. I would freeze and swear under my breath, and when nothing materialized, I would continue, hands out in front, groping the dark. I continued this way for a hundred meters.

---

3. FM 21-77, *Evasion and Escape*, May 1958, p38 of PDF, p35 of manual: https://www.scribd.com/doc/96399177/Fm21-77-Evasion-and-Escape-1958

Then to my right, at about two o'clock and thirty meters away, I heard the unmistakable sound of footsteps. I dropped to a crouch. Silence. Another pair of steps. More silence. Then a few more steps. They were moving away from me and pushing back brush as someone walked slowly through the dark. I was sure it was not a soldier, because they always worked in pairs, or at least that is what they wanted us to believe. The only lone soldiers out here were the ones with dogs, and I heard no chain or growling. It had to be some poor schmuck like me who was out of his mind with fear as he tried to move north.

I took no chances. I settled from a crouch into sitting on my bottom to wait him out. At length he took more steps, continuing away from me, and soon he was far enough away for me to feel comfortable about resuming my own trek.

I took out the compass and checked it again. Even though I was not trying to reach the partisans, I still wanted to move north. I would be following behind the bulk of the captors, covering ground they had abandoned. At the same time, I would avoid remaining in the far rear area, where they might choose to make a sweep to look for stragglers. Staying close to my enemy in this way made sense to me, so I struck out to the north again.

Walking slowly, palpating the darkness ahead, I began to form an idea of what I was looking for. My first safe space had been at the base of a tree, which meant I was not out in the open. A tangle of fallen branches from the tree had given me quick cover. Yet it was a miserable type of cover, with sharp sticks digging into me from all directions.

Three meters ahead was a looming dark patch of brush about four meters in diameter surrounding a large pine tree. The forest floor was full of patches of thick, bushy growth like this that were sometimes waist high and exceedingly difficult to walk through. The path of least resistance was to go around those patches. So if I hid *inside* one of them, soldiers without dogs would be likely to pass me by. Dogs would still sniff me out, but there were half as many dogs as there were soldiers, so the brush still improved my odds.

I groped my way to the edge of the growth I had spotted, listened for any suspicious noises, and dropped to my knees. I burrowed all the way in until I reached the tree trunk and patted it with my hand. Even though it was illogical, I felt safer being next to a tree, perhaps because one had saved me just a while earlier.

Once inside the burrow, I felt more secure but now faced a completely new series of concerns. I remembered the snakes. We had heard there were black rattlesnakes in these woods, but we could not trust everything the enlisted instructors told us. They loved to put fear into young lieutenants at every opportunity. Still, lying on the ground I could imagine snakes and all sorts of other creatures that might not take kindly to my intrusion. Spiders, scorpions, even ants could be a real danger. Plus, for all I knew I was lying in a bed of the poison ivy that was common throughout the Georgia woods. What was I doing in there?

o

OUTSIDE, ABOVE THE brush, the buzzing of mosquitoes was incessant. They had stayed away from me because of all the repellent I was wearing, and they were the last thing I was expecting down here at ground level. They turned out to be the worst problem I faced, constantly dive-bombing into my ear.

I quickly grabbed my bottle of repellent and wiped its liquid into every crevice of my ears, eyes, and nose, putting more on my head, neck, and hands for good measure, stinging my injured lips as I did. It was crude and oily, unlike the light and fragrant repellents that would follow a half century later.

"Take that, you bastards," I whispered.

The repellent stopped the dive-bombing but not the buzzing, which continued unabated. The only advantage was that it took my mind off the snakes and other venomous beasts that might be taking over stalking duty from the soldiers.

I turned over on my back. The stress had exhausted me physically, and even more so mentally and emotionally. Little wounds pricked my arms, legs, and torso, and my lips were throbbing and stinging. I tried to avoid licking them because they had shoe polish and insect repellent all over them. But I kept forgetting and had nothing to clean my tongue on except my sleeve, which also had insect repellent and dirt on it and only made things worse. I did have a canteen of tepid water, but the mouthpiece was filthy. If I pursed my lips, I could get a few drops of clean water and swish it out amid heightened pain signals from my lips.

I listened intently for any sign of activity in the area and heard none. In the silence, I found it impossible to stay alert, and alternately dozed and awakened with a snort when I realized I had fallen asleep.

After a particularly long catnap, I awoke with a start. Jesus, I could hear someone walking *south* towards my position. Determined cracks and snaps of twigs gave a clear sign someone or something was moving towards me from the north. My heart raced with the thought that two enterprising soldiers had decided to loop back to see if there were any stragglers. I heard no dog, so maybe they would pass me by. I trained my ears on the source of the noise, and it shortly morphed into the sound of a branch tapping the tree above me from a gust of wind, then nothing. No one was coming. It had been a bad dream.

I thought of home. Four days earlier, the Watts riots back in LA had ended after close to a week of mayhem that resulted in thirty-four deaths and three thousand arrests. Yet right now, I wished I were in LA instead of in this insect-infested burrow.

I shivered. I had been still for an hour or more and all the perspiration had dried off. The breeze that tapped the branch above me had cooled me off to the point where I was cold. That amazed me, because it had to be at least eighty degrees on this hot Georgia night. However, that was almost twenty degrees below my body temperature, so a shiver was certainly possible.

On our utility belts the only equipment we had that night were the compass, the canteen, the repellent, and a plastic poncho. Still on my back, I removed the poncho from my right side and put it on my chest, unfolding it in the few inches of space between me and the top of the burrow until I got it undone. I managed to get the poncho unfolded but it bunched up between my chest and my knees. There was no room to sit up, so I tried to grab the lower end of it with my boots and pull it flat. But my grip kept slipping. I did manage to cover myself just below the knees and decided that would have to do.

My exertion and the impermeability of the plastic supplied instant warmth, so much so that I had to lie still to avoid sweating again. The heat wave passed, the breeze brought fresh air, and I soon was fast asleep.

Later in the night, I once again awoke to the sound of someone working their way south. I knew it was another dream, but it was so *realistic.* The breaking of brush was directional in orientation and got progressively louder with each crack. I was convinced I was hallucinating like before, but this time no shiver followed the dream. I tried to move but I could not. Paralyzed, I was fully aware of louder and louder noises coming near me but could not even lift a little finger in response.

I had read somewhere that this was a normal part of sleep. During the rapid eye movement or REM phase when the most active dreaming took place, the body went into paralysis to prevent arms and legs from flailing all over. That useful tidbit supplied little comfort, however, because the noise kept getting closer, louder, and now I could hear muffled voices: no words, just incoherent syllables strung together.

I had also read that sometimes it was possible to break out of REM-induced paralysis by moving something—anything—I could extend into larger activity. I tried blinking my eyes. I could do it, but it did not stop the paralysis. I turned my wrists from side to side, or thought I did, but they were not moving. I moved my right ankle back and forth with the heavy toecap on my boot leveraging gravity to accelerate the movement. Gradually, I was able to move my whole leg and then come into full body control.

There were no voices, no people smashing through

the growth, only the wind in the pines.

I took several deep breaths and fell back asleep.

o

THE NEXT TIME I awoke, it was first light. Minute by minute, the darkness lifted, and I could see straight up through the brush of my burrow. I spied the top of my large tree and a small patch of sky that started out gray and gradually turned blue. The distant shouts and growls of the night had disappeared, replaced by a chorus of birds chirping in the trees.

Despite appearances, this was a dangerous time. The exercise would continue through to 0900 hours, and now the captors had the advantage of daylight to flush out anybody who might have eluded them so far. I had no watch and could not recall how they would signal the end of the event, so I stayed where I was. I would much rather fail the exercise than get abused at the last minute.

I had to pee. I had had to go when I first jumped off the truck, but in all the night's drama had utterly disregarded the urge. Now I *really* had to go, and this presented a big problem.

The dogs were urine specialists. Their doggie brains were flooded with all sorts of meaningful information when they got a whiff of another dog's pee, and I imagined human pee was no different. It was acrid and pungent, an aromatic beacon any German shepherd in the vicinity would latch onto and follow.

I considered my options. I could hold it and die a thousand deaths of discomfort until an all clear sounded. I could sneak out of the burrow, run forty meters to pee in a location that would serve as a decoy, and then return to my hiding spot—stupid, given that now the sun was almost completely up. Alternatively, I could turn on my side, dig a trench, fill it with offensive liquid, and cover it up like a cat. I liked that idea the best, but the mosquitoes were still at it in the burrow, and I was reluctant to put insect repellent on my pecker. Moreover, given my luck, I was likely to dig the trench improperly and have it all flow back towards my groin, soiling my fatigues with the unmistakable evidence that during the exercise I had peed in my pants.

After the night I had just spent, all this was too much to think through. I decided to listen to the birds and see if I could fall back asleep. I apparently had no problem doing so because the next thing I heard was the whine of a diesel engine chugging along a forest road, broken periodically by a voice over a bullhorn: "*The exercise is over. Repeat. The exercise is over. Walk to the nearest road and wait to be picked up. Repeat. The exercise is over.*"

This could be a trap, but in looking out at the sun I could see it was too high in the sky for it to be earlier than 0900. Not that I was an expert in such matters, but I had to pee.

I sat up in the burrow, now seeing that the growth was not as thick as I had thought it to be at night. Then I stood up and stomped my way out of the undergrowth to a clear spot where I relieved myself with joyous abandon, mosquitoes be damned.

I found a road and waited. I heard the grind of a diesel in low gear coming from around a corner to my right and suddenly was nervous about the consequences I might face for what I did that night. But the truck was half full of guys like me who had hidden out, and soon a small fleet of other half-full trucks joined us on the trip back to the barracks. The penalties for simply hiding might be severe, but at least I was in good company.

Despite the Army staff telling us that failure to reach the safe zone was not an option, they nonetheless seemed to divide the class into three cohorts. At the top were those who reached the objective without getting caught. At the bottom were those who did get caught. And in the middle were the truckloads of guys like me who got credit for successfully hiding out all night, even if we did not reach the partisan free zone. I figured the instructors had to have been thinking something similar to this because after the course ended, they sent me a letter saying I had graduated in the top ten percent of my boot camp class.

o

I WAS JOYOUS that I had made it through the night uninjured.

But that was no thanks to my winning recipe. I had to abandon it because I knew the only way to succeed in the exercise was to be bold and daring, meaning to be an extrovert for real. I could never have been outgoing enough to triumph in this situation.

As soon as I let go of the recipe and went to the source of the fear—the idea I held that my only option was to take the terrible risk of trying to escape, rather than just to evade—I was able to cope constructively. Reframing the evasion part of the trial to be a huge potential success caused both the fear and the urgency to engage in my recipe to decline.

That was a key shift in consciousness that would stay with me my whole life. From then on, I saw that any meaning I held in my head was only an interpretation. It was not an unvarying truth, and to treat it as such closed off a whole universe of additional possibilities that might support me better as a human being. Knowing that provided me with a deeper sense of security than any recipe ever could.

> *"I saw that any meaning I held in my head was only an interpretation."*

With four girls in a row, I had tried to follow a recipe and done a lot of damage to myself. Even though I was still in contact with the two in Rio, I was completely free of Anabela and Roberta, and was open to whatever girl might come my way next.

Soon after the evasion and escape exercise ended, I was on my way to Baltimore to complete my Army Intelligence School training. In October, I would meet a girl in New York who might help me heal.

# Chapter 8
# Love and War

OCTOBER 1965. DUNDALK, MARYLAND. One cloudy afternoon, I moved into an apartment just outside of Baltimore with Les Gorman, a skinny and toothy second lieutenant I had met at Fort Benning.

The crisp fall air brought a wonderful atmosphere of promise. Would it include meeting a girl? Possibly, because my cousin Angie in Brooklyn had done a lot to set the stage with one of her girlfriends at New York University. The girl, whose name was Ida Bergstrom, was so favorably disposed after a year of hearing about me that when I met her, I was relaxed despite having no process to lean on. I did not need to be extroverted to approach her. I could just be myself.

Ida had a pleasant, attractive face, a slim figure, and beautiful legs. She dressed in good taste and wore her hair long, so that while her femininity was not overpowering, it was unmistakable.

When I first saw her, I had no thunderbolt of chemical desire, but her gentle warmth soon grew on me. Ida was sure of herself, easygoing, and cheerful. She gave a picture of internal happiness that was contagious.

She was warm and inviting, open to touch. It had been six months since I had anything physical to do with Roberta, so the slightest contact with Ida brought tremendous satisfaction.

Ida was just as introverted as I was. Neither of us was adept at playing games. We both had been hurt in the past and saw in each other a sympathetic companion who would not even know how to cause pain. I felt so wholesome in her presence.

o

I SPENT THANKSGIVING 1965 with Ida at her parents' modest house on Lake Candlewood just outside Danbury, Connecticut. It was unfamiliar and marvelous; not since Brazil could I remember having been so careless of time.

In Ida, I had stumbled across just the kind of girl I now realized I valued. As a student of psychology, she had a deep and sincere concern for human life and a desire to discover her own answers about it. She was one of the most gentle and affectionate girls I had known, one highly sensitive to my moods and desires, one who could talk ethics or kiss and hold me at four in the morning, do something for me before I asked or get me to do something for her with a wordless request.

Despite all the positive signs that Ida was different, I felt myself pulling back. For days I had tried to analyze my own feelings, to discover why such a girl did not have me in hand, and I drew a blank. The scars from Roberta ran deep—I would no longer let myself fall in love without an idea of what I was getting into.

Something gnawed at me, but I could not pinpoint it.

In the experiences with Anabela and Ana Maria, I

was focused on the goal of getting or avoiding the girl. But my devotion to the process to achieve that end left me blind to whether the goal was worthy in the first place. That had prevented me from seeing how wrong either one would have been for me as a life partner.

I knew Ida had grown up in a world different from mine. Her family was steeped in reserved communications, conservative morals, and traditional religion. But now I am embarrassed to say it did not even occur to me that one day she might embrace all of that. I was so taken with the warm sense of shelter she provided, that I did not detect the possibility that she, like the others, might not be the person to spend my life with.

Instead, I believed that because we were young, we could overcome the way her parents raised her. And as our relationship developed, I did not look too closely because she was sustaining me through challenging times.

A week after Thanksgiving, I lay in bed back in Baltimore scanning the dots of light on the ceiling that filtered through the curtains from the parking lot outside. I had written her and thought over her reply. Her letter, quiet and gentle, made me realize she was beginning to love me. She said she could sense how much I wanted to be near her, to hold her close to me. And she had asked herself, "What more can I give?"

Ever analytical, I read the letter many times and turned my concerns into a sequential process, ticking them off one by one. She was not the prettiest girl I had ever gotten close to, but Anabela taught me that external attractiveness counted for nothing. Internal beauty was what counted, and Ida's was abundant. Ida was not the most talented girl I had ever met, but Ana Maria taught me that music was no substitute for the kind of intimacy Ida repeatedly expressed. Neither was Ida the most analytical girl in my life, but Sofia taught me that analytics often just got in the way of love. Ida's thinking was clear and direct, and I respected her. Overall she was the anti-Roberta, someone of great stability and self-confidence who made me feel good about myself every time I was with her. She was the first girl I had ever been with who made me feel safe. I felt no need to protect myself from her in any way.

I saw my worries were phantoms. I started to sense there were no restraints, no faults, no shortcomings, no negative factors blocking the possibility of loving her. As soon as I let go of resistance, the love began to shine through. Lying in bed, I began to see all she had to give, and that she, too, was lonely and in search of a tender person to share life with. I cried tears of joy recognizing I had found someone so special I no longer needed to keep looking for love.

Over the next few weeks, my devotion to Ida grew stronger each day, taking on new and deeper roots within me. A new Beatles song called "Michelle" ran endlessly through my head: "I love you; I love you; I love you / That's all I want to say. . ."

o

AFTER CHRISTMAS, I was back at Lake Candlewood. Looking down from the house, I could see that so far, there were no patches of ice around the shoreline that would signal the true arrival of winter.

Ida's parents, Leo and Kate, were good people. They worked hard and only wanted what was best for their four children, of whom Ida was the eldest. That said, a cultural divide separated me from them that was as wide as the gap between the beaches of California and the snows of Minnesota where they had been raised.

Of Swedish descent, Leo had a full head of white hair even though he was only in his forties. He was handsome, outwardly jovial, and inwardly aloof. Kate, perky and happy, looked very much like the future actor Meg Ryan in *When Harry Met Sally*. Kate had Finnish ancestors and often served fruit salad made with little marshmallows.

Immigrants from Scandinavia had heavily influenced the culture in the Minnesota where Leo and Kate grew up. People called it "Minnesota nice." On the plus side, it included reserved manners, gracious courtesy, and friendly politeness. On the minus side, it was truly—at its core—about keeping up appearances, and it could be exhausting pretending to be something no human actually was all the time.

When I walked in with Ida, I likely had three strikes against me. First, I grew up in liberal, anything-goes California, where people simply laughed at the somber attitudes of the Midwest. Second, I came from a family in show business, which went out of its way to ridicule the strictures of Midwest thinking in a public and articulate way. And third, I was a soldier, potentially a love-'em-and-leave-'em Lothario who could ship out at any time. If Garrison Keillor of *A Prairie Home Companion* was to be believed years later, the conservative inhabitants of the Upper Midwest had a dark outlook on life: when things were going well, they knew that if they just waited a bit, surely things would get worse.

The Bergstrom's unpretentious house on the hill overlooking Lake Candlewood was the only place Ida and I could be together, and that was a big deal. I lived in Baltimore, and she lived in New York City with a roommate in a women's dorm. It meant we could not have time alone together unless we were right under her parents' noses.

I wanted Ida to go back to Baltimore with me and brought it up at dinner.

"It will only be for two days, and I'll bring her right back," I explained.

Leo frowned. Kate grimaced. Looking down at the table, she said, "We don't think that is such a good idea, Ben. You hardly know each other."

With two short sentences she succeeded in keeping up appearances and putting me in my place. From their faces, I could see their position was firm.

We should not have been surprised at their refusal, but we were. Ida became wistful and sad. When I saw her sweet face with such a look of pain on it, my own sadness vanished. We retreated to the downstairs bedroom that belonged to her brother, who was away. I took her in my arms, talked softly to her, played the guitar, and sang to her for two hours. When I sang "The Twelfth of Never," a popular Johnny Mathis song, my eyes shone with tears.

o

THE NEXT MORNING, there was frost on the ground. In a quiet moment, Ida and I sat again in her brother's bedroom. It was carved out of the hill and always had a musty smell.

We talked deeply and decided we were so much in love that we wanted to get married. Not right away, but in the future when I had finished with the Army and grad school. The date was three and a half years away, yet we now were committed to each other and felt wonderful about it.

Around Ida, my craving for process was fading into the background. That made intimacy more possible with her than with any girl I had ever known. When we were near each other, we jumped up and down like little kids, hardly able to contain ourselves. The frigid reaction of Ida's parents—such a contrast to the physical warmth of their home—was only driving us closer together. They had not seen my worth, had not understood her love for me, and were doing their best to slow our pace. This caused Ida great suffering.

In February, my father made a surprise business trip to New York. He was as dapper as always, wearing an understated sports coat and slacks that had a California flair to them. Ida and I had dinner with him and could not help telling him about our still-secret decision to get married.

He had already guessed what was in the air just by hearing me on tape recordings and seeing us together. It was wonderful for Ida and me to sit together and talk of our plans with someone who was so dear to me.

"She's exceptional, Ben," he said later when we were alone. "Mom and I hope it works out for you two to stay together."

"I guess after Roberta she's an improvement, no?"

He laughed. "They're not even on the same planet. Ida is wonderful, very solid. Strong emotionally. You couldn't ask for more."

As I drove back to Baltimore, I realized how important it was to have Dad's approval. He legalized us. He proved that the process I went through to dispel my doubts about Ida, going through a step-by-step examination of the concerns I had and methodically discharging them, had produced the right conclusion about her.

A few weeks after Dad's visit, we celebrated our February 1966 birthdays, Ida's twenty-first and my twenty-third, which fell just a few days apart. To commemorate that and make my commitment to her public, I gave her the Phi Beta Kappa honor society key I had earned at Stanford. It meant we were pinned—promised to each other. She put it on a chain around her neck to have something to show to her friends. I looked across the room at her wearing it and felt doubly proud: not only that I had won it, but also that I had such a wonderful girl to give it to.

In an act of stunning bravery, Ida wore the key home and showed it to her parents. They surprised us by receiving it warmly, and we did not know why. Maybe they recognized the academic achievement it represented and realized this kid who was sniffing around their daughter might not be such a schlemiel after all. Or maybe it finally penetrated that she and I were serious. Whatever the reason, we hoped this unexpected high point would be the beginning of a thaw between all of us.

It was not. During our weekend visits to Connecticut in March, Leo and Kate made little effort to reach out to me, make me feel wanted, or even comfortable. Nevertheless, by mid-April, we decided it was time to tell them our secret. I spoke to Leo in the family room downstairs while Ida talked to Kate on the upper level. He was cheerful and businesslike in his acceptance, as if agreeing to something he had seen coming from a long way off. But he never once said anything that led me to believe he thought I would make a good husband for his daughter.

With her mother, Ida ran into a brick wall. Kate refused to face the fact that Ida and I had chosen one another. She had none of the pleasantness and chilly grace that Leo had shown. Ida hardly knew what to say. Afterwards, Kate said not one word to me about having just learned I was going to be her son-in-law.

o

I HOPED I would be able to find contentment in my first Army assignment to match the happiness I had in my relationship with Ida, but soon discovered otherwise.

At the Army Intelligence School, I had received twenty weeks of training in how to conduct background investigations on people so they could receive a security clearance.

Almost one hundred and ninety thousand American troops were now in Vietnam and more were arriving every week, so there was a high demand for clearances. Yet after five months of teaching me a specific skill, the Army assigned me to a job in Manhattan for which I had absolutely zero preparation. I was to be the adjutant—the chief administrative officer of the Northeast Region of the 77th Intelligence Corps Group. It fielded three hundred men from Pennsylvania to Maine who knocked on doors to do background interviews.

As adjutant, I was the first person to know when the Army was ordering someone in the 77th to go to Vietnam. A lieutenant at the Pentagon in Washington would call with the list of names and serial numbers; I would then relay them to my superiors and to the hapless soldier's commanding officer. It was not pleasant, since, for all I knew, I was communicating a death sentence.

Oddly, I had been receiving such phone calls for months with only the vaguest notion my own name might be on that list.

One bright Tuesday in June, I headed into the office as usual. When the phone rang, I answered the lieutenant's call like every other time before, thinking about the poor guy whose life was about to change. But this time, the name and the serial number from the other end of the line were mine.

o

THE ALERT QUASHED any further introspection I might have engaged in about Ida. During the next year, she was to be my lifeline to sanity, and I only had eyes for the love and tenderness she had to offer.

What I did not realize was that even after four relationship failures, I had again lost focus about who a girl might really be. In my room in Baltimore when I was pondering why this sweet young lady had not captured my heart, I used the methodical process of my recipe to analyze each objection to her that I might hold. One by one they fell away, and I ended up embracing her less for who she was than for having successfully made it through the labyrinth of my analysis.

Unfortunately, I had focused more on the process of evaluating Ida than on the vague sense of unrest I had detected. The lack of any identifiable danger signs was a problem. It hid a mismatch between what my heart was saying and the conclusions from my logic. I was oblivious to any concern that a long-term relationship with her might have an unrewarding outcome. Instead, my winning recipe made it easy to put aside my doubts.

It had me rejecting them simply because I had completed a methodical analysis.

Long after Vietnam was over, those doubts would resurface. But right now, I was going to war and even if such thoughts had occurred to me, I would have squashed them. She was a rock, and I desperately sought to anchor myself to her.

In this, I was looking for a relationship to make the world safe for me to live in. The intrusion of the war was crude and life-threatening. The next eight months would force me to be even more extroverted than during that terrible night with the dogs in Georgia. Now, just as then, no recipe could protect me. But this relationship might.

In Vietnam, thoughts of Ida would be a safe emotional space to retreat into when the relentless pressure on me to be extroverted got to be too much. That space would allow me to be more comfortable with my introversion, rather than try to flee from it through a recipe. It was only a short-term solution, but I welcomed it.

o

SHORTLY AFTER THE terrible phone call from Washington, Ida and I met at my Brooklyn apartment. We lay down together and felt the closest thing to despair we had ever known. We held each other and cried as the blackest, most irrational feelings and thoughts wormed into us in an unending stream. I pressed her body against me and felt like I wanted to die. That day, the United States had bombed Hanoi and Haiphong for the first time, and it made the danger inherent in going to Vietnam frighteningly tangible.

My forthcoming deployment to Vietnam aggravated

our already-tense relations with Ida's parents. Events came to a head over the long Fourth of July weekend in Connecticut. Originally, Ida and I had planned to be engaged in a year, after she graduated from NYU, but with eight months of separation facing us we decided to have a ring on her finger in the next four weeks. Leo and Kate were firm that they did not want us to get engaged before I went overseas.

We were at a low ebb when Dad called me at the office few days later. In his gentle, rich voice, he shared that he had been looking into a ring for us. He called to say he found that we could get a beautiful one at a reasonable price with good terms.

"And don't worry about keeping in touch with each other while you're on the other side of the world," he said. "I know buying tape recorders is probably more than you can afford, so let Mom and me get one for each of you. That way you can stay in close contact while you're separated."

He also told me not to worry about getting plane tickets for my planned three-week leave with Ida and my family in California. Even if we could not go on standby status for half fare, he and Mom would bring us out to LA anyway.

On the problem of Ida's parents, he had kind words, sober words of tolerance and patience. Having gone through tough times with Mom's father in past years, Dad said our love was the only thing that mattered. He asked us to just let go of all the issues we could not resolve with Leo and Kate.

When I told Ida about his unexpected call, we nearly cried. My parents' attitude was so diametrically opposed to that of Leo and Kate's that it hit us like a shot of adrenalin. In one chat, he managed not only to clear up the three things that worried us greatly—a ring, tape recorders, and plane tickets—but also to wrap them in love and support that helped to fill the void in us. I was going to war, and he and Mom would do anything they could to make things as easy as possible for us.

o

ON AUGUST 14, 1966, the sun rose over the Pacific at Laguna Beach at 6:14 a.m. Ida and I stood on a rocky promontory splashed by the waves. We looked out and saw each wave rushing towards us, hitting the rocks, then withdrawing with white spray and the sound of gentle sizzling as it passed over the sand.

I placed an engagement ring on Ida's finger and held her to me. We had been betrothed in spirit since last December, and now were engaged in fact for the world to see. The sights and sounds of the receding Pacific had symbolized peace to me ever since I was a child, and in that moment, I was more at peace with life than I could remember. I was openly defying the challenges from Ida's parents and the Army without any formula to rely on.

Two days later, we found ourselves enjoying three hours of delightful, childlike fun in the ocean. The lovely afternoon surf trickled off our backs in big drips. Yet at precisely that time, the fear came back. How could such a terrible thing as our impending separation exist in a world that produced the warmth and beauty of the afternoon we had just spent? We had seen it was possible to live in peace, away from violence and unhappiness, and asked why we had to become a part of so much agony in just a few days.

Adding to my fright was the ocean itself. Especially

at night, when I looked out over the dark Pacific and imagined that I had to cross every inch of it in a troop ship, then be deposited on a hostile shore where enemy soldiers and civilian sympathizers would try to kill me, it became too much to face. Across that black expanse was something more sinister than anything I had ever known, and I might not come back from it. Many men did not, or they came back maimed in some way that seemed to make life not worth living. The moonlit swells of the sea, propelled by the wind and forces deep within the ocean, were a living, moving reminder of the existential threat I faced by venturing out onto the water and landing in a place where life was cheap and could be extinguished with a single bullet.

o

ON AUGUST 29, Ida and I were back in Manhattan in her women's residence hall at NYU. It was early afternoon. We lay on her bed, holding each other. I was not supposed to be there, but nobody was enforcing the rules. At that moment, we had something much bigger on our minds. In a few minutes, we would be saying good-bye for the last time before I left for pre-deployment at Fort Bragg, North Carolina, with no idea of when we would ever see each other again.

The horns and sirens on Fifth Avenue had replaced the crashing of waves on Laguna beach, reminding us every second that we were no longer in California.

What do two people say to each other at a time like that? Over the centuries, many men went off to war and had to leave behind a woman they loved more desperately than anything in life. When the moment came to part, the pain was so searing, so crushing, that all words failed. I have no recollection of what we said to each other. I would never wish such an experience for any of our children, or for any children anywhere.

We held each other so tightly that we felt like we were merging into one. Then the time came to go, and I gently let go of her, kissing her face and her forehead as I moved away to begin gathering my things. Starting in ten minutes, I would be driving straight through Virginia on my way to Bragg and wanted to leave the room before both of us broke down.

We had agreed to say good-bye in her room where we had some privacy, rather than in the lobby downstairs or the street. I shouldered my gear, kissed her one last time, and walked out the door.

When I got down to Fifth Avenue, I walked no more than a few steps when I heard Ida behind me, "Ben! Ben!"

I dropped everything and turned as she ran to me, holding me tightly and trying hard not to cry. It was all I could do to hold back tears myself. It felt like we had done nothing but cry for weeks. It was the only process we had for coping, and except for talking with my parents, we had managed on our own.

I embraced her. "You are so strong, Ida. And so am I. We will get through this. I'll call you from Virginia in a few hours."

She nodded and we parted, my last image of her as I gradually backed away being that of a sad, forlorn girl standing in the middle of a broad New York sidewalk framed by tall buildings on either side.

During the six-and-a-half hour drive to an overnight stop in Fredericksburg, Virginia, I uttered not a word to myself in the car. I dared not turn on the radio for fear that "Michelle" would come on with its piercing lyrics of "I love you; I love you; I love you. . ." The separation ripped out a part of me. I held an emotionless face and looked straight ahead without knowing from hour to hour where I was.

o

AFTER WEEKS IN North Carolina, I received my departure orders. I was to embark for Vietnam on a troop ship that would leave from the docks at the Oakland Army Base near San Francisco.

Dad, Mom, and my sisters—Carla, 22, and Nan, 8—met me at the base the day my ship was put to sea. Mom had on her pointy-ended 1950s-style glasses that somehow still looked cute on her, covering eyes swollen from crying. Dad tried to smile but his eyes, too, were puffy and sad. Both girls were more wistful than I had ever seen them.

I was the eldest child going off to war. When it came time to go, I gave each of them a long, heartfelt hug.

I had never seen my father cry. I will never forget the sight of the tears running down his face after I hugged him and backed away to board the ship that would take me to Vietnam.

# Chapter 9
# Welcome to Vietnam, GI

NOVEMBER 1966. OAKLAND, CALIFORNIA. I hauled my duffel bag up the gangplank towards the guts of the ship that loomed in front of me.

The smell of saltwater and diesel fuel filled my nostrils. The air was crisp, only in the fifties despite the afternoon sun high above. After losing my way several times on board, I eventually found my cabin. I was the first man in so I pushed my duffel bag up onto one of the top bunks.

The USS *Gordon* was a World War II troop ship that the Navy had pressed into duty to transport soldiers from the West Coast to Vietnam. Over six hundred feet long and seventy-five feet wide, it was a self-contained universe that looked inward to create a sense of reality as it moved through an environment of nothingness.

As I walked through the ship, I could see this humming, pulsating world of compartmentalized steel slabs was able to light, wash, and feed itself in an uncanny deception of self-sufficiency. After we pulled away from the dock, it rocked gently from side to side as a condescending gesture to the flat sea that bore it.

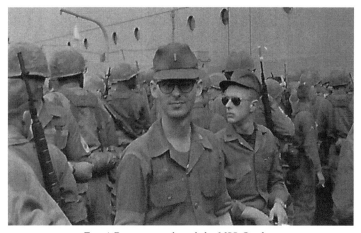

*Fig. 4 Preparing to board the USS Gordon.*
*Oakland Army Base, CA, 1966.*

From Oakland, the *Gordon* sailed under the Golden Gate Bridge and down the California coast to San Diego, where it took on more troops and supplies. We then put out to sea again, all of us pressed against the portholes with our transistor radios, trying to pick up rock and roll music from the San Diego stations. The music got fainter and fainter as we headed west.

Fittingly, one of the last songs I heard was "The Sounds of Silence" by Simon and Garfunkel. The echoes of the familiar America we all knew and loved were slipping away, replaced by the incessant crashing of the sea against the hull of the ship.

This was a Navy vessel, but we were still in the Army—an insane world of rank and authority, of duty and abundant free time, of work ostensibly justified by its relation to higher purpose but its present context relating only to survival. We wore uniforms, spoke of the time in hundreds, saluted, begged each other's pardon with respect, and stood in line to use the head. The

Army functioned as it did everywhere else in the world, and I took a bit of comfort in these rituals. I ate, read philosophy, and occasionally played a guy's guitar, oblivious to where I came from or where I was going.

Soon physical malaise underscored everything I did. The sea had become more self-expressive, and while not stormy or unduly rough, it churned with life and rocked the ship. Boredom and constant motion made me too sleepy to keep my mind occupied with positive things; I felt sluggish and worthless. My appetite vanished; all I could eat was just enough to keep hunger away.

The reality of the move to Asia became clearer with each day we spent at sea. Along with the other lieutenants who were shipping out with me, I was getting worried.

"Hey Dubchek," I said to one I had gotten to know, "do you ever think about getting hit or getting killed?"

"All the time," he said. "I can't get it out of my head. And for what? I could go home in a basket, and it wouldn't make a damn bit of difference."

Day by day, as the ship sailed further from America, I wanted a reward for having completed the initial step of the journey. But all I had was a purposeless daily routine. I tried to turn it into a process, but there was no meaningful outcome that it could produce. I felt cheated. Such thoughts swirled through my mind for hours until I was sick of them.

o

TEN DAYS WEST of San Diego and four days before Thanksgiving 1966, I was sitting at a table in the recreation room still trying to accustom myself to the rolling of the ship.

A Navy lieutenant came over and told me softly that there was a radiogram for me upstairs in the communications room. In the days before widespread satellite communications, the best way to get a message to a ship at sea was by radio. I followed him topside to a small chamber crammed with electronic equipment, signed for the message, and stepped into an exterior passageway. I looked out to sea to steady my stomach on the horizon before glancing down at the paper in my hand.

"Ben—I love you, Sweetheart. All my love, Ida." The stark, block letters moved me beyond words.

That afternoon I had listened twice to one of the tapes she sent me to hear on board. By some uncanny faculty of projection, she was able to foretell my needs three weeks in advance, offering me help as real as if she were standing beside me. She knew that I would listen to her in my bunk, that I would be conscious of the rocking of the ship and be sad about how far I was from her and my family.

Tears welled up in my eyes when she told me in words and by the ardor in her voice that she loved me. She said she was with me in thought every day and night, and she wanted me in her bed. She said I was strong; everything was all right in our world, and this separation would end before we realized it. I knew those things but still needed to hear them.

And the mail! She reminded me there would be a pile of goodwill and love waiting for me in Saigon. That gave me something concrete to look forward to on arrival.

A FEW DAYS after an unexpectedly sumptuous Thanksgiving meal on board, we made landfall in Vietnam at Da Nang. We then headed south for our second port of call, Qui Nhon, but a tropical depression blew in. It prevented us from docking, so we rode out the storm in the bay.

Being captive inside an enormous steel container that moved according to powerful forces of nature was terrifying beyond words. The ship would list to the right, then more to the right, then so far to the right that bodies and belongings would slam into the opposite wall. The great steel plates squealed as they twisted in ways beyond their capacity and took a final tilt to the right, each of us knowing that surely, this time, we would capsize and die as water rushed in and drowned us where we stood.

Then, after an eternity of no further movement, in a neutral zone between righting itself and tipping over, the ship would creak, shudder, and slowly, imperceptibly, begin to tilt to the left. The whole drama would begin again on the other side of the vessel, terminating in long moments of paralysis while the *Gordon* decided, contrary to the beliefs of everyone on board, it would not tip over that time either. Then it would start to the right again.

The delay left me uncomfortable, cooped up, and thwarted in my assault on Vietnam, for which I had summoned every ounce of my courage now that we were there. I turned into a bundle of nerves as I waited for the shipboard nightmare to end and the onshore ordeal to begin.

When it did end four days later, I prepared to disembark with my shipmates sixty miles southeast of Saigon at the port of Vung Tau. As I gathered my gear, I was in decent shape emotionally. Through her tapes Ida had given me the reassurance I needed.

I wrestled my heavy duffel bag off the top bunk and dragged it with scores of other men towards the enormous disembarkation door on the lower level. A landing craft was waiting just outside to take us ashore. Its big diesel engines emitted a menacing growl so loud we could hear it through the ship's hull. As the door slowly slid open, the sound became deafening. I reflexively squeezed the handle on my duffel bag until my fingers turned white.

o

AFTER SHELTERING US for over four weeks within its thick panels of gray steel, the *Gordon* discharged us into the open sun at Vung Tau on December 6, 1966. It was a sweltering Tuesday morning.

Along with several dozen other men, I stepped onto an open barge and looked across the water to see a tall, green jungle bobbing on the horizon. We felt naked—the barge exposed our chests to any small arms fire the Viet Cong might send our way.

Thankfully, there were no bullets. Once on land, we shuttled to a nearby airfield and avoided the dangers of the sixty-mile route into Saigon by flying to nearby Bien Hoa air base in a military transport.

As we drove from Bien Hoa into Saigon in the back of an open truck, I saw a vast, disorganized complex of crooked streets, swamps, canals, and tumbled-down buildings made of everything from reinforced concrete to tin cans. The place was absurdly gaudy and shabby from the destruction and hasty reconstruction of war.

Streets were in poor repair, yet hundreds of

thousands of Vietnamese dressed in plastic sandals and lightweight clothes scooted deftly around chug-holes on Japanese motorbikes. Bombed-out bars stood next to new ones thrown up overnight. Buses and homes had wire screens over them as protection from grenades. Women shuffled by in the ancient dress of long-sleeved, Mandarin-collared silk gowns topped with coolie hats. Downtown, modern office buildings towered skyward with concertina barbed wire surrounding every inch of ground considered worth defending. Ruined buildings, armed men patrolling the streets, barbed wire and sandbags at major establishments, and military vehicles zipping back and forth made the war visible everywhere. The stench of garbage and putrid water seized my nose.

The compound where we had our temporary quarters in the northeast suburb of Gia Dinh was no better. Once an old villa set at the junction of the Saigon River and a major tributary, the place now had hastily built barracks, latrines, offices, and guard posts surrounding it on all four sides. Cheap red adobe tiles and cracking walls characterized the outer structures, while lofty ceilings, inlaid tile, and iron grillwork showed what remained of the former splendor of the central building.

Thirty of us moved into the second floor in what must have been a palatial dining hall. Despite its size, each of us had little more space than on board the *Gordon.* Our bunks were comfortable enough, but the heat, the filth on the ground outside, and the unreliable running water made the space foul.

I thought of Ida. I could not wait to get my hands on the pile of tapes and letters from her that I knew were waiting for me somewhere in the compound.

I was organizing my gear on my bed when KA-BAM!!! A violent, concussive explosion ripped through a bridge just outside, deafening us and pushing compressed air against our chests. I hit the floor and pulled my mattress on top of me as they had trained us to do, terrified at not knowing if the blast was the extent of the attack or only the opening round. I was thankful my reaction had been so automatic.

All the lights on our floor were still on, and somebody's radio was blasting out "Turn! Turn! Turn!" by the Byrds.

Guys were screaming, "Kill the lights! Turn off that goddamn radio!" The lights and music persisted.

"*A time to be born, a time to die. . .*"

"The lights! The lights!"

We had only been there for a few hours, so nobody knew where the switch was. After more screaming, someone did manage to darken the room, but the radio continued on with the maddening normalcy of its tune and lyrics.

"If you don't shut off that fucking radio, I'm going to blast it!" someone yelled. We all had been issued .45-caliber pistols and ammunition and were in a culture where shooting a radio out would have been just fine. The threat was real, and it did the trick. Silence now filled the darkness in which we lay, sweat accumulating under our backs from the unaccustomed weight and warmth of the mattresses on top of us.

The Viet Cong had loaded a river barge with explosives and rammed it into a piling supporting the bridge located adjacent to our building. The blast did not disable the bridge. Nor did the attackers follow up. But they scared the living bejesus out of two-and-a-half dozen young American lieutenants on their very first night in the country. This gave us all a taste of what was in store.

o

WITH MY EARS still ringing from the blast, I started observing my mind. I noticed that as soon as I arrived at the compound, I became complacent. I was on dry land, would be eating fresh food, and soon would finally have a job to do. As an introvert, I mostly lived in my head anyway, and the newfound pleasures of a less cramped setting than at sea made me blind to the world I had just walked into.

The explosion remade my attitude. Instead of being content, I was now wary; instead of trying to ignore the present circumstances, I dove into them with a critical eye. When I went back to unpacking, I stopped daydreaming about a fresh meal, and made sure I could quickly get my hands on my ammunition if needed.

The result was a unified consciousness unlike any I ever had. I still pondered a lot, because that is what introverts do. But I also checked every sound, every smell, and every sight around me for danger. I felt like an exterminator looking for rats.

My gut told me that in Vietnam, it was critical to stop skewing my thinking towards my internal environment and instead to unify it with the outside world. That resulted in a dual awareness that stayed with me and brought me at least a little sense of security the whole time I was in the war zone.

Good thing, because at my new duty station in Pleiku, I would soon have an acute need for it.

# Chapter 10
# Pleiku

DECEMBER 1966. PLEIKU, SOUTH VIETNAM. After weeks in Saigon, I was thrilled to step down the ladder of a military transport five days before Christmas into the cool air of a sunny morning in Pleiku. This was my new duty station in the Central Highlands—three hundred miles north of Saigon.

I was now on a high plain surrounded by distant mountains, making it possible to see for miles in all directions. Clumps of trees did exist along the perimeter of the base where I would live and work, but even so, it was a huge improvement over the congestion of Saigon and the nearby jungle that could harbor the Viet Cong.

Here, many large combat units were in the area, including the US Fourth Infantry Division. I was no longer in an isolated compound. If anything happened, the Fourth would respond. Blankets and freedom from mosquitoes were the rule. My bed was comfortable, the water was pure (even hot on occasion), and the food far surpassed the fare at the squalid compound in Gia Dinh. And because of Ida, I had a wonderful Christmas. Her many presents, letters, tapes, and pictures all brought her presence to my side. I dreamt of her every night.

Best of all, I now had a job to do. I was working at the II Corps Headquarters of the Army of the Republic of Vietnam (ARVN), one of only four such operations centers in the country. The work was clean, safe, and mildly challenging. All I did every day was combine disorganized scraps of information into larger wholes in order to produce military intelligence. Working with maps, written reports, and common sense, I tried to figure out what was happening in our area.

Sometime after midnight in the early morning of January 7, 1967, the other three officers in our room and I were sound asleep when we heard the ka-*whump!* ka-*whump!* of incoming mortar rounds blowing craters in the ground so close by that we feared they would hit us next. More rounds landed, and an air raid siren started to wail, directed at the thousands of men in the Fourth Division and the two hundred or so in our compound.

Our facility was in the shape of a square. The rooms formed the four sides of a grassy courtyard in the center, and each room housed four officers. The building sat right next to the Fourth Infantry Division, but rather than being enclosed within that unit, we were on the side of it, sharing a common front with the forest. A perimeter fence separated the US installation from the trees and growth just beyond.

Bedlam ensued in our room. The commander had assigned all of us defensive posts in a ditch facing the forest behind the compound, but before we could get there, we had to find our pants, our helmets, our flak jackets, our weapons, and our boots. It was pitch black, and nobody could find anything. The incessant screaming of the air raid siren and the booms of the growing mortar response from the Fourth Division made it hard to think.

I found my pants and shirt and got them on quickly, then put on my heavy steel helmet to protect my head in case a shell landed nearby. My flak jacket was hanging off the end of my bunk, so I easily slipped that on, but my boots were a problem. At first, I could not find them in the dark, and then when I did find a pair, I wasn't sure if they were mine.

"Hey, whose boots are these?" I said, as if anybody could see them in the dark.

"Doesn't matter!" said one of the men. "Jam your feet in and get the hell out of here!"

They *were* mine, but in the rush, I could not get my feet into them easily and had to unlace them first. Between all the noise outside and the frantic cursing of my roommates asking where the fuck was this or that, the stress was unbearable. At length, I got dressed, grabbed my .30-caliber machine gun and two magazines of shells, and stumbled out the door into the darkness.

My post in the V-shaped trench behind our compound faced the perimeter fence. I threw myself into the depression and rested my body against the side that faced the fence, with only my helmet and carbine above ground, thankful that once again Army protocol meant I did not have to invent what to do. Every few meters, men positioned themselves along the trench the same as me. In the daylight when they had assigned us to these points, it all seemed like a good plan. Now the location exposed us to any round that might be coming down upon us from beyond the fence, making where we lay feel like a death trap.

Exposing us even more were parachute flares that

the Fourth Division was spreading across the sky. Those bright beacons went up a thousand feet, deployed their parachutes, and descended slowly, ever so slowly, swinging back and forth in a way that made every shadow seem to move with a life of its own. The silhouettes they created scared me out of my wits, making me see things moving in the semi-darkness.

The flares illuminated a wide area of the ground on behalf of the helicopters that the Fourth was now scrambling into the sky. The gunships had searchlights and rockets of their own. I looked left and right and saw the flares also illuminating our pitiful little defense line. If anybody in the forest wanted to pick us off, they would have had no problem.

But then the Fourth Division fully opened up. In a colossal response, they began to pump tons of ordnance into the area beyond the fence. The flashes of light and deafening booms of shells hitting the earth showed what a systematic response of an all-Army approach looked like. I felt joy and pride. But the all-consuming fear did not leave me.

The experience was doubly cathartic. First, it revealed that my recipe of handling life with stepwise processes was useless against fear, because when the fear got big enough, the recipe simply disappeared. Until that moment, I was used to having a crisis spur my recipe into begging me to launch a process. But now I realized the recipe was no match for an existential threat.

Secondly, in the trench, the attack made me believe I *was* the fear, that it was my very identity. But when the all-clear sounded I realized I was actually the person *having* the fear. This made it easier to back away from the recipe a bit; I was able to watch it in operation from the outside and not be so stuck inside of it. In that way it helped me to escape from the prison of my own mind, something that, as an introvert, I regularly inhabited. By changing my identity in this way, shifting from fear-as-myself to context-as-myself, I got enough distance from the fear to stop shaking.

o

ON AN OVERCAST afternoon the day after the attack, I was sitting in the Order of Battle section where I worked. Operation Cedar Falls had just launched in the Iron Triangle area just west of Saigon with thirty thousand American troops, and we hoped an operation that massive would shorten the war.

"*The attack made me believe that I <u>was</u> the fear, but I was actually the person <u>having</u> the fear.*"

I was thinking about how I still was not used to the smell of the crisp, dry air coming in through the window when I noticed an unfamiliar captain walking by in the hall. Paunchy and dark-haired, he looked vaguely like an owl. I learned his name was Derek Quigley, and he had been in the country even less time than I had.

Major Muntz, who oversaw us, came in shortly and asked a volunteer to transfer from Order of Battle to the Target Center, the other team in our unit and the one Quigley was going to supervise. After some thought, I went for it. I knew I was not essential in my current role and did not want the commander to send me to the dangers of Kontum to the north or Ban Me Thuot to the south.

The transfer was the right decision. But it put me in conflict with the two active and experienced lieutenants who currently ran the Target Center. They resented the fact that someone new, the hapless Captain Quigley, was now above them, and that another lieutenant, a greenhorn and their peer, was now joining their team.

They were enthusiastic about their work—locating targets for the Air Force to bomb—and excellent at it. Lieutenant Neubauer, compact and thickset, was from Montana and wanted to be a rancher. He had the hands and the attitude for it. He could drive cattle or men; it was all the same. Lieutenant Beadle, from Maryland, was tall and thin. He had perennially pursed lips and was strict in his work. He always gave the impression that he was hiding a riding crop behind his leg and might whack it across your backside if you gave him any lip.

The oversized room where the two lieutenants sat had one long desk running along the back wall and another along a side wall.

"Where do I put my stuff?" I asked.

"You need to find someplace else," said Neubauer.

"Yeah, someplace else," said Beadle.

Four people could have worked in that L-shaped space, but I felt like I was in *Alice in Wonderland*. The Mad Hatter and the March Hare were telling me there was no room at the tea table.

Incensed at such pettiness, I put my things down and walked down the hall to a storeroom. There I found a small, Army-issue, dark green folding table that had nicks all over it. It would do nicely. I walked back into the Target Center, unfolded the table, and slapped it down on the concrete floor in the exact center of the open space of the L behind these two jackasses. I brought out my nametag, snapped it onto the table, and arranged my papers behind it. Another trip to the storeroom produced a wooden folding chair, which I set up behind the desk. That made it official: I was now a part of the team, whether these guys liked it or not.

I walked next door to meet the Vietnamese Army officers who worked there. Recalling that Vietnam had been a French colony for over sixty years, I dredged up some phrases from my days in France three years earlier and greeted them in French, which they spoke better than English. I made an ironic joke about how elegant they all looked in their dirty boots and hoped their laughter was loud enough to carry out into the hallway so that Neubauer and Beadle could hear it. I wanted them to understand that I was a person they had to reckon with.

A few weeks later, on an unusually chilly afternoon, I was sitting in the Target Center doing my work when I saw Neubauer get up from his table and walk towards me. The hair rose on the back of my neck.

He and Beadle had been relentless for days. Even though we were all first lieutenants working on the same team, they continued to badger me, insisting I had no idea what I was doing. The more it went on, the more I thought of lashing out. But I managed to step back and see that their aim was probably to provoke me into doing exactly that so they could pressure Quigley to transfer me out of Pleiku. At first, I was not sure how to defend myself, but I soon saw the solution could be for me to build a data retrieval system.

The device was simple. In the days before personal

computers, there was no way for the three of us to store and retrieve the large amount of data that came in each day. That did not matter too much because the reports were time-sensitive; the location of the Viet Cong two days ago was of little value today. But by breaking the reports down into categories, creating an index, and jotting down a one-sentence summary of what each report contained and where they were filed, I gained a complete understanding of the situation. When challenged, I could support myself with facts and shut my detractors up. The new process allowed me to be self-confident and more outgoing.

At times, what these predatory lieutenants told me was constructive, so I accepted the content even if the delivery was caustic. But if they made an error, I recorded it into my little database. The screw-ups were valuable insights into how they thought. It also gave me more ammunition for shutting them up.

At age four, I could never have faced anybody down about anything—I was too introverted. Now I needed to confront my two peers, and I believed I could not do it unless I used a process, namely organizing intelligence into a database. I had no love for it. Maintaining it was tedious, boring, and spirit-destroying. But I knew no other way to cope. And it avoided my having to call out their behavior directly.

When Neubauer arrived at my desk, he wore both a scowl and a smile at the same time, a specialty of his.

"Plumb, you've been here for weeks and you still have no goddamn idea what you're doing. This is crap," he said as he threw a memo of mine on the table.

I stood up. He was more muscular, but I was an inch taller, so I was able to look down at him. "Look,

Neubauer, remember last week when you thought the aerial photography was the problem, and just like I said it turned out to be the infrared reports? You looked like a real dumb ass in front of the captain. So, you might want to listen to me on this one." The scowl disappeared, leaving only a sheepish smile.

In addition to direct confrontations such as this, the duo had perfected a "stealth assault" on me. It was to champion hard opposition on something, saying, for example, that doing things my way was worthless and stupid, yet later coming around to my way of thinking. They expressed repeated, grave doubts about the value of experiments I was conducting with intelligence information, yet when they needed something in a hurry they came to me for the data, because no one else was organizing the intelligence the way I was.

They slammed me so many times and I stood my ground with facts so often that they gradually backed off and my relationship with them improved. By outlasting their nitpicking and acid remarks, I turned myself into an authority on things they wanted to know.

Slowly, the three of us discovered we were moving onto common ground on some things. For example, I now agreed with them that our Captain Quigley was a jerk. He pretended to know things that he did not, seemed more interested in observing report protocol than guaranteeing good content, and did not have our backs. Despite that, Neubauer and Beadle had tired of baiting him; so while I now got along with him a little worse, they got along a little better, and we met in the middle.

This happened just as the room assignments in the compound changed, and I had to find a new home. The two of them were looking for a roommate so we talked,

*Fig. 5 In front of quarters shared with Neubauer and Beadle. Pleiku, South Vietnam, 1967.*

and soon I confidently moved into their quarters. From that point on, we got along fine. True to form, a process, my database, had again produced unintended consequences. But this time they were positive: good relationships with my peers and a new place for me to live.

o

AS MY ATTENTION shifted away from those two clowns, I learned one of the duties of each officer in our compound—lieutenants, captains, and majors—was to serve as Captain of the Guard. This happened on a rotating basis every few months. As was often true in the Army, the activity involved combining elements that were harmless and those that were terrifying.

One benign item was known as the "guard mount." It involved calling to attention, at dusk, the twenty or so enlisted men who would move out to their guard posts around the perimeter of the compound and spend the entire night awake looking for signs of infiltration or attack. You had to be a real manly man to do the guard mount right, which as a bespectacled intelligence officer, I was anything but.

Calling out "atten-*chun!*" in as throaty a voice as I could muster, I heard the sound die away in the late afternoon heat as soon as it left my lips. Ideally, I would have done this in a canyon so I could produce a series of echoes: "atten-*chun! –chun –chun...*" But on the plains of Pleiku, there was nothing for the sound to bounce against. After my command, the troops stood taller but did not stiffen their backs one iota.

That first step under my belt, my next task was to inspect the guard. This was the other benign item of the afternoon, but it was tricky because I had no idea what I was looking for. If it were up to me, I would just check to make sure they had fully loaded their extra carbine magazines with rounds and gotten enough sleep the night before so they could stay up all night tonight.

But it was not up to me, and I had to go through the charade of standing in front of each man, looking him from head to toe and finding something negative to say. I had to address the shine on his boots, the wrinkles in his uniform, or the closeness of his shave, all of which were of course essential to our mutual defense during the coming evening. Somebody who was really good at this would do it with such passion, such conviction, and so many obscenities that he would touch the core of each man to let him know he was a truly vile human being for daring to present himself for this guard duty in such a condition. But that was not me.

After the inspection, the scary part began. I stood in front of the group and said "at-*eeze!*" The men relaxed, spreading their legs apart and putting their hands behind them.

"You have all been advised what the password for tonight is. Do not forget it. I repeat, do not forget it." I could not say it aloud because only we twenty-one soldiers were supposed to know it for that night, and who knew what spies might be lurking about. The code was usually something like "*Red Dog.*" I was always concerned about the quality of these passwords. They were bland, unoriginal, and simple, so the men could easily remember them. However, that also made them quite easy to forget. I favored passwords like "*Rectal Thermometer*" or "*Yo Mama,*" but had to deal with "*Red Dog*" and the likes every time.

Why was this scary? Because if any of these fine gentlemen forgot the password, and I approached him on my rounds in the dark with a word he did not recognize, or did not acknowledge back to me, we could end up killing each other on the spot. I only had a .45, so his chances of survival were good. But he had a fully loaded automatic carbine and could plug me full of holes in seconds.

I dismissed the troops, and they fanned out to their posts. I retreated to the underground bunker where the Captain of the Guard hung out, along with the mosquitoes that seemed to appear nowhere else in the entire compound except in that hole. Unlike the soldiers, I could sleep. The cot and pillow in that concrete hovel made it look homey and inviting. However, before I could lie down, I had to wait for dark, and then make at least two trips around the entire perimeter, hearing "Halt! Who goes there?" twenty times and answering, "*Red Dog,*" before perceiving, "You may advance," rather than a hail of bullets coming my way.

The truly frightening part was that I was not supposed to announce my presence in the dark, but rather walk normally and see if the guard detected me. The Army supposedly designed this to keep the men alert, but more likely to reduce the number of surplus lieutenants. If a soldier panicked and forgot to ask me who went there, or thought the password was maybe *Green Rat* instead of *Red Dog*, I was toast.

Fortunately, I survived the forty encounters of my two nerve-racking trips around the perimeter and was able to go back to my insect-infested cell. Yet before I could sleep, I had to complete one other essential duty of the evening.

I had to go into the Non-Commissioned Officer's Club with a bucket and withdraw all the coins out of the slot machines. The Army provided them as a diversion for the troops, but only trusted officers to collect the money out of them. I carted the coins back to my hole, spread them on an aging, green folding table like the one I had carried into the Target Center, and counted them. The tallies done, I had to certify the amounts, put the money in bags, and turn them in. I conjectured that the funds were probably enough to buy a single nylon string on one of the hundreds of parachute flares that the US fired into the sky every time a Viet Cong stepped on a twig somewhere outside the fence.

I slathered mosquito repellent on my face and went back down into my dump to sleep, laughing at the madness of all this and trying to remember how many days were left before I could go home.

o

FOR SIX MONTHS, the rest of my tour passed with relatively little excitement. I thankfully faced no more attacks, and went to Singapore for a week on leave. A steady diet of tapes and letters from Ida kept me sane during long days of boredom, unappetizing meals, and post-nasal drips provoked by a string of cool and humid days.

A month before my tour ended, I climbed up to my bunk in the compound and grabbed the short-timer calendar that hung over the top of my bedpost on a string. I could smell the fresh evening air coming in through the open windows below me on the other side of the room.

Every soldier in Vietnam kept such a calendar, and mine was now getting short indeed. I had created a grid of over two hundred squares on a single piece of paper and numbered them backwards to stand for the days I had left before returning home for good and getting discharged from the Army. Crossing off each day was hugely satisfying, even when the progress seemed to be excruciatingly slow. One by one, the days fell away, and this evening there were only thirty left. Nice!

When I was down to nineteen days, I began to feel overwhelmed with everything I had to do before I could get out of Vietnam. There was another depressing all-night tour as Captain of the Guard, the assumption of all Neubauer's duties while he was gone for a few weeks, and the impatient wait for the port call paperwork that would take me home. In the days before email, I then had to figure out a way—quicker than the regular mail—to relay my arrival date to my family and Ida. And, at the very end, I had to spend three miserable days in Saigon to complete exit procedures.

I also needed to get mentally prepared for the huge transition that would await me when I got home. I had to get ready to be a civilian again and to be close to Ida physically, not just metaphorically. I had been admitted to the Harvard Business School in the class entering in September 1967, which meant I would only have two months to make the psychological change from Pleiku to Boston.

The nineteen days passed quickly. At work, the entire office turned itself upside down. We left the old South Vietnamese Army building where I had sat for so many days and moved into a new US facility complete with florescent lights and the smell of fresh paint. Neubauer had not been in for two weeks, Beadle was in Bangkok on leave, and in their places were two new second lieutenants whose focus and bright outlook were a refreshing change. To top it off, the weather had been beautiful, with plenty of sun after so many months of cool weather, a wonderful portent of the California warmth waiting for me.

On my last night in Pleiku, July 4, 1967, I recalled the final night Ida and I had spent in Laguna before beginning our long ordeal almost a full year earlier. The white fluff of the tide and the golden descent of the sun had captivated me. Sitting at my writing table back then, I thought about how subjective the experience of time was. I had written, "... [P]erhaps our long separation will be made short if we can adopt the proper attitude...[and] live at peace in the long months ahead."

It was hard to wrap my mind around the knowledge that we had traversed virtually every day of that huge monolith of time. So far, I had not suffered any of the harm I had feared I might, and had done so with no process to guide me other than the small database I had used to defend myself from Beadle and Neubauer.

Ida and I had triumphed over our separation, and now it was time to go home to her. The only remaining obstacle to our being together was that her parents still had the upper hand, but I was confident we would eventually find a way to change that.

With only a few days left, I flew to the Bien Hoa airbase near Saigon. The hassle of processing wore me out. I rushed about, carrying my bags and records from place to place, then found myself sitting with not a thing to do for hours on end, waiting for a ride to somewhere else. Luckily, I ran into Les Gorman, my skinny, South Georgia roommate at intelligence school in Baltimore.

"Les! I can't believe it! Why aren't you in jail?"

He laughed. "*Je suis moi, d'ailleurs,*" ("It's me, by the way.") He said it with his toothy grin, as if putting that nonsense into French made it have deep meaning.

Cooperative as always, and swearing in his South Georgia French, he joined me in working through the out-processing, and we got it done a lot faster. But it still came down to what we all said: "You're never short enough," meaning as long as you had one hour to go, you were still a prisoner of that wretched war and had to suffer all the attendant discomforts of being there.

After two more days of waiting, my short-timer calendar expired. At dusk, I stood on the tarmac in a long line of soldiers pinching themselves to make sure they weren't dreaming as they saw a gorgeous Continental Airlines Boeing 707 jet waiting just ahead of them.

A beautiful American girl—the first any of us had seen in months—stood at the top of the stairs by the open door in her crisp flight attendant's uniform, smiling and beckoning us to come aboard, and my eyes welled up with tears. Our job was over, and America was calling us home.

The flight from Saigon to San Francisco took seventeen hours. When we touched down on American soil, every soldier on the plane erupted in cheers and high-fives.

o

I TOOK A plane to LA, and as soon as I stepped off the airstair I saw Ida running out onto the tarmac with tears in her eyes, joined by half a dozen other young women who were rushing to welcome their soldiers home. Ida and I kissed and cried, finding it hard to believe our long separation was finally over, and I had come home safely.

Inside the terminal, I had a joyous round of hugs and kisses with my parents and sisters. Above our smiles and laughter, we were all choking back tears.

I had experienced no fears about going back to Ida; it felt good to be with her again. But after we spent several days together at my parents' Van Nuys home, I began to feel a bit distant from her.

Part of that was my fault. In Vietnam, to cope with the ever-present possibility of a Viet Cong attack, I had shut down my emotions more than I realized. Now, sitting next to Ida on the side of the small swimming pool at the house, our feet in the water, I realized that I had little spark. She saw that. We talked about it and decided it would just take time for me to abandon a war mentality and re-enter the civilian world.

But another part of the distance was due to Ida's having grown. The whole time I was gone, she was finishing up her senior year at NYU. She had now graduated and seemed more self-assured than before. She had been on her own for so long that she had firmer opinions and was more willing to speak up.

The distance was not due to a re-emergence of my doubts about her; those would appear much later. For now, we gradually got used to each other without being gripped by the passionate level of neediness we both felt when I was preparing to go to war.

o

ONE MONTH LATER, Ida and I sat on a quiet, secluded picnic ground just outside Avalon, thirty miles off the coast of Southern California on Catalina Island.

She looked radiant, her complexion pink from the sun and her eyes squinting with happiness every time she smiled at me.

After arriving on the steamer from Long Beach, we cycled to the picnic grounds on a contraption made for two and were enjoying long moments of rest on a hill overlooking the Pacific. As we gazed out to sea, the water and the air were crystal blue. The sun was clear and hot, the ocean breeze fresh. The searing brown California countryside was dotted with olive green patches of oak and palm and somehow reminded us of how free and alive and in love we were. We owned the world now. Our lives together were just beginning, and at that moment we felt washed and clean.

I had come so far since the last time I sat and looked out at the natural beauty of California with a pretty woman. Back then, she was Anabela, and the only connection was physical. That proved to be tenuous and unsustainable. The connection with Ida was deep and rich, made strong by the separation and despair of war, and renewed with passion when we finally held one another again.

Three weeks later, we were in Boston. We were busy getting Ida into an apartment in Brookline and me into an on-campus dorm at the Business School.

Ever since we returned from California, her parents had been meddling in our affairs, telling us how to go about getting set up in Boston and voicing disapproval at our modest achievements as we got one thing settled after another.

One afternoon, when we were at the house in Connecticut, Ida's mother came to us unexpectedly and asked us to sit with her at the dining room table. The house had no air conditioning, but a breeze was blowing in off the lake, cooling us despite the heat outside.

"I'm beginning to see," Kate said while looking down, "that I've been trying to slow the process of Ida leaving home. The thought of my first child going away really made me uneasy."

She paused and looked up at us. "I'm sorry for being such an obstructionist."

We were floored. In so many words, she said she realized Ida's going away was not a rejection of her, but rather an affirmation of Ida's healthy self-expression. She asked us to bear with her while she readjusted her thinking.

Her self-analysis required not only profound care and skill, but also great courage and no small amount of humility to voice. We never expected such a positive approach from her and were overjoyed at what this could mean for the quality of our relationship with Kate and Leo in the coming years. We had vanquished not only our long separation, but also the opposition from her parents that had troubled us for so long.

o

MY WINNING RECIPE had been a big success in dealing with Neubauer and Beadle. It spurred me to create a database process that not only earned me respect from them, but also the beginnings of friendship. After so many failures in using processes with women, this was the first time a procedure had actually improved relations with people I was trying to influence. Under the right conditions, the recipe could work outside of academia.

But as a guide to living, it had been powerless to provide me with safety. It was no help in reducing my terror during the evasion and escape exercise, my anguish after the Vietnam alert, my fright after the blast in Saigon, or the scare of the night attack in Pleiku.

During all of this the recipe had short circuited and almost prevented three realizations from coming to light. Instead, fear itself had forced me into a crash course in self-awareness. I now had three powerful insights to draw on for the rest of my life:

- *The Source of Meaning:* Evasion and escape taught me that all the meanings in my head were merely interpretations, and that to support my well-being, I was free to change them.

- *A Unified Awareness:* The Saigon explosion embedded in me the desire and ability to increase my own safety by unifying my internal focus with the external world.

- *The Self as Context:* The mortar assault in Pleiku

taught me to see myself not as whatever emotion I was having, but rather as the context for all of it. I was not the emotion. I was the person who was having it.

Underlying all these understandings was my growing skill in being able to step outside my mind and simply watch it operate. Overall, the Army had provided a sobering and maturing experience, one far more valuable than any winning recipe I could have listened to.

I had survived the war and now faced a whole new problem—one potentially more perilous for my self-esteem than anything I had just faced in Vietnam: how to survive the Harvard Business School.

# Part 3
# Danger

# Chapter 11
# The Snake Pit

SEPTEMBER 1967. BOSTON, MASSACHUSETTS.
On a crisp, chilly morning, my sixth day at the Harvard
Business School, I approached the entrance to Aldrich
Hall. The one-hundred-and-five-thousand-square-foot,
red-brick behemoth in front me had heavy double wood
doors that must have been twelve feet high. It was all I
could do to pull one of them open.

Inside, I reported to the classroom for Section C.
Like the sixteen other amphitheaters in this cavernous
facility, it was horseshoe-shaped and held about one
hundred students. Seven rows of swivel chairs and
continuous writing surfaces descended into a hollow at
the bottom. Each row was broken by two aisles that ran
from the top down to where the professor stood.

Students called it the Snake Pit.

Every weekday, the school assigned three business
cases, each one a sanitized real-world situation typically
described in twenty to forty staple-bound pages of text
and financial data. We picked them up from a cave in
the catacombs under the school. For a guy used to the
bright sunshine of California and Vietnam, the place

was uncomfortable and foreboding.

There was no assignment other than, "What should Mr. Brown do?" The case rarely even identified what the problem was; you had to figure it out for yourself.

There were no textbooks or lectures, just a relentless flow of cases five days a week. Occasionally we would get a note on production or some other topic that might describe a few general principles, but that was it.

In each of the three daily classes, the professor cold-called on a student to present his or her analysis of the case. Half the course grade was based on class participation, which meant that when called on, you needed to give a cogent, convincing analysis of what the issue was and how to solve it. And when not the presenter, you had to join the snarling, noisy debate that immediately followed the student's presentation. At that point the class became a pack of hyenas ready for a kill.

This was introvert hell. The loudest, most incessant voices often prevailed, regardless of how shallow the thinking might be. Whether presenting or commenting, the premium was on projecting certainty and confidence even if you barely had time to read the case the night before. Because even when you did read it, there was rarely enough information in it to justify much confidence in a decision. Appearing unsure of yourself, or worse, rarely speaking, shunted you to the lower reaches of the class and put your social status in the cellar.

The school purposely designed the workload to prevent students from ever being prepared. I could not take my time with anything or think through a problem in any more than the most superficial way. A slow and steady approach was a recipe for disaster.

The shock of all this drove me deep into my shell. I sat all the way at the back in the very top row of the Snake Pit, just inside the door as if ready for a quick escape. I prepared for each case by trying to resurrect the safety of the same process I had used so successfully in my undergraduate days: taking notes, memorizing them, and rehearsing what to say. But in the end, I never spoke a single word into the cacophony of unrestrained extroversion all around me. I watched it from my perch high above the brawl, looking for—but never finding—a way to say anything at all. As I sat up there, my heart pounded. Every time I thought I might raise my hand, I trembled.

o

IN CONTRAST TO the stress at school, being with Ida after so long a separation was soft and comfortable. I had now fully made the transition to civilian life, so I loved being with her again. Jointly we were able to smooth out the rough edges of the new world we faced in Boston. And given the threatening environment I faced in grad school, she provided the only security I had.

She lived in a nice hillside apartment in Brookline, and I had a small dormitory room on campus so I would have a place to study between classes. I spent every night at her apartment, enjoying the taste of her delicious home-cooked meals and going back to my room only the next morning before class.

Ida could not find anything that would make use of her psychology degree, so she bought a new skirt suit and took a job as a receptionist at Liberty Mutual Insurance Company. I bought a pair of tan wingtip dress shoes to complement the suits and ties I would be wearing to class each day so I would fit in with the formal dress code in the 97% male atmosphere.

Outside of the Snake Pit, I kept to myself, getting to know none of my classmates. The one exception was an Englishman who had observed my comings and goings from the dorm. He was bunking down the hall with a roommate and had no place to spend time with his fiancée, so he asked if he could use my room at night. When I gave him the key, he was the happiest Brit I ever saw.

o

"MR. PLUMB, PLEASE present today's case."

It happened in Marketing two months into the term. I had not uttered a word in that or any other class. A bolt of fear pierced my midsection when I saw I was on stage with a hundred faces turning up to look at me.

My college-based study process had been sputtering. It was a high-performance engine that relied on a steady flow of textbooks and lectures as fuel to drive my notetaking. At Harvard, any notes I could get from cases were thin and sporadic, making my engine close to useless. But I knew no other way to cope, so I kept at it.

A few days earlier a background document on marketing had shown up, and I devoured it using my standard techniques.

Fortunately, I had applied what I learned from the note to the case the professor asked me to present. It was about market segmentation, figuring out how to divide the customers for a product according to their preferences for things like convenience, reliability, selection, and service.

An occasional feature of my old approach was to

create little tables of information as a mnemonic device. I had done that here, creating a matrix of sixteen cells, four columns of preferences for four categories of customers that I could discern in the case.

As I reeled them off, the professor turned to the blackboard and kept up with me, frantically writing to capture the contents of every cell as I spoke. He filled the board, then with an audible *swoosh* pushed it way up to reveal a second board beneath it and kept writing. He was silent the whole time, except for questions about what I meant, so I thought for sure he was setting me up for the hyenas. They were already restless.

"What kind of numbers would you put on each of these segments, Mr. Plumb?"

More stirring from the audience.

"That's as far as I got, sir."

A stern look in my direction. "All right, who has done the numbers on this?"

The room erupted. That was normal, but in the case that I was presenting, numbers were central. In contrast to the qualitative thinking many people had trouble with, and I excelled at, they had all run the numbers. As different students spoke, all with characteristic bravado, the professor kept writing.

I noticed that nobody was challenging my matrix. When the professor had had his fill, he ended the discussion, reached the back of his hand up to me and said, "Mr. Plumb, that is the kind of analysis we want to see in this class." In two months, the professor had never acknowledged anyone in that way. The guy sitting in the row just below me looked up and said, "Wow, roses!"

IN THE FOLLOWING months, I was never able to duplicate that win in Marketing or in any other class. Instead of helping me, my undergraduate study process was so far off track for this environment that in almost every class it made me virtually unable to function. The tension was almost unbearable.

One valuable takeaway from the experience was to pay attention to the numbers of a case, and thereafter I always did. But otherwise, even though I understood the material, I still did not have the confidence to speak up in class.

I came away with exactly the wrong message: I doubled down on trying to take notes, because doing so had saved me here and might again. That reinforced my dependence on the now-gasping system that had served me so well at Stanford, and it blinded me to any possibility of change.

I knew many of my classmates were meeting for an hour before class to hash out the day's cases. But from afar it just looked like more grandstanding and the thought of joining them turned my stomach. I continued alone, reinforcing a lifelong pattern of staying comfortable as a loner, prioritizing my own process over benefitting from collaborating with others.

The stress of the caseload became intolerable. The more I took notes, the further behind I fell. In Written Analysis of Cases, I was pulling all-nighters to turn in my reports by the 6:00 a.m. deadline, sliding on the ice in the pre-dawn darkness to reach the designated turn-in chute before it closed. In Decisions Under Uncertainty, I got called on and had to admit I was not prepared—I did not read the case the night before.

Everyone felt pressure; it was part of the teaching

model. What I did not know was that it also affected the assistant professors who were trying to gain tenure. I discovered this when the young leader of our Human Behavior in Organizations class went into the attic of his residence, put a shotgun into his mouth, and blew off the top of his head.

In January 1968, I crunched across the snowy walkway to my dorm and found a letter from the dean waiting for me. It was courteous but blunt:

"Mr. Plumb, if you do not significantly improve your performance by the end of March, the university will have no choice but to ask you to leave the program."

My undergraduate study process had failed me so disastrously that I was now in danger of getting thrown out of Harvard. By yielding to my winning recipe in such an inappropriate way, I had stuck with something that was utterly unworkable. I was now more concerned about my ability to survive as a person than I ever was in Vietnam.

I considered giving up and seeing if I could re-activate the admission to the Stanford Business School that I had received while in Pleiku. But on reflection, I saw that if I could not make it at Harvard, the other school was not likely to let me in.

When I calmed down, I decided there was no way for me to improvise my way through this. So, over the next few days I met with every one of my professors. I walked up and down the long, dark halls of the school seeking advice. My Managerial Economics professor was particularly candid.

"Stop being a loner, Mr. Plumb. You need to go join a discussion group with some other students. You have been here for four months. Why haven't you done that yet?"

"It's hard for me, sir. I'm not used to learning that way."

He pulled back and took a long look at me.

"Well, you better get over that. Otherwise, you'll never make it. Your isolation from the other students is unhealthy both academically and socially. Maybe you don't belong here."

I left in despair. Joining a group was so far outside of who I was that I could hardly stand to think about it. I *was* a loner, and they were asking me to pretend to be somebody else.

I agonized over this, but only briefly. If I wanted a Harvard MBA, I had to do it. Otherwise, I would have to drop out. Within that stark frame there was no choice. I held my nose and approached a guy named Lloyd who had been nice to me once. He was happy to have me join his group.

o

THE FIRST FEW times I met with Lloyd and his group, I felt awkward and said little. I was preoccupied. The recent deaths of Gus Grissom, Ed White, and Roger Chaffee were on my mind; they had just been killed in a fire that swept through the Apollo 1 command module in Florida. I shuddered at the unimaginable pain their families were going through and at the management failures that likely caused such a disaster. It showed that if we got something wrong in the profession we were being trained for, it could have life and death consequences. This was personal, because for all I knew I might end up in mining, construction, healthcare, steel manufacturing, or some other industry where people's lives were at risk every day.

I looked from man to man in my group. I saw that some, like me, wore suits from JC Penney and sounded like they went to public school. Others wore silk ties and tailor-made Italian ensembles and talked like prep-school patricians.

As I had feared, a few in the group did beat their chests and waste everyone's time. But I noticed that overall, what mattered most to these guys was quality, not volume.

We continued meeting day after day, and I started making two important contributions to the group. The first I expected: being able to make insightful, subjective analyses, much as I had done that day in Marketing. The second was a surprise: I found that I had an easy facility with numbers and could use them to distill points that some of the others had missed. I also was able to use figures to bolster the qualitative arguments I was already competent at making.

By listening to the group, I got deeper insight into cases and as a bonus, went through them faster than on my own. Most importantly, I received the confidence I needed in order to speak up in class. I became surer of my arguments after trying them out on the others because I learned of any pitfalls before looking like an ass in front of a hundred people. And best of all, I had dry runs of speaking before a group. I slowly learned to condense my sharing down to a few key points and make them with more confidence than I actually felt.

The impact on my performance was measurable. By March, my grades had come up so fast that there was no more talk of asking me to leave. And by June, I had had a strong finish to the first year.

All the while, I was doubly uncomfortable with the

frequent and intense experience of being around others and with having to fly blind so often, just as I had that night in the Georgia woods.

But as the year drew to a close, I saw that while I would rather work in a cave with a single light bulb hanging from a wire in the ceiling than go to group meetings, those guys were not so bad. They were smart, committed, and occasionally funny. I was learning more from them than from the professors.

I also saw that far from being without a process at this school, I now had a shiny new one. It was different from anything I had ever built. Now the only notes I took were scribbled reminders of things the other students in my group said. Unlike at Stanford, my fuel for achievement was no longer memories gleaned from textbooks and lectures, but memories of the insights from my peers. The system geared itself to their perceptions, as well as their reactions to my own thoughts and number-crunching. In just a few months, all that had reversed my slide into disaster and positioned me for even more success in my second year.

The good news was, it made me feel safer. The bad news was, I was ignoring a danger even more serious than expulsion: the reality that unlike many introverts, I was not temperamentally suited to be either a senior executive or an entrepreneur. To succeed in the executive suite or in the marketplace, I would need to repeat my Harvard peer group experience every day for the rest of my career. If I had realized this, I would have had to admit that with my temperament, I simply did not have the stomach for it. For now, I certainly felt more secure. But for decades afterwards, the mismatch between my disposition and the realities of the business world would prevent me from ever feeling completely okay with myself.

I belonged in research or writing, but with such slavish devotion to my recipe, I could never have chosen those careers. The processes leading to success were far too amorphous; by comparison those in business were crystal-clear. The solution to the danger would have been to tell the truth about who I really was. But I was so focused on getting through business school—and so immature and unaware—that I did not even stop to think whether business leadership was the right career for me.

o

ON JUNE 8, 1968, in the glow of a good Harvard report card, Ida and I were married in a little New England church resplendent with white flowers. By now, her parents had accepted me. But a major wrinkle was that one week before the wedding I missed a step while rushing down a flight of stairs at Leo and Kate's house and broke the outermost metatarsal bone in my left foot. Ida's father took me to the local hospital where an osteopath set the bone. I limped out on crutches and in a plaster walking cast that extended up to my knee.

Another issue was that despite the success of my new peer-based system, I could not find any groomsmen among my classmates. I had no friends, even among our discussion group, because I did not participate in the drinking and dining they all enjoyed at night. Ida and I had devolved into an unhealthy dependence on one another; my wanting to spend every free moment with her justified my not socializing with classmates. I learned years later that I was not considered to be a wholly successful HBS graduate because I had not used after-hours socializing to build a robust social network.

At length, Sam Horowitz from my Brazil group, Lieutenant Beadle from Vietnam, and Ida's brother Leo Junior as best man, all kindly came as groomsmen to Ida's church in Connecticut for the ceremony. Beadle in particular surprised me. Now that he was out of the Army, he was friendly and supportive. In Vietnam I was so focused on running my little intelligence-gathering database that I had completely missed seeing that side of him.

I split my pants leg to accommodate the cast during the wedding ceremony and did a passable job with a cane to peg-leg my bride down the aisle.

We had a brief honeymoon in the Poconos, then boarded a flight, cast, cane, and all, for the wilds of northeastern Brazil. For months, I had planned to go there to do research for my second-year master's thesis at Harvard, and was damned if a broken foot was going to stop me.

# Chapter 12
# A Testicular Engineer

JUNE 1968, 10:32 P.M. SOMEWHERE OVER THE AMAZON. Ida and I clutched each other's hands so tightly that our fingers were white.

Our Boeing 707 was on its final approach into the Atlantic port of Belém near the mouth of the Amazon River in Brazil. The thunderous lightning storm outside our window had buffeted us to the point of nausea.

We could not look at each other or even speak. It took all our concentration to just keep breathing and avoid losing the dinner we had eaten on board an hour earlier.

We hit an air pocket. The plane plummeted twenty feet, stabilized, then plummeted another twenty. It felt like twenty thousand. My mind raced with the thought that below us were two possibilities. Either we would try to land on the river and hope the incoming water did not include the flesh-eating piranhas that swam in the Amazon, or we would crash into the jungle, and a fire would race through the cabin to kill us all where we sat.

The plane whined, creaked, and shuddered, making snapping noises that sounded like pieces of it were falling off.

I thought back to the map of Brazil I had looked at months earlier when choosing a destination for my master's thesis. The chart was clean and pretty, immobile on a tabletop at Ida's parents' house in Connecticut. It was simple to trace a route from New York to Belém and then on to São Luís further east down the coast. It looked like an easy trip.

I had chosen São Luís because it was so godforsaken. It was the small capital of one of the poorest states in Brazil, and I saw opportunity there. It sat between the Amazon proper to the west and the Northeast rump of the country to the east, two regions investors had been targeting for years. I was hoping I could launch an agribusiness project halfway between them based on oil from the *babassú* (ba-ba-*soo*) palm tree. It would help to transform the economy, put money in the pockets of poverty-stricken people, and in time provide a good living for Ida and me. As such, this could turn out to be more than just a research project, so I was glad Ida had made good progress in learning at least a conversational level of Portuguese.

To go into a foreign city where I knew no one and come out with measurable results, I needed to be more extroverted than I was used to being. Today, I am surprised I chose to put myself in such a situation. To meet key people, I would have to improvise, which meant I would be uncomfortable. But I guessed that my success with the peer group at the Harvard Business School would give me the energy I needed to reach out once we got to São Luís. I was sure I could figure out a process that would bring a good outcome. And thankfully, my Portuguese was still good.

I had chosen agribusiness because it was central to

*Fig. 6 Maps of South America and Brazil showing locations of Belém, São Luís, and Rio de Janeiro. 2022.*

the pet theory of my thesis advisor, Professor Nelson Pettigrew. He believed helping people produce and sell agricultural products could lift them out of poverty. Tall, lanky, and handsome, he was the Brahmin son of generations of Massachusetts congressmen. Pettigrew had left Harvard to run for the House himself in 1958, but he lost and was now back at the university.

"Ben," Ida cried, her voice shaking as she shouted above the roar outside, "shouldn't we be there by now?"

I had made the same calculation. "Yes, we should be. Maybe we have to land someplace else."

"Oh God, I just can't stand this," she said. "I really think I'm going to be sick." She withdrew her hand and put it on her stomach.

With my newly freed hand, I reached down to scratch the top of the cast on my left leg, trying to relieve a persistent itch that jabbed me from deep inside.

I forced myself to recall once again why we were there. One of Professor Pettigrew's consulting clients was Herbert Cornuelle (pronounced "Cornell"), the

CEO of the United Fruit Company (UFC), a firm headquartered near our campus in Boston. UFC was one of the largest corporations in the world, the iconic owner of the "Great White Fleet" of refrigerated ships that for decades had brought fresh bananas from Central America to the US.

United Fruit was massively unpopular in Latin America. The company owned land, railroads, and company towns. As such, it had a reputation as *El Pulpo*—the octopus which took more out of each country than it put in. Cornuelle desperately wanted to change all that and was looking for a novel approach. Knowing this, Professor Pettigrew convinced him to grubstake me for a summer of research in any poor location of my choice. I chose São Luís with a goal of building a revolutionary new model that UFC could scale up.

One of the things the business school drilled into every student was a concept I called "Environmental Scanning 101," even though there was no actual course by that name. It meant that an integral part of any decision-making process needed to be a visceral, aggressive look at the business setting a company was in. What forces were on the horizon that might upend the current situation? What threats existed, and what opportunities? What strengths did the firm have in the face of those, and what weaknesses? In my excitement to get to Brazil and get on with the research, I skipped over doing that for United Fruit. Instead, in thrall to my recipe, I focused on all the steps I had to execute between now and the time my thesis was done. And I never for a second thought my broken foot would be a reason to abort the trip.

I had happily bought two suits, one blue and one

dark green, along with white shirts and a few ties, all of which could be thrown in the sink and washed to rid them of the tropical stink that would no doubt saturate everything we wore in São Luís. I was an experienced international traveler, but this was Ida's first trip outside the country. She no doubt was wondering what she had gotten herself into.

## "What forces were on the horizon that might upend the situation?"

A plunge through a third air pocket made us gasp. We lurched down, and down, and down. Ida was close to tears, and I was close to vomiting. We heard the wheels screech and felt them hit the runway. The engines roared to reverse thrust and slow us down, pushing the smell of kerosene through the ventilation system. Weak applause rippled through the cabin.

o

SHAKEN, WE TOOK a cab to a modest hotel in Belém. In our room, I was surprised to find glorious, dark hardwood doors and cabinets that normally would grace a much more expensive inn. No doubt they were products from the rainforest that surrounded the city.

Ida was in no mood to appreciate them. She was disoriented and frightened, her discomfort made more acute by the exhaustion of the long trip and a terrifying landing. She wanted to talk but I was impatient, silently wondering why she could not suck it up like I had. I forgot how unsettling an alien environment could be to a first-time foreign traveler. In retrospect, I was a real shit. She just wanted to be held and comforted, and I could only think about getting us both to bed so we could catch our early flight to São Luís in the morning. Just a few minutes of caring from me could have made such a difference for her, but I was too small and immature to offer it.

Decades later, I realized this was an unintended consequence of my devotion to my process-driven approach to life. All I could think about were the steps I needed to follow for my thesis. We had to get to São Luís, meet people who could provide me with data, and capture the information. I then had to organize it, run numbers based on it, prepare a business case, and so on. I was thinking about all of this so constantly that in Belém, it put the first crack in our relationship.

The next morning, she felt better. We boarded a small, two-engine plane for the three-hundred-mile trip east to São Luís. The day was sunny, but the heat welling up off the land below us kept battering the small craft. Once again, we felt nauseated.

When we landed, we found our hotel to be even more modest than the one in Belém, but it still had a full ration of gorgeous hardwoods on wall panels, armoires, and doors. Spare but clean, it had a decent bathroom, plenty of space to spread out, and an effective but noisy wall unit air conditioner that kept the room cool.

First thing the next day, Ida donned a nice dress while I put on a coat and tie, and in the blistering heat we walked to the local library. This was long before the days of the internet, and there was not even a copy machine in the building. So we spent hours writing down production and sales figures for babassu palm oil on lined notepads. This gave me data on the size of the market that at the time was available no other way.

We then walked over to the Brazil-United States Institute in search of data. The Institute taught English and promoted understanding between the two countries. As soon as we arrived, the staff treated us like heroes—here were real live Americans, and in São Luís! Olivia, the administrator, gushed all over us in decent English, asking dozens of questions and wanting to help us in any way she could. She had no statistics I could use but did know of two people who had given her a standing invitation to house any Americans who might need a place to stay, a professor and a businessman.

Never expecting such a windfall and happy at the thought of being able to live more comfortably than in a hotel, we readily agreed to move into the businessman's home if he and his family would have us. Soon, we and Olivia were in a cab driving towards what passed for an upscale neighborhood in this humble town and found ourselves outside the gate of a fortress: a large, two-story concrete block house surrounded by a high wall. We rang the bell, a housemaid answered, and Olivia explained to her that she had brought some Americans who wanted to speak with the owner.

The young woman nodded and led us through a spacious courtyard that had a mammoth hardwood tree growing in the middle of it to block the broiling sun. An upstairs balcony loomed over the space; from beyond its open French doors, we could hear yelling and scurrying around. The housekeeper told an unseen senhora who we were. The lady called her husband at work, and within minutes, he joined us in the living room.

Tall, swarthy, and well-built, William Nagem (na-zheng) was an affable, outgoing, fortyish entrepreneur of

Lebanese-Brazilian descent. He spoke excellent English that he had learned when studying engineering at a textile institute in England in the early 1950s. He owned a cloth-making factory in São Luís that obviously supplied a good living. He introduced his small, attractive, and garrulous wife, a son about eight years old and a daughter about five, all of whom said hello and then left us alone with William and Olivia. An air conditioner on the wall growled into life, pushing a delicious, cool breeze onto our faces.

When Olivia told him that we were from Boston doing research on babassu oil for a program at Harvard, his eyebrows went up. She said we were looking for a place to stay and knew he had expressed interest in helping any Americans who might show up at the Institute. He nodded and quickly offered us our own apartment—a bedroom and bath located above the detached garage on the other side of the courtyard.

We thanked him for his generosity, shook on it, and were about to return to the hotel to get our belongings when he expressed keen interest to know the nature of the project I was working on. I told him it would be a venture to use US capital to fund a babassu oil processing plant as well as any other agricultural ventures that might make sense. This heightened his attention even more, and it was only when Olivia said she needed to get back that we left—in William's car, no less, with his personal driver at the wheel.

o

OVER THE NEXT few days, I thought a lot about William. When I started on this trip, I was not looking for a local venture partner, but after meeting him I began to entertain the idea. It would smooth things politically, bring in local knowledge, and in general get us off to a faster start.

That said, I concluded that William was not the guy. I would want someone who was a disrupter, a development-oriented partner who would not focus on earning money to the exclusion of supplying social benefits for the local people. This, William was not. On the contrary, I saw him as having all the signs of a patriarch, a man with an entrenched interest in the status quo.

He owned a factory that used an ancient technology; textile manufacturing had been around for two hundred years. In his home, he had at least four full-time, live-in servants—a maid, a cook, a driver, and a houseboy. And he was something of an outsider, although as a Lebanese Brazilian, he did have a wide network of Middle Eastern contacts.

Yet he had good political connections. A childhood friend was Edison Soares, the governor of the state of Maranhão where São Luís sat. And William was a funny guy. He told me that in this city, people were not familiar with *engenheiros têxteis* (textile engineers) and he sometimes got mail addressed to *William Nagem, Engenheiro Testicular*. So, I now considered him to be our friend, the Testicular Engineer.

The apartment William kindly offered made our grubstake go a lot further. He would not accept a penny for rent or food, even knowing that United Fruit was footing the bill. But the place had its challenges. Foremost was the lack of air conditioning or any screens on the windows. To stay cool, we did have a ceiling fan, and we could get a cross breeze by keeping the windows open all night long. But to do so, we had to sleep under a mosquito net. That cut down the air circulation and was a pain to get in and out of in the dark.

All the odd night sounds of São Luís came directly into our bedroom. Motorbikes buzzed on the street outside. Vendors cried, "*Jornal do Rio!*" announcing the arrival of newspapers that had just come in by air from Rio de Janeiro fourteen hundred miles to the south. Roosters crowed at 4:00 a.m. Competing roosters crowed at 4:01 a.m. But otherwise, the apartment was clean and comfortable, and Ida was content with it.

She continued to go with me to the library, which had a surprising amount of useful information for us to copy. She had studied Portuguese at NYU before we came down and tried to speak with William's wife. But with language issues on both sides and the woman insisting on simply speaking louder when Ida did not understand something, there was not much companionship. Especially when Ida saw the lady standing on her balcony every day screaming at the housekeeper and houseboy in the courtyard below. Ida hated that.

To help ease her isolation, I read to her in the evenings, translating articles about America from the Rio newspapers. That July, Vassar College began admitting men, the first Special Olympics were held, and Virginia Slims launched a new cigarette brand using the slogan, "You've Come a Long Way, Baby."

Since the day we arrived in Brazil, Ida had had an upset stomach from the unfamiliar bacteria in the food. Fortunately, a test showed no infection, and eventually her discomfort passed.

Each morning, we had breakfast with William and the family on a picnic table in the courtyard, under the giant hardwood tree; for lunch and dinner we ate inside by ourselves, with the cook or the maid serving us. At Sunday breakfast, we all ate a huge spread of eggs, fruit, and wonderful Brazilian coffee. For some reason, the meal always included tapioca pudding, a delicious but strange addition. Sunday evenings, William treated us and the family to dinner at the best restaurant in town, which improbably was at the airport. Our favorites were broiled chicken and a dessert of chocolate or vanilla ice cream covered with *ameixas cozidas* (stewed plums). William ensured us with a grin that we could eat as much as we wanted, because nothing we consumed on a Sunday would make us fat.

William often spoke of "the interior" as if it were a place of mystery. São Luis was a civilized little city of two hundred thousand people on an island just yards off the Atlantic coast. But the rest of Maranhão was a wild and untamed wilderness where most of the state's 3.75 million people lived. Periodically, he drove his pickup there to buy cotton for his cloth factory and see to some of his other ventures. He always came back filthy, with red dust on his truck and his clothes from having driven for hundreds of kilometers over washboard dirt roads. Once, he lent us his truck so we could go to a beach that could only be reached by a half-hour drive over the washboards.

Ahead of time, he told me how to drive on them. "Go slow," he said, "and it jars your teeth loose. Go fast, and you skim over the top of the bumps."

"Won't that hurt the truck?" I asked.

He laughed. "It hurts it worse if you go slow. If you drive fast, it's bumpy but still smoother."

His was the voice of experience. I tried it, and it worked.

One night, William took us to an astonishing *macumba* ceremony in the backlands. *Macumba* was an Afro-Brazilian form of witchcraft widely practiced in the interior. He was not sure where to find the event because it moved around from night to night. So just after 10:00 p.m. he drove into the darkness with Ida and me sitting beside him in the pickup. He cut the engine and lights and listened. After doing this three or four times, we all heard the syncopated rhythm of drums beating, and by homing in on that, we soon found a wooden structure where the ritual was taking place.

We were nervous about interrupting a quasi-religious ceremony, but William assured us nobody would even notice we were there. We walked into a sizeable room and looked across it, seeing thirty or forty people milling around in a circle with a large opening in the middle, and he was right—we were invisible. Four African-Brazilian women dressed in white linen were in the middle, spinning, their eyes looking straight up as if hypnotized. A fifth woman lay on the floor, rigid and quivering. Shortly, a woman standing next to us let out a yelp and threw herself into the circle on the floor, rolling and shaking as if in the grip of an epileptic fit. William said they were all being possessed by spirits but would be fine in the morning.

o

OVER THE ENSUING weeks, I spent many hours with William and gradually came to see him in a different light.

He had been born and raised in São Luís. Twelve years earlier, when he returned from England, he started his own small textile factory from scratch, using his technical knowledge to compete in a way new to Maranhão, one based on low costs, thin margins, and high volume. As his business grew, he generously offered technical and financial aid to friends and competitors alike. Now, just about anyone of influence in the state was indebted to him in terms of gratitude or money.

He was fascinated with my project and asked me many questions about it, offering suggestions that made sense.

"Why just focus on babassu oil?" he asked. "It's true that we have over a billion babassu palms, and there is strong demand for the oil. And yes, supply bottlenecks are keeping the market artificially small."

He paused, looking at me intently. "But there is a lot more you can do here."

"Such as?" I asked, my curiosity piqued.

"Well, rice milling. And cotton ginning. I have small operations in the interior doing both of those, and they are very successful."

This struck a chord in me. In my research, I had learned that Maranhão cotton was of low quality and improperly cleaned, but that the soil would support high-grade varieties. It had done so in colonial times until it began to overshadow the industry in Portugal, leading the colonizers to shut the Brazilian industry down. Rice, too, could stand to have its seed quality and handling improved. William's local knowledge seemed right on target.

As he spoke, I thought of the families in the interior who were gathering the babassu nuts and growing the rice. I had discovered that they lived in almost total deprivation, earning under one hundred dollars per year. They were semi-nomads, moving their families every two years because the slash-and-burn technique that they used to clear the land depleted the soil. They were constantly in debt to local traders, which was another reason for moving. The traders were intermediaries between producers and customers; they worked for the *grande comerciante* or big business owner who controlled the economy of the municipality. Because Maranhão was so isolated, the families still regarded the *comerciantes* with some affection; elsewhere in Brazil, rural violence had been directed against those oligarchs.

Among the families, illiteracy was close to 100%, and health was staggeringly bad. Their diet consisted of rice, beans, and manioc—a great deal of starch. They drank polluted water and walked barefoot. Worms, malaria, and schistosomiasis were the main conditions they suffered from, but they also had to deal with tuberculosis, pneumonia, leprosy, gangrene, and snakebites.

I contrasted their health situation with my own, which at that moment consisted of only one problem: how to get my cast off now that the required six weeks had passed. I was leery of a doctor in this town using a circular saw to remove it, so I plunged it into the bathtub until it got soft and ripped it off with my bare hands.

I began to see that William was more of a disrupter than I had imagined. He did not do business like a *grande comerciante*. One of his best friends was a French-Canadian priest named Edmund Pouliot, a man who had been working in the interior for over seven years organizing and motivating the families to form self-help groups. Pouliot used a painstaking process of "self-inventory" to help the locals become agitated about their poverty and self-organize to fight the conditions they lived in.

After learning about how people lived in the interior, I could not wait to add a community development piece to the project. When I told William, he got excited and said Father Edmund would probably jump at the chance to lead it using techniques he had already mastered. Recently, the padre had risen to program coordinator for twelve interior parishes and seemed to be looking for a bigger challenge either with local families or back in Canada. We went to see him, and he, too, became thrilled over the possibility of doing work on a larger scale than he had been. A serene man with curly brown hair and a cherubic face that belied his interior drive, he surprised us a few days later by reporting that his archbishop had already given him tentative approval to work with us.

I say "us," because by now I was convinced William was indispensable to this project. We had talked further, and he was now openly willing to join me in any way he could be helpful. As if to make good on that promise, he asked if I would like to meet Governor Soares. I said yes since I was on a roll. I had already reached out successfully to William and Edmund and did not shrink away from visiting the Governor despite my typically introverted self. The energy of dealing with my peer group back at Harvard still pushed me forward.

"Edison is the first development-minded governor we have ever had," William said. "He is looking for projects that will bring money, technology, and good management into Maranhão."

"That sounds too good to be true," I replied.

"In a way it is. Soares does not like private foreign

investment. Most of his power comes from the *caboclos* (the subsistence families in the interior), not the *grandes comerciantes*, so he may not be too enthusiastic."

William went on to balance out his advice. He said the governor had the power to grant virgin land to us in the interior, reduce taxes, and cut red tape. "The first year of the project, he would probably make us build dirt roads and drill freshwater wells," he said. "But that would not be a big deal."

William reported that despite Soares's progressive interests he still had some old-time oligarch ways about him. I knew from photos in the paper that he had slick, black hair and eyes set close together that peered out over a bushy black mustache. He certainly looked the part. I laughed when William said that whenever Soares called a *caboclo* to speak with him at the governor's residence, he brought the man into his bedroom and sat with him on the bed. This was intimidating in the extreme since most people in the interior did not have even so much as a mattress to sleep on in their mud and stick shacks.

When we met Soares—not in his bedroom, but on the second-floor veranda of the governor's mansion under a slowly turning ceiling fan—I found that William had correctly sized him up. The governor was mildly interested, but openly skeptical that I could do anything. I looked out across his manicured grounds, then watched a trickle of sweat drip down the side of a transparent glass pitcher of iced tea on the table in front of us. I assured him we would have the backing of United Fruit. But he said he had heard many promises of such foreign largesse before and would have to be shown our project was real. He would not oppose us, but we had our work cut out. After we left, William said once our deal was more mature, he was sure he could bring his friend Edison around.

Now we went to work on the project in earnest. Based on William's cost and revenue figures, I built financial projections for an $8.5 million venture: $2.5 million from UFC and the rest from local investors and government incentives. A synthetic cloth manufacturing facility in São Luís would take 70% of the money, and a self-supporting complex of agricultural projects in the interior—a babassu oil mill, a cotton gin, a rice mill, and a community development program—would take 30%. The textile factory would provide a nice return on investment for UFC, while the other projects would help to transform people's lives.

At a one-hundred-and-twenty-five-acre site, Father Edmund would organize and train one thousand families to change from subsistence to commercial agriculture, raising crops that they would sell to our company, the Maranhão Development Corporation. At Edmund's suggestion we would supply only roads, fresh water, and training via seventy-five full-time professionals in health, literacy, home economy, agriculture, and community organization. It would be up to the families to stop slashing and burning and fix themselves to the seventy-five acres of land they would buy over time.

I would be Managing Director for up to five years, and William would be President. Initially, I might have been concerned that William was taking part only to enrich himself and would pocket much of the investment money. But there was nothing in his background or his personality that remotely suggested he would be dishonest.

It came time for Ida and me to leave Brazil. William, Edmund, and I agreed that we now had to put everything on hold until I got back to the States and could work with Professor Pettigrew to get the funding we needed from United Fruit.

o

BY LATE AUGUST, Ida and I were back in Boston and moved into married student housing in a tower on the Charles River. My foot had healed. We got a gray tabby kitten that we named Babassu, and on his first night with us, we laughed as he curled up in one of my tan wingtip shoes to sleep.

Soon, we settled down into a normal life as I went back to my second year at the business school, and Ida got another job. She was relieved to be back in the US, but neither of us realized how hard the summer in Brazil had been on our relationship. She craved stability, and with me she was getting anything but.

Professor Pettigrew was thrilled with the progress William and I had made on the project. It showed how private business could change centuries-old ways of doing things and lift people out of poverty.

He wanted to meet William. One freezing night in October, I welcomed the sturdy Brazilian at Logan Airport, finding him shivering in the light topcoat he had worn. The next day, we met Pettigrew in his office on campus, and the chemistry was excellent. William's sincerity, passion, and executive presence were obvious. The next step was for the three of us to meet with Cornuelle, the CEO of United Fruit, to present our case and convince him to present the project to his board.

It never happened. Unknown to the three of us,

United Fruit was being pursued by companies that wanted to take it over. Just as we were ready to meet with Cornuelle, he revealed that he was in late-stage negotiations for UFC to sell itself to AMK Corporation of New York, a conglomerate. He could not focus on our project any longer and refused to meet with us.

We were devastated. William returned to Brazil. Professor Pettigrew and I continued on, meeting with the new owners in later months, but found they had none of Cornuelle's social consciousness. Their only interest in Brazil was to see if their A&W subsidiary could open root beer stands there.

o

I HAD BEEN so focused on the internal processes needed to get the Brazilian project off the ground that I failed to be curious about the danger existing in its external environment, the political situation at United Fruit.

It was clear that before going to Brazil, I should have looked at the company's balance sheet. United Fruit was a public company. The records were easily available at Baker Library, and it would have been a simple matter to walk in and review them. Their current assets would have shown me immediately that because the firm was awash in cash, it could be in peril as an attractive takeover candidate. Armed with that knowledge, I could have gone to Pettigrew with a concern, and we possibly could have lined up a backup sponsor.

As it was, I got blindsided when AMC showed up. Now it was too late to do anything about it. I had forgotten the painful lesson I learned after the explosion that first night in Saigon: that despite being an introvert,

I always needed to take the external environment into account. In this case, it was not a matter of failing to be omniscient, just one of failing to do the homework I had been trained to do.

In 1969, Nelson Pettigrew published the Maranhão Development Corporation as a Harvard Business School case study. He taught it to students to illustrate his view that business could have a productive role in helping societies advance. He retired from Harvard in 1997, and is 94 years old.

Cornuelle resigned within a few months and moved to Hawaii to work for an international construction firm. He died in 1996.

The main shareholder in AMK Corporation—UFC's new owner—was a man named Eli Black. He mismanaged the company by crippling it with debt and in 1975, committed suicide by jumping out of his office on the 44th floor of the Pan Am building in New York.

Edison Soares left the governorship of Maranhão in 1970 and was elected President of Brazil in 1987.

Father Edmund Pouliot returned to his home in Victoriaville, not far from Montreal in Quebec. Ida and I drove up from Boston to visit with him there while we were still working with AMK to continue the project. But we had little hope of success, and our lunch was melancholy. We lost contact with him, and I later learned he died in 2017.

William Nagem continued expanding his local businesses. He was diagnosed with Alzheimer's disease in 2001 and died in 2014 at the age of eighty-four.

o

THANKS TO MY peer-based study approach, I

graduated in the top third of my class in June 1969.

Given where I had stood just eighteen months earlier, that was a joyful outcome. But the successful process I had followed concealed an inconvenient fact: I had gotten short-term results by joining a peer group and ended up feeling safer at Harvard by doing that. But I simply did not have the outgoing personality required to survive long-term, let alone prosper, in the aggressive and confrontational world of top executive leadership in business. Far from giving me financial security, a business career would put me in decades of economic jeopardy.

I now had an MBA but had done no interviewing because I had felt so reassured by the way the project was coming together. Consequently, I was in a dangerous financial bind for months. I eventually landed a job as Assistant Director of Planning for Castle & Cooke, Inc. in Hawaii. As the owners of Dole Bananas, they were the main competitors of UFC. After I joined them, I saw first-hand that a project such as mine would have sparked zero interest there, so I let go of it.

Ida was ecstatic that we were not going to be roughing it in the interior of Brazil; in retrospect, I see a life like that would have been tough on both of us. Instead, Castle & Cooke had hired me for a whopping $11,000 a year, and soon the three of us, Ida, Babassu, and I were on our way to company headquarters in Honolulu.

I was now twenty-six years old. It was late 1969, and we were excited about the new world that lay ahead of us in Hawaii. But moody clouds surrounded the plane as we descended into Oahu.

# Chapter 13
# Chaos in Chile

OCTOBER 1969. HONOLULU, HAWAII. When Ida and I stepped off the plane with the other passengers, a line of women in brightly colored dresses placed leis of live, fragrant flowers around our necks and welcomed us to the islands.

Our cat Babassu received no lei. Instead, the airline shipped him and his cage directly to the airport quarantine facility and a few days later, to the permanent quarantine station just outside Honolulu. The islands were free of rabies, and to keep it that way, the state required pets to be held for one hundred and twenty days.

The animals lived in luxury. On our first visit to our cat, we looked up and saw that his outdoor, screened-in enclosure was at least ten feet tall and big enough for both of us to walk around in. A leafless tree trunk led from the concrete floor up to a platform and a covered box where he could sleep. Every day, Ida went to see him by herself; on weekends we went together. He was her baby, and she could hardly stand to be away from him. This was a sign that she was not getting everything she needed from our relationship, but it did not concern me enough to do anything about it.

My own obsession was my new job. I worked for Elijah Chan, a native of Hawaii and the Director of Planning at Castle & Cooke (C&C). Ours was the largest company in the islands, the owner of enormous pineapple plantations whose output they marketed under the Dole brand. Our office building rose far above the nearby Aloha Tower. When I mentioned that to my parents, they were amazed—that old tower had been the tallest building in Honolulu when they honeymooned there in 1939.

Elijah was fortyish, handsome, intense, and brilliant. A chain smoker who often had small white clouds of smoke wafting up into his coal-black hair, he was also kind and mildly introverted, committed to developing me in a gentle way. On my first day, he took me to a Chinese restaurant and introduced me to *dim sum*, a Cantonese dish of steamed dumplings that I had never heard of and found to be deliciously exotic.

In one week, he taught me more about financial forecasting than I had learned in two years at Harvard. Our department's main job was to evaluate companies for acquisition, so it was critical to build an accurate model of how much cash we would have to invest and when it would come back to us.

We did everything by hand on buff-colored, thirteen-column sheets of accounting paper. The only tools we had were electronic calculators and slide rules; personal computers powerful enough to do the job were at least fifteen years in the future.

The work was excruciating, but Elijah made it come alive. He likened each analysis to a detective story. When we projected income into the future and subtracted expenses, we exposed precisely when the acquisition would run out of money, and by how much. But that information was hidden and had to be dug out.

Elijah had two approaches for doing that. A private learning experience with him was salve to my heart after so much forced extroversion at Harvard, and I was eager to absorb both of his methods.

First, he said, project everything weekly. If you did it monthly, you would not uncover the actual cash shortage that lurked inside the month. Second, keep a running total from week to week. If you simply picked the week with the biggest *one-week* shortfall you would likely be wrong, perhaps fatally for the business.

I was thrilled. Here was a robust, practical process I could use to face the real world head on as my primary contribution to success. I latched onto it with steely-eyed determination.

One of the acquisitions Elijah had already decided on was Erdesa, a builder of earthquake-resistant, steel and plaster houses in Chile. The struggling, two-bit operation belonged to Art Kipke, the manic-depressive president; Bill Warneke, the perpetually angry field manager and the only one of the owners currently living in Chile; and Bruce Fraser, the grounded and energetic Executive VP. Bruce was of Scottish descent and had a twinkle in his eyes above a graying beard; I took an immediate liking to him. It was mutual: he probably saw in me an ally who could help him provide coherent thinking in the small company.

Elijah wanted his own man in Chile on the inside of Erdesa as VP and Controller, and after I had been in Hawaii for just nine months, he gave me the job.

My first task before I left was to buy a money belt. As soon as I had it, I went in to see him.

"Here's a present for you," he said, reaching into his desk. He took out $55,000 in negotiable cashier's checks and handed them to me, saying, "Fold these in half the long way and see if you can get all of them into the belt."

"What is going on here, Elijah?"

"You're going to smuggle these into Chile when you and Ida move down there. The clowns at Erdesa illegally took that much *out* of the company by using Chilean escudos to buy US dollars on the black market. So, there is a gaping hole on Erdesa's local books. The only way to fill it is to reverse the process—black market and all—and you're the only one I trust to do it right."

He watched as I crammed the heavy, bulky checks into the belt. If I had needed to burn off fat around my midsection, that would have been a great way to do it.

o

CASTLE & COOKE had shipped our household goods and our blue 1965 Chevy Nova coupe from Boston to Honolulu and now had to ship all of that again from Honolulu to the port of Valparaiso, near Santiago in Chile. In preparation, I had heavy-duty shock absorbers and springs added to the car so it could survive the local roads.

C&C also paid for us to ship our long-suffering cat on the plane with us when we departed for South America in June 1970. Babassu was only a few months out of Hawaiian quarantine after his five-thousand-mile trip from Boston. Now he found me once again propelling a tranquilizer pill down his throat before we all got on the eight-thousand-mile flight to Chile.

We stopped in LA during the day and again at night in Lima, Peru. There we had his cage lowered onto the dimly-lit tarmac amid the roar of jet engines. Every hair on the cat's body was sticking straight up, but likely not from the noise: a bear was also in the plane's animal compartment. Babassu seemed unusually eager to accept the tranquilizer I offered. On arrival we had no worries about going through another quarantine because there was none; rabies was widespread in Chile.

Our living situation was far more comfortable than it had been two years before in São Luís, and Ida adapted well. The nice, wood-frame, furnished bungalow we rented in the Pedro de Valdivia section of Santiago felt to me like it was in a middle-class part of Los Angeles. The warm, dry weather was similar since the two cities were roughly the same distance from the equator. Except here we were in the shadow of the towering and snow-capped Andes Mountains, and June was the start of winter instead of summer. On cold days, we were thankful for the kerosene stove in the hallway. It smelled of fumes but heated the whole house nicely.

We hired a full-time housekeeper named Conchita. Squat, good-natured, and cheery, she called us *Don Benjamín* and *Doña Ida,* which she pronounced as ben-ha-*meen* and *ee*-dah. She cooked, ironed, shopped, and laughed a lot, smoothing our introduction to local life. Ida especially appreciated help in running the house and having someone friendly to practice her Spanish with.

Only three of the four executives of Erdesa moved to Chile. Art Kipke remained in California. Bruce Fraser and his wife moved down to Santiago when Ida and I did. Bill Warneke was already living seven hundred miles to the north in Antofagasta to run our project there. I was glad he was so far away because he was a pain in the ass to deal with. Bruce, on the other hand, was upbeat and great fun to be around. He and I set up a small office in the leafy Vitacura section of town. He focused on chasing new projects while I managed the cash flow and kept Elijah Chan up to date on our progress.

Another bright spot was Maximiliano ("Max") Soto, our lead civil engineer. A Chilean in his thirties, he had extraordinary competence and a gentle, patient air about him that made him a natural leader. Squinty-eyed from the smoke of the frequent cigarettes in his mouth, he was slightly extroverted and always a source of fun and good advice. Once, when I proposed that we postpone paying a bunch of small bills instead of a few large ones, he said, *"Son las cuentas chicas que friegan, Ben,"* meaning it was the small accounts that grated on us. I took his suggestion and paid them, letting the big ones fester instead. I did not regret it.

I quietly got the $55,000 into the country and contacted our insurance broker, a Brit in his sixties, to convert the funds on the black market. Jolly, overweight, and a bit befuddled, his name was Jerry Bell. Before each transaction he liked to receive a phone call with a coded request. Exchange controls were not yet being enforced, but he was nervous, so he asked us to call ahead and let him know how many holes of golf we wanted to play for how many days (the amount of US dollars to exchange, in thousands), as well as the hour we wanted to start (the exchange rate we would accept).

"Hello Jerry, this is Ben Plumb from Erdesa."

"Hello, Ben! Bruce told me you might call today."

"Yes. We'd like to play eleven holes of golf for five

days [meaning $55,000] and are looking to start at about eight p.m., which is twenty hundred hours [meaning a rate of twenty escudos per dollar]."

"Fine. That is fifty-five holes. Could we play them all today?"

"Ummm. . . sure."

"Give me a minute to see what I can do." Long pause. "Good news. I can play at twenty-one hundred hours. Is that okay?"

"Sure Jerry, that's even better." The escudo was already depreciating, so we were getting a few more of them for each dollar than I had expected.

"OK, fine. Bring it in, Ben, and I will make a deposit to your account."

If anyone was listening in, that last comment exposed the whole call as a farce. I told Bruce about it, and he fell over laughing.

Early on, Bruce had five new projects in the pipeline. I calculated the expected revenue, costs, and cash flow for each one using Elijah Chan's method, then prepared a summary into which I fed the results of each project. This took weeks and filled more than a dozen thirteen-column pages of accounting paper. I shipped them air mail to Honolulu, and Elijah was astonished. He pinned all of them to the wall of his office so that as he looked from left to right, he could trace the money flow from each project into the summary. He approved only a few of the investments, but now at least he and his boss no longer saw Erdesa as a flaky outfit run by guys who didn't know what they were doing.

The exercise also proved to Bruce that I was the financial authority in Erdesa. Both Bruce and Art Kipke were highly extroverted and therefore prone to have less patience with detail than I had. My financial forecasting work focused their attention on the specifics in an engaging way.

o

IT WAS NOT long before an unfamiliar, dark side of Chile started to appear. Overall, it would require more extroversion to confront than I could muster.

The triggering event occurred in November 1970, six months after our arrival, when Salvador Allende became President. A far-left socialist who got only 36% of the vote, he rapidly nationalized US copper operations and gave zero compensation to three of the five companies.

The action was popular with voters, as were the achievements of his first year in office—economic growth, lower inflation, less unemployment, and increased pay for workers. But Allende professed Marxism. A visit by Fidel Castro gradually led many Chileans to fear the president was putting the country on the same path as Cuba. Soon, sporadic riots started to occur.

Despite that, Chile was a beautiful place. The cost of living was extremely low, the food and wine delicious, and the scenery magnificent. At one point, we drove the Chevy six hundred miles south on the Pan-American highway to Puerto Montt, the capital of Chilean Patagonia. The forested mountains descending towards fjords made us think we were in British Columbia. We boarded a moored fishing boat owned by a local artist and bought an original oil painting called "Merienda," meaning lunchtime. It showed a family gathered in the dark hold of a small boat like the one we were on, their faces illuminated by a lantern in the center of their mealtime circle.

From the day we arrived, Erdesa struggled to survive. My cash projections helped us to stay afloat, but for me, the work soon became miserable. Our main projects were in the Atacama Desert in Antofagasta and even further north in Arica. When I went up there and looked across the terrain, it was so dry that I felt like I was on the moon.

To put correct forecasts together, I had to go onsite and in so doing, clashed regularly with the white-haired, irascible Bill Warneke. He did not appreciate my long sideburns or the bell-bottomed suits I had bought in Singapore when I was on leave during my Vietnam days.

Copper was Chile's main export, and during 1971, President Allende's first year, the world price fell. That, plus Allende's populist policies, soon led to rampant inflation, shortages of consumer goods, and more riots.

The stress of all this was acute, especially for Ida. I was totally focused on the business and was in Antofagasta for days at a time. She was now pregnant, and at one point, things got so bad we packed up our household goods and planned to leave the country. The situation calmed down and we did not leave, but around that time, Ida developed a pain in her abdomen. During a visit to a local clinic, she bled a great deal and ended up losing the baby. To add to the growing public chaos around us, we now had to deal with our own private grief as well.

Strikes and demonstrations became so common that Ida and I each fell afoul of them separately. One morning, she was shopping downtown when a riot erupted in the street, and police used tear gas to disperse it. She fled into a nearby shop just before the owner rolled down the heavy steel curtain that usually protected the store only at night. Tear gas fumes found their way inside under the bottom of the curtain; Ida, the owner, and his salesladies retreated as far as they could to the rear of the building as the fumes kept advancing. There was no back door. Fortunately, the tear gas stopped just short of where everyone had huddled. When Ida finally was able to leave, she was shaking.

On another day, I was driving by the University of Chile on my way downtown for an appointment when students dragged a coiled row of barbed wire in front of my car. I quickly looked along the length of it and saw it crossed all four lanes of the two-way boulevard I was on. I wheeled the car to the left, bumped up over a curb, drove across a grassy median, dropped into the street on the other side, and high-tailed it out of there with screams and shouts following close behind me. The tension kept my heart pounding until I got miles away from the scene.

These incidents terrified Ida and left me unsettled. Neither of us had ever been through anything like this. The unrest threatened our safety and left us with a feeling of helplessness. We did not want to think about what would have happened to Ida if she had not been able to escape the tear gas, or to me if I had not been able to outrun the mob.

We talked about the physical side of what happened to us, but rarely spoke about the psychological impact. Fortunately, she had majored in psychology and knew she needed help. She started seeing a local psychologist every few weeks, and it eased her mind a bit.

The cat was a lifeline for her, a link to happier days in Boston, but she worried about him. He loved to sit on an eight-foot cinder block wall in the back yard, hissing at a ferocious German shepherd below. It drove the dog so insane that when he growled and jumped up at the wall, the whole thing shook, and we were afraid Babassu would fall off.

He never did, but once he got stuck in a space between the roof and the overhang on the outside of the front of the house. I was in Rio de Janeiro with Bruce chasing new business. Ida managed to get a call through to my hotel and was in tears, asking me to come home to get him out. I was so concerned for her that I packed up and flew back, getting to Santiago the next day. By then, the cat had freed himself and all was well. But imperceptibly, the incident rekindled my initial concern about whether she was the right girl for me. My chosen career was in international business, and Ida needed more stability than I could provide. I did little to address that.

The loss of the baby weighed much heavier on Ida than it did on me. We kept trying for another one but so far were having little success. I was either out of town or so preoccupied at the office that we had little time together for intimacy or even to talk.

She spent every day going out to shop for necessities. That was a challenge in an economy where supermarkets were rare and supply shortages were starting to appear. So, it took her hours to find the simplest things. Otherwise, she was at home with Conchita, whose chattiness and good humor did help Ida's sagging morale.

o

IT WAS CLEAR that because of the political unrest, our business would not last long in Chile. The economy was sinking fast and taking us down with it. Despite support from C&C, our business had never been that strong to start with. By now, supplies were getting short, skilled labor was hard to find, and inflation grew every day. The currency seemed to depreciate by the hour.

Meanwhile, Bruce somehow discovered that a small construction company in Buenos Aires, Argentina was looking to partner with a US firm, so we flew over the Andes to meet with the owners.

The CEO was Eduardo Castro-Sanchez—a retired general in the Argentine army. Tall, dignified, and with piercing eyes, he spoke with precision. Number one, he was impressed with the patented building method we were licensing from Ohio Steelworks in Cleveland. Number two, his firm had secured a contract to build houses in Paraná, a five-hour drive north of Buenos Aires. Number three, his company, América Construcciones, wanted to partner with us on the project.

This, of course, was madness. We were barely surviving. We were having trouble running our own distant projects in Chile, and Paraná was even more remote and difficult to reach from Santiago. C&C was not happy with the events in Chile and might put us out of business at any moment. But we thought this deal could be our ticket out of Chile, so amid handshakes and hugs all around, we agreed to do it.

From the start, the project was doubly doomed. For one thing, Argentine labor was in the grip of Peronism, a populist movement that strongly supported unions and was highly nationalistic. For a foreign firm such as ours, both policies made the workers difficult to engage with. This mattered because the key to our profitability, such as it was, lay in using a mechanical concrete pump to spray a high volume of plaster onto walls covered with steel mesh. The workers opposed such a labor-saving device, and instead insisted on flicking small gobs of plaster onto the mesh by hand using pointed trowels. Labor costs using that method were unsustainable.

In addition, just keeping my cash projection process going consumed a great deal of time. It was an important source of security for me, so I hired an exceptionally competent jobsite accountant. A pudgy, courteous man, Isando Duque worked hard to carefully capture the data I needed to build forecasts. But in the days before email, and in an environment of increasing governmental paralysis in Chile, the only way for me to get current information was to take down data from him over the phone—provided I could get through to him using the unreliable telephone systems in both countries. It was either do that or spend an entire day traveling to Paraná.

The phone worked for a while. But one day in Santiago, we got an urgent call from the General saying the job had run out of cash and could not make payroll; a strike was imminent if we did not come up with half the money. We had none to give, so the General and his financial guy had to walk into gas stations all over Buenos Aires and cash scores of personal checks to get the money. In his book, we were now pariahs.

Around that time, we traveled to Caracas, Venezuela to meet with a developer about a new project. He had checked up on us and neatly summarized our Argentine experience: "*Se fueron al otro lado de los Andes, y se cagaron*" ("They went to the other side of the Andes, and crapped all over themselves.")

o

WHEN THE ONE-YEAR lease was up on our little wooden bungalow, Ida and I moved into a modernistic concrete home in the Vitacura section of Santiago, not far from the office. It was more spacious and sat on a beautiful half-acre lot. The rotund and obsequious owner, Orlando Marcos, turned out to be a construction manager who, like so many in Chile, had fallen on tough times. Ida and I felt sad that he had to move himself and his six children elsewhere, but Bruce ended up hiring him to fill a vacancy on one of our projects.

Ida loved the new place and decorated it well. She was homesick, so we brought her youngest sister Naomi down to Chile from Connecticut for a two-week visit that helped Ida's spirits immensely. Unfortunately, her optimism did not last.

A few weeks later, in the middle of the night, the sound of an approaching freight train woke us up. At this house, we had never heard a train before and there were no railroad tracks near us. What we heard approaching was an earthquake.

The roar grew so loud we could hardly talk over it. We jumped out of bed and groped our way barefoot across the undulating floor to an archway just outside the bedroom. It was a strong point likely to endure if the ceiling started dropping around us. We huddled under the arch; the noise became deafening, and we could barely keep our balance. We heard crashes across the house as plates and knick-knacks fell to the floor.

The movement stopped as quickly as it began. The electricity was out, so I got a flashlight from my night table and surveyed the scene. I happened to point it upwards at a heavy ceramic teapot that was on a shelf jutting halfway out of the arch we had stood under. The pot had turned completely around. If it had fallen, it would have thrown shards of glass all over our legs and bare feet. In addition to all the violence in Santiago, it scared us even more to realize we could not even count on the ground beneath us.

Not long afterwards, Ida had a sharp pain in her groin that doubled her over. She was pregnant again and we feared it was another miscarriage. We rushed to the closest hospital. The doctor told us it was her appendix and that he needed to operate immediately. Ida was so frightened that before the staff took her away, I asked him if I could be present. To my surprise and Ida's relief, he said I could. He would give me a complete surgical getup and introduce me to the operating room team as "Doctor Ploom."

I suited up and came in just as the anesthesiologist was injecting an intravenous needle into Ida's arm. Duly introduced to the staff, I went to her and held her hand until she became unconscious. Shortly afterward, and before the doctor began cutting, Ida started flailing her arms and legs so violently she almost fell off the table. Nurses rushed to contain her; she was still out and thankfully unaware of what was happening. The surgeon was relaxed, saying that happened sometimes, and he would wait until he was sure she was calm before operating. At that point, my faith in Chilean medicine was pretty shaky. But the operation went well. The baby was safe, and in a few weeks, Ida was mostly back to normal.

In the middle of the night, a month or so after the operation, someone broke into our house. We heard it;

I grabbed a flashlight and rushed towards the living room. Footsteps hurried out the kitchen back door. I flipped on the outside floodlights just in time to see a man scaling the side wall and jumping onto the property next door. I recognized him as one of the workers our housekeeper Conchita had recommended to do some repairs. When she found out, she was mortified. He was a relative and she never thought him capable of such a thing, no matter how bad the economy was getting.

We believed she was telling the truth and we never had another break-in. But with the public violence, Ida's surgery, the earthquake, and now the burglary, I felt great anxiety, and Ida descended further into fear. With a trembling voice, she asked if we could get a golf club to put under the bed to defend ourselves. I got one right away.

Today, I am aghast and ashamed that I let things get to that point. We talked little about what really mattered, namely our emotional safety, which was threatened almost daily by the events around us. Instead, I saw to her physical comfort as best I could but rushed about dealing with urgent problems at work by running my financial projection process. I hoped it would fix everything in the business and by extension, fix everything at home. But it did not, and we gradually became more anxious and more distant from one another.

o

ONE OF THE biggest problems in our business was making payroll. Coming up with the money was only part of it. We received a trickle of supporting funds from our parent company in US dollars, but they had to be converted into Chilean escudos for the workers.

For that purpose, I became skilled at dealing with two black market moneychangers. One was Jerry Bell, the jolly English insurance broker who worked at the downtown stock exchange; another was Dr. Enriquez, a physician who had lost his wife and broken multiple bones in a car accident. He was living at home and always came to the door in a leg cast and an arm sling.

I alternated between them, delivering dollars in cash in exchange for literally suitcases of Chilean currency. The biggest denomination was one hundred escudos, which at one point was worth about four US dollars. They folded the escudos in half and bound them with rubber bands into ten-thousand escudo blocks, each worth about $400. They would put twenty or thirty of the blocks into my waiting suitcase, which I would haul away, limping and leaning heavily to one side. I would then put the suitcase in the trunk of the 1965 Nova, drive to our Santiago jobsite, and make payroll out of the back of the car.

In mid-1972, it became too difficult for Erdesa to function. We could not get materials. And the workers, egged on by the socialist Allende government, expropriated our most valuable piece of equipment, the high-volume concrete pump we had imported at great expense from the United States. Unable to build, and under pressure from C&C to get out, we made plans to abandon everything.

Because the government had implemented strict export controls, we had to leave with only the clothes on our backs plus the contents of one suitcase apiece and just a few hundred US dollars. A trip to the black market netted us several thousand dollars in hundred-dollar bills, so a most important question became how to get the money out. Ida was now six months pregnant, and we would need the money wherever we went to make a new start.

We knew Allende had inspectors at Santiago's Pudahuel airport who went through everyone's luggage and presumably checked their wallets before they boarded an international flight.

So, to get around that, I improvised and came up with a way to take the money out. It was risky because, if caught, I could be detained and funneled into the Chilean justice system. But out of desperation, I devised a little process to hide the funds.

In the office, I flattened the bills into two stacks. I put each one in a letter-sized envelope and folded the sides to reduce the envelope to the size of the bills. I then took off my shoes and socks to do a trial run. I placed one stack on the bottom of my right foot and put my sock over it and did the same with the left foot. I then put my shoes on and stood up.

My Chilean partner Max was watching this whole charade. "What do you think?" I asked.

"I don't know. Show me one of the packets," he said.

I retrieved it from my sock and handed it to him. He put it up to his nose.

"*Oooofff*," he said with a frown, squinching his face up like it was the worst thing he had ever smelled in his life. Then he broke into a huge grin.

On the day of our flight, Ida and I headed to the airport in a cab. Once we were there, the inspector searched our suitcases. When finished he stood in front of me and looked me up and down. The bills were so hot against my feet that I was sure steam was rising out of my shoes. He must have decided I looked too geeky to try anything risky, because after a long moment he waved us on to the boarding gate.

o

OBSESSION WITH MY Elijah-Chan-inspired cash forecasting model had not prevented our demise in Chile. Instead, it had distracted me from seeing how bad the situation outside our door really was. Far worse, I was so deeply into the model that I failed to provide enough psychological comfort to a wife who was enduring terrifying experiences thousands of miles from home.

In all of this, the relentless demands of my winning recipe kept me focused on the future instead of on the daily reality we were facing. The solution to the danger would have been to be present, to pay attention to the current situation instead of always concentrating on a future state that never came.

What is so devastating for me to realize in retrospect, was that the two giant issues I missed were right there in front of me. Ida and I could not even go downtown to shop or do business without potentially having a run-in with a mob. What was I thinking? How could I possibly assume my cash flow machinations could overcome the train wreck that the Chilean economy had become? As it was, we were lucky to get out with a few clothes and some US dollars hidden in my shoes.

Ida's stress was right on the surface. She had trouble sleeping; we lived in a nice part of town, but she feared another home invasion. When her sister Naomi had flown down from Connecticut and then returned to the US, I had been sure Ida wished we could be on that plane with her. Yet I plodded on, continuing to hope my cash management process would provide the financial security the business needed. In the end, we simply had to flee.

The Chilean story illustrates a truism: even when the whole world is burning down, you will die in an effort to save your winning recipe.

o

BY NOW, MY family back in California owned a little house on the beach in Malibu, and they offered it to us as an interim stop after Chile.

That meant I had three choices: quitting Erdesa and trying to find a job in the US while living on the beach, transferring within C&C to an opening they had for me on a banana plantation in Honduras, or going with Bruce and Max to the Republic of Panama for a new project he had secured on the Atlantic side of the isthmus at Colón.

Given all Ida had been through, she wanted to have the baby in the US. But my career ambitions based on my financial forecasting method eclipsed everything else. Art Kipke, the president of the company, was ill, so Bruce was now leading Erdesa and reporting directly to Elijah Chan in Honolulu. The prospect of riches—baronial splendor, as Bruce described it—by building steel-based housing in a stable and prosperous country like Panama captivated my heart. I was sure in that setting, my financial forecasting method would finally pay off.

Even though it further increased the distance between Ida and me, I selected the third option. She had very little say in it. It was cruel and unforgivable of me to treat her like that. It might have extended our marriage if we had gone to Malibu. But we did not, and we would pay a harsh price for my choice.

*"Even when the whole world is burning down, you will die in an effort to save your winning recipe."*

We took off from Santiago with the cash still in my socks. I did not remove it until we were safe in Panama some seven hours and three thousand miles away.

With us also, were Babassu the cat and a stray black and white cat named Baba Junior who had adopted us in Chile. With them in tow, we were eager to make a fresh start.

We had no idea that in Panama, we would face a new and even more serious physical threat to our safety.

# Chapter 14
# The Noriega Incident

JUNE 1972. PANAMA CITY, PANAMA. When we came off the plane at Tocumen airport, a hot blast of tropical heat hit us in the face, telling us we were now in a place totally unlike the temperate Santiago where we had lived for the past two years.

Around 2:00 p.m. each afternoon, it rained with such fury that the water bounced off the streets to a height of two feet, creating a knee-high horizontal line of water to walk through if we were foolish enough to go outside.

There was no public unrest and no inflation. The economy was bustling, and the American influence was everywhere. The city butted up against the American-controlled Canal Zone, a strip of land five miles wide on each side of the Panama Canal in which thousands of Americans lived. Life there was like in any small community on the US mainland. In Panama City itself, many people spoke English, and shops accepted US dollars, which they called *balboas*. When Ida and I saw all of this, it greatly relieved our minds.

That said, I was so desperate to get out of Chile and

get a new forecasting process set up in Panama, that I jumped at the chance to move there without looking closely at the business environment I was stepping into. Manuel Noriega, the country's hidden puppet master, was a grasping, venal thug who unofficially sat atop the national bank that was to be our paymaster. I was so frantic in service to my recipe that once again, I had not scanned the environment as I was trained to do in business school. If I had done so, I would have seen that while Panama looked stable on the surface, its underbelly was rotten. I might have insisted that Bruce try to locate a new project somewhere else, or at the very least have thought about how we could protect ourselves if Noriega tried to extort money from our company.

That said, Ida was thrilled to be in a place that felt so familiar it was almost like home. We rented a brand-new, two-story townhouse off Calle 50 near the upscale Punta Paitilla part of town, and she loved it. Our venerable Chevy Nova was stolen by the Chilean employee we had asked to sell it for us there, so we bought two new cars, a tiny green Datsun hatchback for me and a silver Mitsubishi mini station wagon for her.

Like Hawaii, Panama was free of rabies, so Babassu and Baba Junior went into quarantine, this time for ninety days. The feline digs were not as sumptuous as in Honolulu, but they were adequate, and Ida got to see them every day.

As soon as we left Chile, C&C bowed out, transferring the stock to Bruce, Max, and me. We formed a Panamanian company, Erdesa International, Inc., so we could continue to do business. In running it, the three of us got along great, balancing each other's skills well—Bruce promoted new business, Max oversaw

*Fig. 7 Bruce Fraser and Myself. Panama City, Panama, 1973.*

the construction work, and I managed the finances. Bruce bought a little Alpha Romeo sports car, He was happy that in Panama he did not have to worry about it being damaged in a riot.

Despite our debacle in Argentina and the disruptive effect on my relationship with Ida while we were in Chile, I at once started running the cash forecasting method again. I believed that surely in this more familiar, more American context my financial processes would thrive and provide the security I sought. Bruce had made a deal with an American developer for us to build our earthquake-resistant housing in Colón near the Atlantic entrance to the canal. It was only an hour away from the Pacific side where we had our office, so I was sure I could easily get the data I needed to keep my process fed.

The developer, Al Oberlander, was a short, middle-aged and confused American salesperson whose signature possession was a six-foot long, four-inch-wide tan leather tube that held rolled-up plans of the project. In the tropical heat it smelled like fresh cow dung. He took it everywhere, often in the company of his partner, Tito Vazquez, a thin man with a heavily creased face whose level of incoherence fluctuated hourly depending on how much scotch he had just nipped. The two were so incompetent that they bordered on being morons. In the company of such fine gentlemen, what could possibly go wrong? I was too focused on the numbers to care.

o

WHEN WE EMIGRATED to Panama, we knew the medical care would be excellent. The country boasted of many US-trained physicians and had hospitals with good reputations. This put our minds at ease as we waited the three months after our arrival for Ida to have our first child.

With steam rising from the streets of Panama City after an epic downpour on the afternoon of October 2, 1972, Ida gave birth in the Clínica San Fernando. She endured nine hours of labor followed by a Caesarian section to deliver a girl, whom we named Hannah. We were out of our minds with joy. The baby was beautiful, healthy, and a portent, we thought, of many wonderful things to come.

After we took her home, our first responsibility was to get her registered as an American citizen. I completed the paperwork at the US Embassy and the Ministerio de Relaciones Exteriores of Panama, secure in the knowledge that she could now live permanently in the US.

We had hired a full-time housekeeper named Cora, a skinny African-Panamanian woman who cooked and cleaned but would not iron because she was convinced that doing so in the heat made people sick. She loved Hannah and was an immense help to Ida in caring for her.

Ida blossomed like I had never seen. She adored being a mother, nursing the baby, cooing and talking to her in a little voice that previously she had reserved only for the cats. We alternated nighttime feedings, with me heating up the formula in the kitchen when it was my turn.

A month after Hannah was born, my father Neely flew down for a few days. She was his first grandchild, and he was entranced. We took a now-graying Neely to the canal at the Miraflores Locks, sat in the bleachers there, and looked across the concrete to see a massive ship slowly rise up, up, and up right in front of us. He had spent several years at Georgia Tech and marveled at the engineering that made it all possible. When he saw a sign that said "Miraflores Locks—1914," he noted that he had been born in 1912. "Geez," he said, "I'm older than the Panama Canal."

Shortly afterwards, Ida's mother Kate came down for a week. Hannah was her first grandchild as well and completely captivated the new grandmother. Having her cheery, perennially smiling mother there kept Ida's spirits high.

When little blonde-haired Hannah was old enough to walk, she followed Cora around the house saying, "*¡Chuletas, Cora, chuletas!*" *Chuletas* were pork chops, one of Cora's specialties. Hannah's dietary preferences were broad. For example, she loved to go onto the patio and eat dirt out of a potted plant before grinning through a large patch of soil around her mouth.

We had to be careful about our back yard. Our patio faced a small lawn that had six-foot concrete walls on three sides and backed up to an overgrown creek. Near the water were iguanas so huge we feared they might be a threat to Hannah. One day, a reptile a yard long came across the patio and through the open sliding doors into the house, flicking its forked tongue in all directions to see what might be available to eat in our living room. I grabbed a broom. When it saw me coming, it turned around to run but struggled to get traction on the terrazzo tile floor. It finally did, swerving its tail back and forth until it hit the grass. It went straight up the wall and disappeared into the growth on the other side.

One of our favorite pastimes was to take Hannah to the beach on the Pacific side of the isthmus and stay in a rustic cabin for a few days. There was no bathtub, so Ida bathed her in a plastic dish tub.

During the day, we put a beach umbrella in the sand just at the water line so Hannah could hold onto the pole as the gentle surf came in. She would squeal with joy as the cool water hit her, and in seeing that, we bathed ourselves in happiness.

o

AT THE START of our project in Panama, the company did well financially. We always did so at the beginning of construction jobs, because at that point they were flush with cash. But as soon as the work advanced a little, we began surviving from one progress payment to the next.

The initial bloom of optimism we felt after moving to Panama gradually wore off in other ways as well.

The heat was stifling, and we had no central air conditioning in the townhouse. The window units were too expensive to keep turned on all the time, so we only fired them up when we needed them. Cora lived in a four-story wooden tenement with arcades around each floor, and I felt terrible taking her back to such a place each day. Once, we went to a wedding in a nice part of town and came back to find that the left rear tire of the Datsun had been stolen right off the car, leaving it and us in a lurch.

In quick succession, I caught both amebic dysentery and malaria. The dysentery had me ejecting material at both ends and so thoroughly emptied me of fluids that all I could do between episodes was lie on the bathroom floor. To get help, Ida had to run next door carrying the baby because Cora was off that day. An elderly neighbor put me in the back seat of his car and drove me to the Clínica San Fernando, where an intravenous solution of glucose soon made me feel better. I recovered in a few days.

The malaria, however, was insidious. It appeared not long after I left the hospital, causing spikes of fever and shakes every few hours. I could work but I never knew when the fever would hit. As I began to feel it mounting, I would rush home to sweat it out, then possibly go back to the office. The case turned out to be light. My doctor had treated it at once with antimalarial medication, and after a year, it disappeared.

No amount of financial process work on my part could make Erdesa International survive in Panama. The project was too small, and payments tied to progress came in too slowly. Al and Tito constantly inserted themselves, gumming up our efforts to make headway.

Bruce was unfazed. Somehow, in 1973 he connected with people in the Middle East who expressed interest in our earthquake-resistant building technology. We still had some cash in the bank, so we left the work in Max's capable hands and bought plane tickets for the seventy-three-hundred-mile trip to Beirut, where we picked up a flamboyant promoter named Farid Shaheen. The three of us then continued to Bahrain and Saudi Arabia.

Thanks to Shaheen, we met with two Saudi princes. One was an elderly man who listened to our pitch with dignified respect, nodding and occasionally saying, with perfect diction, "I see." He said that about forty times. Later we learned he did not understand a word of English.

Then we met with a young prince who did speak English and was excited to go into business with us. He was obsessed with the idea of opening an office in London, which we saw no purpose for but did not oppose. Afterwards, we found out he just wanted to get away from the strictures of Saudi society to a place where he could drink and whore to his heart's content.

After returning from such a pointless trip, we decided to look for work closer to home. Bruce again beat the bushes and in 1974 came up with a real project—a big one—in Jamaica. It was with the Ministry of Housing, which like all our former customers, loved our earthquake-resistant construction.

They wanted to build several hundred units in Port Antonio on the western tip of the island. Some were single-family structures like we were used to building; the rest were multi-story units that we had never constructed but figured we could build if we modified the technology a bit.

Still smarting from the mess we created in Argentina, which had been too far away for us to manage, we decided to hire a third party, a New York construction management company called ADA, to keep a project manager onsite in Jamaica and do all the reporting.

I worked overtime preparing the financials. This was by far the biggest job we had ever bid on, and I did what I could to make sure the numbers were right. I traveled to Kingston several times to meet with Ministry of Housing officials in musty offices piled high with yellowing paper files. Thanks to Bruce and Max's meetings on the technical side, we got the contract.

Unfortunately, the project manager ADA sent was an alcoholic more interested in consuming gin than generating correct data. ADA just added overhead without improving performance, so the burden fell on Bruce, Max, and me to get things done.

This was difficult because of the distance and because Jamaica had become a gangster economy. A mobster once approached one of our own project managers from Panama and said he was going to slit the man's throat and suck his blood if he did not pay a bribe. Somehow, we scraped through without the thugs cutting anybody's throat.

o

BY MID-1975, my cash forecasting systems in Panama and Jamaica needed a great deal of attention just to keep my partners focused on the money so we could stay afloat. In focusing on all of that so fixedly, I continued to be inattentive to Ida and damaged the relationship even further. I also completely missed a sinister, looming threat that would soon consume us.

Manuel Noriega put the squeeze on us. Jowly, pock-marked, and ruthless, he was the power behind General Omar Torrijos, the Panamanian president who had overthrown his predecessor seven years before. Noriega was a key information source for the CIA, as well as an operative who quietly supplied illegal guns, equipment, and cash to CIA-backed counter-insurgency groups in Latin America. He had made a fortune in drug trafficking, ran the gambling business in Panama, and despite being largely hidden from public view, was the most important man in the government.

Noriega's power affected our business as an everyday, indirect threat because as a small foreign firm, we were a visible target. He had his hand in everything in the country, and soon it reached out to grasp us.

Our Colón housing contract was with the government, via the Banco Nacional de Panamá. To make sure funds got to us in a timely way, instead of via the unreliable mail service, I stuffed down my introversion and reached out to the bank's paymaster, a diminutive, mustachioed bureaucrat named Señor Bonilla. He was always pleasant and received my detailed progress reports with courtesy and interest. Disbursements to us were based on the physical progress of the job. We were often behind schedule, so it took some convincing to get him to release partial funding if we did not qualify for the full amount.

One day, I went to see him for a $50,000 disbursement we had legitimately earned the previous week, but he balked. He said there were irregularities. The bank was looking into them, and until they finished, there would be no more money.

Confused, Bruce and I tried to get an appointment

with the president of the bank. He would not see us, and Bonilla would not tell us what the problem was.

At first, we thought it might be related to the Panama Canal negotiations between President Carter and General Torrijos. But that made no sense. The last thing Torrijos needed was the bad publicity of appearing to pressure a small American company.

We then thought the bank might be having financial problems and needed an excuse not to pay us. But again, that would not have been smart. The bank wanted the houses and the windfall of positive news they would generate for the people of Colón.

In the end, we concluded that it was simple, heavy-handed extortion. The bank would refuse to pay the $50,000, thinking we would be too intimidated to stop the job, and they would still get their houses. Because little happened in Panama without Noriega's consent, we guessed that he had to be behind the ploy.

The accuracy of this interpretation came home to us one evening around 7:00 p.m. when Bruce, Max, and I were working in the office. Two Panamanian soldiers with crew cuts, thick necks, and green fatigues pressing tightly against their biceps walked in and demanded my passport. With no smiles on their faces and outsized revolvers hanging from their Army-issue web belts, they were serious.

Shaking, I opened my briefcase, took out the passport and handed it to them. They left with it as quietly as they came.

They had not taken Bruce's passport, nor Max's, because I was the face of Erdesa International at the bank. We at once called our lawyer, a young man named Jorge Antonio Rojas. Slick, mustachioed, good-looking,

American-educated, and the grandson of a former president, Jorge Antonio was politically well-connected. Although now that the soldiers were running everything, we were not sure how much that still mattered.

He came right over. With the relaxed air of an aristocrat and sporting a fresh coat of Old Spice on his cheeks even at that late hour, he told us not to worry. He would fix it. Seeing we were not convinced, he walked over to the window and pulled back the curtains to reveal the darkness outside.

"Uh-oh," he said in a somber tone. I looked at Bruce and Max. They had turned as white as I had, thinking the police had come back to haul us off to rot in a Panamanian jail.

Jorge Antonio whipped his head around. "Gotcha!" We gave him a nervous laugh.

"Look, you guys need to loosen up," he said. "I will look into this and get it handled quickly if I can."

On the way out he chuckled to himself and winked, saying, "Better keep a watch on that window. . ."

He came back a few days later wearing a silk tie and one of his many Italian suits. After doing some checking, he was convinced not only that Noriega was behind it, but that the best way to get out of the situation was to sue the man, personally, before the Supreme Court of Panama. Noriega was not expecting that and would not want the media frenzy Jorge Antonio gleefully expected to launch just as the canal negotiations were becoming critical.

The easy confidence with which the words rolled off Jorge Antonio's tongue made it all sound so simple. But my mind raced with images of sitting forever in a

Panamanian jail while the legal system made glacial progress. I told him I needed to think about it.

When I related all this to Ida, she asked what our options were. I saw two. The first was to follow Jorge Antonio's advice and embark on a risky course in a country where the rule of law still existed but was shaky. The second was to flee. We would not need a passport to get back to the US since there was free passage from Panama into the Canal Zone. We would find a way to get ourselves on a military flight to Florida.

She did not like either choice, especially running away, and the more we talked I saw why. Fighting Noriega was hugely risky but trying to escape might be even more so. For all we knew the government was watching me and could arrest me if we tried to cross into the Canal Zone. We would have to leave everything behind except what we wore and two suitcases, just like in Chile. Plus, there was no guarantee that the American military would let civilians on a flight, particularly if one were under a cloud in Panama and had no passport to prove he was an American. We had a little girl who was not two years old, and Ida was six months pregnant again.

I listened to what she said and the next day talked it over with Bruce and Max. I told them that for Ida and me, the only way ahead was to take Jorge Antonio's advice and bull through. They agreed, and soon Noriega had a case pending against him in the Panamanian Supreme Court.

o

THAT DID NOTHING for my peace of mind.

A pang of fear went through me every time I saw a police officer. They all wore military uniforms that were like those of the Panamanian Defense Force goons who had taken my passport.

Weeks passed, and we heard nothing. Jorge Antonio made the rounds of his contacts, letting everyone within earshot know he was going to create a huge stink about this case if Noriega did not return my passport and pay us the $50,000 we had justifiably earned. The canal negotiations were continuing. We hoped Noriega was getting the message, but Jorge Antonio could detect no movement from the other side.

One Saturday, we put Hannah in her car seat in the Mitsubishi and drove towards Colón for an outing. The shortest route to the Atlantic side was a two-lane highway through the Canal Zone, but while we were still in the Republic, a police car appeared behind me with its red lights flashing.

If this was it, I stupidly decided I was not going to let them catch me when we were all so close to freedom. Without thinking it through, I punched the gas and went as fast as the curving jungle road would allow. We drove for five miles before I noticed the cop was gaining on me. There were still ten more miles to go before reaching the Canal Zone, and I knew he would not follow me in there, so I kept on. But the cop was a more experienced driver, and after another few miles, he pulled up right beside me and pointed for me to pull over.

I did so. He came up behind and stood by the door. He had the familiar green Defense Force fatigues, bulging biceps and huge hip pistol. I rolled down the window. The pungency and humidity of the surrounding jungle air flowed into the car.

In my best Spanish, I asked what the problem was. He asked me to step onto the road. My heart pounded.

I got out and looked up and down the highway. No cars. If anything were to happen, there would be no witnesses. The police officer motioned for me to come with him to the back of the car.

Once there, he pointed to one of the taillights.

"Señor, this light is not working. It dangerous. You must have it fixed. Have a nice day." He turned his car around and sped off. I wished there was a good place to clean out my pants.

Now more rattled than before, I almost fainted from a hyperactive heartbeat a week later when our secretary told me a lawyer from the Corte Suprema was on the phone. He would not give his name and said one of the justices wanted to see me, alone, that very morning at 11:00 a.m.

I had no idea where the Supreme Court building was, and as I drove, looking at the directions our secretary had given me, I could not find a building that was stately enough for such a facility. At length, I matched the address to a squat, aging structure that could have been a warehouse. Waist-high dirt and scuff marks colored the yellow walls on both sides of the door.

I walked in and told the man inside who I was. He ushered me into a small office where a middle-aged gentleman in a black robe was sitting. His desk looked like it had just been delivered from a garage sale. His manner was grave and dignified.

"Señor, there has been a misunderstanding," he said in Spanish. "Please accept this."

He opened a tiny drawer and pulled out my passport.

He held it towards me but did not release it. He looked straight at me, and with every ounce of gravitas he could muster said, "This did not happen."

I looked back at him and agreed wholeheartedly that none of this had ever taken place. My passport resting in my pocket and a huge release of breath now exiting my lungs, I walked out, silently thanking Jorge Antonio Rojas and his aristocratic ways.

Because of him, we also recovered the $50,000 Noriega had unfairly withheld from us. We had applied the law and used the magnetic pull of possible adverse publicity at a time when Canal negotiations with the United States had become critical. Jorge Antonio was masterful.

o

WHEN HANNAH FOUND out that another a baby was going to come out of Mommy's tummy soon, she started calling us by our first names. "I want a cookie, Ida," or "Ben, I have a poopy." We read that was normal behavior for a two-year-old, so we did not make a big deal about it, and eventually she stopped.

Panama was causing much less stress for us than Chile had. But the Noriega episode made us acutely uncomfortable, because now we had so much more at stake with one and soon two little children to care for.

Bruce and I had also soured on the place and on overseas living in general. The Colón and Port Antonio jobs were winding down after having supplied an adequate, but not baronial, level of financial returns. We now looked to Miami for our next venture.

In Panama, we had set up an international trading arm within our company to bring in goods in bulk, break them down in a duty-free zone in the Republic, then reship them to customers throughout Latin America. The venture was prospering and had generated a comfortable cash cushion for the three of us. Max loved that business and would stay behind to run it in Panama, while Bruce and I would set up a branch in Miami to do the same kind of work. We looked forward to doing more trading deals and leaving the problems of the construction business behind us.

The prospect of returning to the US after the baby was born made Ida happy and excited. In that mindset, she scheduled a Caesarian delivery on September 22, 1975, in the brand-new Paitilla Medical Center just a few blocks from our townhouse. I was not allowed to be present, so when I saw the obstetrician wheeling the baby out at the end of a long hall, I ran up to him and asked in excited English, "What is it?" A little flustered since English was his second language, he hesitated and said, "It's a baby!"

In Spanish, I clarified what I meant. "It's a boy," he said, "and look how pink and beautiful he is. He did not have to go through the birth canal."

We named him Conor and were beside ourselves with happiness at having two such beautiful children. After Ida and Conor came home, I made the rounds of the embassy and the ministry again to collect the paperwork for registering him as an American citizen. And in December, as soon as Ida was well enough to travel, the six of us, two adults, two kids, and two cats, flew the eleven hundred miles to Miami. I was thirty-two years old, and Ida was thirty. For the first time in five years, we would be living again on American soil.

o

SOME MIGHT SAY that in Panama, I was a victim of circumstance and coercion I could not have predicted.

While it is true that I could never have foreseen the exact form in which events would unfold, from the perspective of today, it is more probable that *something* rather than nothing would have happened to us.

In addition to lobbying Bruce to move us elsewhere after seeing how dangerous Noriega was, I could have implemented a risk mitigation plan, something else I had been trained to do at Harvard. In Jorge Antonio we had a powerful spoiler, a well-connected political operator who probably could have thrown an effective ring of protection around us. Through intermediaries, it would have been easy for him to let Noriega know to keep his hands off us. "Touch these gringos," he could have said, "and I will sue you, publicly, before the Supreme Court. They are not worth it. Go somewhere else to make your money." That was exactly what he ended up doing. Only he did so *after* Noriega made his move, not beforehand as we might have preferred.

I again suffered from an extreme case of selective perception, seeing only the accounting ledgers in front of me and thinking they represented the whole situation.

Psychologists suggest that many things can cause such a narrow view—beliefs, past experiences, mood, gender, age, race, and religion among others. But for me, an introvert, my winning recipe surpassed all of those. It had me willingly relying on a step-by-step cash flow process to ward off danger instead of looking beneath the surface to detect the real peril.

Paradoxically, getting insight into underlying facts often requires not a microscope but a telescope, stepping back to get a wider view. I could have only done that by going outside of my recipe to assess the nature of the man who ran the swamp that my partners and I were in, and then using the potent political force represented by our lawyer and his contacts. But I did not, and as a result, we again were abandoning a country for which we formerly held high hopes.

o

THE RECIPE HAD performed no better with danger than it had with fear.

I escaped from the peril of expulsion from Harvard only by being blind to my unsuitability for a top-level role in business. The Brazil project got canceled because I was more focused on the weeds than on the environment at United Fruit headquarters. Physical danger in Chile and Panama threatened us because I paid more attention to my recipe-induced financial forecasting system than to the hazardous circumstances we lived in, or to a marriage that was falling apart bit by bit.

In all these situations, the recipe itself had been one of the main reasons I failed to find security. It had actually helped to *increase* each of the dangers I faced.

In Miami, we would no longer have to be so preoccupied with danger. The move there was the shortest we had made yet, but despite our best intentions, it would not be the sweetest.

# Part 4
# Vulnerability

# Chapter 15
# Upside Down in Miami

DECEMBER 1975. MIAMI, FLORIDA. We arrived full of hope. We rented a pretty little house on Key Biscayne for a few weeks, and had two white cribs brought in, one for three-year-old Hannah and the other for one-month-old Conor. Even though we were in a subtropical climate, the air was drier and cooler than we had felt in years.

Bruce and I and our families loved being back in the United States, but over the next four years we would not be able to make a go of the trading business. As a construction salesman and a financial guy, he and I did not have the instincts or the skill sets to broker deals that would provide value to all parties.

For me, the worst part was that there was no new methodology that would make a difference. My financial projections were useless because we had no cash coming in.

The impact on my marriage was heavy. After leaving Key Biscayne, we moved into a nice rental home with a pool in the Kendall area of Miami and started to build our own house based on the promise of trading deals that had not closed yet. Babassu, who had survived Boston, Honolulu, Santiago, and Panama was now in Miami but soon disappeared; we looked in nearby vacant lots reeking with dead grass clippings that people had dumped but could never find his body. By the time the new house was finished we could not afford to close on it and had to move out of the rental into a much smaller one. While there, Baba Junior got deathly ill, and we had to put him down.

Ida now focused on our two toddlers and took the pet losses in stride. But the forfeiture of the new house broke her heart. She had worked for six months to make selections for it, and to have to move into an old place that had none of the conveniences she was looking forward to, was hard.

By 1977, we had exhausted our savings. Big trading deals always looked enticing, so we kept chasing them, but there was no income. To keep going, I started borrowing money from my family every few months.

Bruce and I had an office in the Dadeland Towers office complex at the southern end of the Palmetto Expressway in Miami. At one point, we could not pay the rent. In fear of the landlord changing the locks, I moved all the files to my car. I had a 1976 Cadillac Coupe de Ville and was always amazed at the size of its trunk. Each day I opened it and panned my vision across sixteen large open boxes of files, four across and four deep, before selecting the papers we needed for the day. When the management eventually told us to leave, we set up in Bruce's house and moved all the files there.

Ida openly questioned my business judgment at staying so long with Bruce. She did not blame him for our troubles, but me for not recognizing that despite his best efforts, and mine, we had failed. I could not hear this and angrily let her know. I did not say it to her, but I was a Harvard Business School graduate, and what did she know?

Despite that, in the spring of 1979, I told Bruce I could no longer continue with him, and he understood. Max was doing reasonably well in Panama, and at his request, I signed over my shares in Erdesa International to him.

Bruce and I parted as friends and sought income elsewhere. He ended up hiring on as international VP for a company that made interior folding panels. He had a successful twenty-year career there that took him all over the world signing up foreign licensees. Now in his 90s, he is happily retired with his wife in central California.

Meanwhile, Ida and I were now living in a third Miami rental. The events of the nine years since we left Honolulu had so badly shaken my self-confidence that in trying to get a job, I did not even try to trade on my Harvard MBA degree. Ida had been right; my business judgment was terrible. Any large employer was bound to see that as well; for almost a decade I had produced no track record of achievement whatsoever.

By 1980, our marriage was falling apart. Long-dormant issues—ones I had detected when I first met her—now came up to complement the money problems that increasingly divided us. She wanted our kids to be exposed to some kind of traditional church, and I did not. I was interested in occasional sex, and she was not. And neither one of us wanted to talk about it.

To distract from my problems, I started watching a twenty-four-hour news station called CNN that began broadcasting as the first ever such network. One segment covered the premiere of the movie *Urban Cowboy* and its launch of the "mechanical cowboy" craze in country and western bars across the nation. I wondered why anybody would go to such places. Another segment covered the former B-movie actor and governor of California, Ronald Reagan, who was gunning for the Republican nomination for president.

One day in early 1980, I met a guy my age who owned a business called Filterco that made oil refiners for truck and car engines. Short and wiry, with thinning hair, Grant had invented the device himself. It avoided oil changes by constantly cleaning the oil as the engine ran. He was having trouble managing his cash flow, and when he heard what I could do for him, he hired me.

Instantly, I was back in business. In the front office of the company's cavernous factory, I stocked up on thirteen-column paper, resurrected the Elijah Chan cash projection process, and despite not being familiar with manufacturing, I put the finances of the company in order in just a few weeks. The company attorney and two board members took note, thanking me for turning things around and privately confiding in me that the owner was in over his head. Until they said that, I was too focused on finance to think much about the owner. But on reflection I had to agree.

I enjoyed the security of successfully being able to keep food on the table at home. But the income was less than we needed to pay our debts. My singular focus on handling creditors and keeping my job kept my attention from Ida and our relationship.

I was also not focusing on the children. I was not as close to them as my father had been to my sisters and me, and it hurt. I did spend time with them, taking them on rides with Ida on little seats on our bikes, going to the beach and even joining a father-daughter club known then as the Indian Princesses—since adopted as part of the YMCA Adventure Guides program—where Hannah and I had loads of fun. One of our favorite games was when the fathers bent over, put their foreheads on baseball bats that rested perpendicular to the ground, walked in three complete circles while staring at the ground, then stood up dizzy and staggering around like drunk men until they fell at the feet of their giggling daughters.

I loved that Hannah and Conor were getting acculturated into the US instead of Panama. But my preoccupation with my new job and our continuing lack of money despite having some regular income, had to have had an impact on them.

When I got out of survival thinking long enough to look at my life, I saw unmistakably that it was not working. The company I had been part owner of for the better part of ten years had recently failed. Any sense of intimacy with Ida, my wife of twelve years, was gone. On both accounts, my self-confidence was in the cellar.

One of the board directors at Filterco was Dick Bertram, owner of Bertram Yachts and a legend in the boating industry. Silver-haired, craggy, and fit, he invited me to lunch one day but would not say what he wanted to discuss. I was in such grief that I jumped at the invitation. I thought it might be a promotion that he and the other directors were engineering at the company. But it was something far different.

OVER MAYONNAISE-RICH tuna sandwiches, Dick told me about a personal development program he had recently completed called the Erhard Seminars Training (known as the est Training, with a lowercase "e"). It had been founded in 1972 by an ex-car salesman named Jack Robinson who had changed his name to Werner Erhard and become a sensation on the seminar circuit.

Dick was a hard-headed, successful businessman, and I respected him a great deal. He said the four-day training showed people how to put their past in the past instead of using the past to drive their present. In so doing, things they had been struggling with would clear up just in the process of life itself.

Despite admiring Dick, I was skeptical. The New Age movement was in full swing, and this sounded like pure woo-woo.

"Will this help me be a better manager?" I asked.

He nodded. "Absolutely. My experience is that whatever you have not been able to overcome will clear up."

"But how? You can imagine that sounds a little glib."

He looked right at me. "You will be able to take a position outside of yourself and see how you are making choices. That gives you the ability to make changes rather than be on automatic pilot all the time."

I had discovered something like that during the evasion and escape exercise back in 1965. I saw then that I could make a new choice: to just evade rather than automatically try to escape. I was intrigued that a whole program was now being dedicated to mastering that skill. My life was a mess, and I definitely had been on automatic pilot with everything I had striven to implement since Vietnam. When Dick said the program was for people who were well and wanted to take their experience of life to a higher level, he sold me.

I took the course in June 1980 with about two hundred other people of widely different educational, income, and age backgrounds in a hotel seminar room on Miami Beach. The training consisted of the participants holding a microphone and relating experiences in their own lives that connected to points the seminar leader was making. It also involved eyes-closed, guided "processes" that asked everyone to consider times in their lives when X or Y had happened. Those two vehicles exposed cascades of insights for me.

We all sat in chairs tightly packed together facing a raised platform where the trainer stood. From there, he delivered the meat of the course, its "distinctions"—a dozen or so key insights about human behavior that had an unsettling impact on me. They were not intended to do so, but they challenged my default position of being a loner.

I already knew that at age four I had invented myself to be an introvert. I did so before I ever knew the word, based on a judgment that I did not want to be around other people because they were so loud and disruptive. Ever since then, that past decision had governed my present. In the est Training, I realized that even though I was afraid of being more open to stimulation, I could have my fear and go ahead with things anyway.

All this got triggered inside my head as I sat in my chair and listened to the seminar leader and the other participants talk about things that were seemingly unrelated to me. It gave me a pounding headache that lasted for days, both during and between the two weekends of the training. On breaks, I went outside and stood at a railing watching the surf hit the beach between our hotel and the next, hoping the cool salt breeze and negative ions would relieve the pain. They did not.

For me, the distinctions were a new way of thinking, a novel approach to life and to interacting with other people. Just to take part in this training was an exercise in extroversion, because it instilled an irrepressible desire to share insights with the group. I did so twice. I took a microphone that a runner handed to me and looked out across two hundred expectant faces, strangely unafraid of making eye contact with so many people. For a guy as reluctant to be in a large crowd as I was, this was momentous. For the first time, the stimulation involved was not painful but exhilarating. It was opening me up to other people and another way of being.

I went back into the session, and more realizations hit me. Things between Ida and me were not good, and I had not taken steps to address them. I had not yet decided that the marriage was unworkable, nor that I wanted a divorce.

But the more I sat in the training, the more I did see the possibility of being completely blown away in a relationship with a woman. I realized I did not have a relationship like that with Ida and needed to work with her to make a change for the better. Ida was a fabulous mother, but any sense of intimacy or partnership between us was long gone.

I saw I was directing a great deal of anger towards my mother for her drinking while I was growing up. This came up when we were asked to pick the parent we felt most distant from and write down one hundred things they had done for us. As I wrote, I got in touch with how deeply she loved me, how tenderly she cared for me, and how gladly she would have given her life if it would have saved mine. I was crying so hard the ink started to blur on the paper. I resolved that no matter what it took, I was going to clean up my relationship with her.

I took responsibility for my failures in business. I saw that the past decade had been less about the circumstances themselves than about how I had not faced up to them. In Chile, I put my attention on plans and processes instead of admitting that the chaos we were in was unworkable and getting out sooner. In Panama, I did the same thing, focusing on my ledgers instead of using my business training to ferret out the risk Noriega might pose to us and putting in a plan to mitigate it. I saw that given the nature of the owner of Filterco, where I now was working, the unwillingness of the board to remove him, and the precarious cash flow coming in, my current job was a dead end.

Further, the course astonished me by putting my reliance on processes into perspective: *Everybody* did something like that. Not specifically to be methodical, because that was just one of the thousands of different paths people chose. Rather, they did it to overcome their childhood belief that they were not already good enough to succeed in life in some way.

The trainer referred to the phenomenon as having a "winning formula."[4] It was one or more ways of being that we all had hit on to be successful in life, to "make it." The formula could be anything and was compensation for something we could never be when we were young. It often prevented us from relating to

4. Today the successor to est, the Landmark Forum, calls it a "strong suit."

people, since it was about achieving success, not getting close to others. Even though I was not sure all of that applied to absolutely everybody on the planet, I noted that it eerily described exactly what virtually every one of the two hundred people in the seminar room and I had experienced.

o

BY THE TIME I emerged from the four days and a follow-up evening session a few days later my world was upside down. Despite my headache and having to take two five-hundred-milligram Tylenols every six hours to deal with it, I was joyous. I saw the possibility of inventing a whole new life and felt I had the tools and the motivation to make it happen.

> *"The formula was compensation for something we could never be when we were young."*

I soon realized, however, that the distinctions I got exposed to during those four days were a two-edged sword. On one hand, they provided an alternative to my winning recipe as a source of security. They called me to focus on integrity, commitment, responsibility, and engagement—things that could alter my reality for the better if I delivered them well. But on the other hand, the trainer specifically called us to be "unreasonable," meaning not to settle for the status quo or let anyone or anything stop us by offering a "reasonable" argument. For someone as safety conscious as I was, that tended to undercut the very distinctions I had just learned.

That said, the training woke me up. I realized I was victimizing myself, beating myself up over having terrible judgment in choosing a business opportunity and in choosing a woman to spend my life with.

The solution, I came to realize, was to take responsibility for where I was in life. The program leader said three things on that issue that struck me:

- Responsibility begins with a willingness be the cause of a matter, meaning to admit your participation in the issue.

- Responsibility is something you take on by declaring it.

- Once you take responsibility for a complaint, it will disappear completely.

These realizations turned my head around.

I called my mother in California and told her how deeply I loved her and appreciated everything she had done for me. I acknowledged I had been a shit to her and asked if she would forgive me. We both cried, and from that moment on, I had my mother back for the last fifteen years of her life.

I took responsibility for my business judgment by quitting my dead-end job and starting to seek whatever was next for me. After I resigned from Filterco, I called Dick Bertram to let him know I was sorry that had to be an outcome of the training he had recommended. He laughed and said he guessed that might be a possibility but knew whatever I decided would be best for me. He supported my leaving.

I took responsibility for my relationship judgment by trying to rebuild my marriage with Ida. A particularly powerful exercise we had done in the training was to sit knee to knee with a stranger and look into their eyes for ten minutes, only blinking and not averting our gazes. We did that with multiple people and in each case were so moved by them, that we hugged and cried when it was over, even though we had never met until then.

Ida agreed to try that while the kids were asleep, so we set up two chairs in front of a pile of dishes drying on the kitchen counter. About a minute into it, she said she could not continue; it was too hard for her, and she got up. Years later, I realized that at that point, she probably did not recognize me. For a decade and half, I had enrolled her in my being a hard-driving introvert, and now I was more relaxed and outgoing.

After I did est, Ida lost me as her partner in introversion. My genetic makeup had not changed; I was not now an extrovert. But after the training I gained self-confidence and felt less inclination to withdraw from others. That, plus the scars from many years of financial struggle and inattention from me, made it almost impossible to reconnect with her.

Not long afterwards, she said she wanted a trial separation and took the kids to her parents' house for six weeks. They now lived in the Del Water Gap area of western New Jersey. After the est Training, I felt more love for Hannah and Conor than ever before and missed them terribly, even as I was relieved to be away from Ida for a while.

A few weeks into her trip, I got a call at work from our brother-in-law Rob, who was a Lutheran minister.

"Ben, Ida and I have been talking. I just wanted you to know that if you and she are to stay married, things are going to have to change."

"I agree, Rob. What things did she mention?"

"I'd prefer not to get into that. Ida will let you know when she returns."

A month later, she and the kids came back. Her thinking had apparently evolved since the day she spoke with Rob, because now she said she wanted a divorce. I had not seen this coming so soon, but readily consented. Her reasons included our inability to communicate; her having to join a church without me, because she knew I was not interested in doing that; and her exasperation that I was not using my education to get hired by a big company.

The conversation was cordial. We agreed that the well-being of the children was paramount in this, and that no matter what happened, we would never disparage each other in front of them.

We called them into the living room and sat with them on the cheap green carpeting that covered the floor in the rental where we lived. Conor was now five, busy playing with a toy truck. Hannah, eight, was looking down at the floor. When we said the word "divorce," she whipped her head around to look at us. She knew extremely well what that meant. We hugged both children and told them we would always be their Mommy and Daddy, not sure in our own minds how we were ever going to do that successfully if I did not live with them.

This was only the start of the changes I was beginning to make in my life.

# Chapter 16
# On the Brink

APRIL 1981. MIAMI SHORES, FLORIDA. The divorce from Ida was finalized on April 28, ten months after I completed the est Training.

At first, I reveled in the freedom of my new life. I picked up the kids twice a week—on Tuesday night and on Saturday—and loved spending time with them at the mall, the library, and anyplace else that did not have an entrance fee. Oddly, I felt closer to them now than when I lived with them, helping to assuage some of the guilt I had whenever I compared myself to my own dad as a father.

I found a place to live just north of the city in Miami Shores, a single room in a trim stucco bungalow built in the 1950s. I had a nice tile bathroom and a private entrance from the side of the home. My only furniture was a burgundy velvet sofa bed on one wall, a door supported by wire legs that I used as a desk on the opposite wall, and a futuristic leather armchair beside a sliding glass door that looked out on an overgrown back yard.

My landlords were two guys who kept to themselves

and had decorated my space with tuck-and-roll padded walls. It was clean and comfortable, and I made sure I kept it that way.

Beyond the weeds in backyard was a tiny, in-ground swimming pool under some shade trees. Twelve feet long, six feet wide, and four feet deep, the kids believed it to be the best pool there was. On Saturdays, they would spend the night, sleeping in my sofa bed while I slept on the floor. They had a ball splashing around Saturday afternoons and again on Sunday mornings before I took them back to Ida.

Now a ten-month veteran of the est Training, I had stayed enrolled in weekly seminars that solidified the insights I had gained during the event. They also helped me adopt a less reserved, more open approach to life. The desire to invent processes to compensate for being an introvert went underground as glowing embers; I still felt them but did not act.

At a post-training meeting, I met a young guy named Henry who owned one of the first Apple computer stores in Florida. Curly-headed with fleshy cheeks and a growing midsection, Henry talked about the power of these new devices in a way that excited me. I drove the five hours from Miami to his store in Tampa to check them out and see if I could get a job there.

He was not hiring, but his talk captivated me with what personal computers could do for a small business. Out of that realization, I resolved to learn how to sell them. When Henry told me about a new computer store called International Computer Systems (ICS) that had just opened in Coral Gables back in the Miami area, my brain started working intensely on how I could join them.

I came back to Miami Shores just as the long Memorial Day weekend began. After so much exuberance in Tampa, I was disappointed to return to my empty room. After a few hours, it hit home that I was now totally alone, and I started to sense my newfound sociability might be only a veneer. As more long hours unfolded, I realized I had nowhere to go and nothing to do and slowly descended into what would turn out to be the most devastating depression of my life.

o

WHEN IT WASHED over me, I rolled a blank piece of paper into my portable typewriter and began to write.

"I run my life out of 'take care of me,'" I wrote. "I want people and companies to tell me how great I am and save me. I'm always looking for someone or a formula to rescue me. The world doesn't care."

Stunned, I lifted my fingers off the keyboard. This was a new insight. I had never thought of my processes as something I had invented to take care of me. But when I looked, I saw that awareness to be blazingly accurate. Processes provided security, and from the very beginning I had sought to use them as a shield against intrusions from an extroverted world.

I continued. "The lack of intention in my life is staggering."

I was thirty-eight years old and had been out of work for over a month. I was not keeping agreements about money. I had no sense of direction. I reacted to every newspaper ad about a job and every acquaintance who had a deal. I tried to fit everything together, to figure it out, to force it to work. I resisted participating with people. I blasted them for being how they were being. I looked only for comfort and rest. I had no satisfaction whatsoever from my life. I feared I would not survive. My mind absolutely dominated me from the early morning until I went to sleep, and even in my sleep, it ran me. I was physically thin but emotionally heavy. I was no fun to be with.

I had a tremendous sadness about my money situation. I was sad that I could not support the kids and Ida. I could not put food on their table. I could not give them any advantages in life. They were barely making it, and I was so broke that I might have to discontinue providing what little I had been giving to them.

I was sad about my relationship with my father. It was emotionless and filled with survival. I was perpetuating my own dependence and bleeding his resources. He would absolutely have given me the last dollar in his pocket and starved, and I was causing him to do it because of my own lack of intention. I loved him so very dearly. I loved my kids so very dearly.

My most cherished images were when I was little, and Dad would hold me. He took me everywhere. He took care of me at the barber, picked me up from the school bus stop with a towel when it rained, went to bat for me in high school when I almost got screwed out of being co-valedictorian, and brought me hot water bottles to lessen the joint pain when I had rheumatic fever.

My mother was absent from those memories. She was small and beautiful and wore high-heeled shoes. When I was two years old, she crossed her legs and bounced me on her free foot. She scared me. She was so vibrant, alive, talkative, and pretty, and she was coming after me. I could not stand it and ran to Daddy to save me from her. He would take care of me no matter what.

Mom's taking care of me had a hook in it. She wanted me in some way, and I could not deal with it. Yet she stayed with me in the hospital when I was fourteen and had my appendix out. She scratched my back countless times at night to relax me. She took care of me at home when I was sick with measles.

I got up from the table and walked over to the sliding glass door at the back of my room. I looked across the back yard and saw the grayness outside. A slow drizzle was coming down, putting circles all over the surface of the tiny swimming pool and a sprinkling of droplets on the tufts of weeds and the scruffy St. Augustine grass that my landlords had not cut in months. Somewhere in the neighborhood, a dog on a porch barked to be let in.

Back at the table, I went on typing. The cups of the keyboard letters felt comforting on my fingertips.

I closed up inside when Mom came at me. I shut down and turned to Dad for love that was pure and unconditional. Only his had a hook in it too—his desire to play the role of the Daddy he himself never had. He could not be just himself, and that was all I ever wanted him to be. Sometimes he *was* himself, but most of the time he was acting out of his conscious role of giving me the attention he never had.

He rewarded me for needing him. We played an elaborate game and were doing it now. I created circumstances where he needed to take care of me so he could care for me like no one ever cared for him. My whole life had been about this and my processes.

Dad took care of me because he needed to be the father who was missing from his own life. Mom took care of me because she wanted to give me the kind of nurturing that would prevent me from ever becoming like her father. He was a successful businessman, but he drank, neglected her, and physically abused her mother.

Because of those agendas, I did not get that they took care of me for *me*. I did not get a sense of safety out of all that. I spent my whole life trying to find it by having another person or some kind of a process take care of me so I could feel safe.

I saw that the only times I had money were when I successfully found situations where others could care for me. At Castle & Cooke in Honolulu, I had a big company to take care of me. Then my partner Bruce took over, and my other partner Max made a big pile of money for all of us. It was only when the party was over and I had to contribute on my own, that the money stopped. I drove deeper and deeper into Bruce and Dad to take care of me. They played their roles magnificently. They took care of me, isolated me from the world until they could not do it anymore.

Now for the first time ever, I was completely alone. After ten years, my close partner Bruce was gone. After twelve years, my wife Ida was gone; I married her to take care of me, and she got tired of it. She was her own person now. Only the kids were around to take care of me, and I was using them for that purpose every weekend. Rather than contributing to them, I was setting things up so they would take care of my emotional need for love. I was not making a damn bit of difference in their lives.

o

I WANTED TO die. I wanted to end this and get on with something else.

I was holding onto my crummy circumstances by my

fingernails so that the person I was would not die. Yet what I really wanted was for all this to go away. If I just let go of everything and allowed it to be, a new person would emerge. If I had intention, living would become purposeful. Intention would allow a hidden self to emerge from the ruins I was walking through.

The more I wrote, the more I began to feel the stirrings of a nascent willingness to take responsibility for my life again. With a clear intention, the circumstances would be okay enough for me to face them. If I had a framework of intention, then declaring bankruptcy, being cited for contempt of court for nonpayment of child support, and losing my car—all of which were staring me in the face—would be merely content.

The key to the whole thing, to my life, was to have intention. What did I intend?

I got up again and looked out the sliding glass door. It gave me a CinemaScope view of the wet gloom outside. I panned my eyes across the weeds and overgrown grass. The thousands of tiny droplets of water clinging to their sides somehow made them look hopeful. I opened the door a crack and got a whiff of fresh rain on grass, but quickly closed it to keep out a blast of humidity.

In that moment, I realized my intention was to have influence in the lives of people around me. But how?

Back at my familiar typewriter, I wrote that I had always thought making a difference had to look a certain way.

"But I could make a difference at any time," I wrote. "And in any place if that were the framework of my life. Whether I sell encyclopedias door to door, sell personal computers in a store, or work for a construction company in an office, I can make a difference if that is what I intend to do."

For me, making a difference meant empowering other people to become all *they* could be. It would be unique in each situation. I would do whatever they wanted and needed so that I could contribute to them.

Satisfaction all around would be the main product. Money would flow out as a byproduct.

What was wanted and needed that I could provide? I thought of my experience with Henry in Tampa on the previous day and re-phrased the question.

"How could a personal computer make a difference in the life of a small businessperson?"

Traditionally, people used the machine for the dog work of keeping track of the general ledger, payables and receivables, inventory, and sales. How could it be used to transform the business and blow it off the map?

The small business owners would figure it out. When they bought an Apple II and had the experience of making better decisions, they would empower themselves to transform their businesses. My job was to show them how to use that small computer to blow away themselves and their companies.

o

THROUGH MY WRITING that weekend, I got to the point where I was ready to experience what I intended to be: a person who would make a profound difference in the lives of small business owners. To do that, I would need to become an ace salesman for personal computers, even though I knew nothing about them.

I visualized myself learning the products—not how to program them, but how to get them to produce output.

I saw myself focusing on the key decisions business owners regularly made and on showing them how a computer could improve their thinking and their self-image in the bargain.

I then looked down, as if I were hovering high above the floor of a computer store. I saw myself talking with walk-ins, sitting down and doing demonstrations, listening actively about their decisions, collaborating with them to figure out how the computer could improve those choices, and encouraging them to share themselves. I saw myself writing up the order and shaking the customer's hand, then following up after the sale to learn about their experience.

I created a meaning around all of this: it meant that I was *already* an ace salesperson. I already had it within me. All I needed to do was to manifest it in a place where the product and service were right, and my customers and coworkers supported what I was doing. This was not about them taking care of me. It was about me empowering myself to have influence.

This was not noble, it was not a crusade, it was not "right." It just was. It was a vehicle for satisfaction in my life and in the lives of my customers. It was desperately wanted and needed in the uncertain and chaotic business environment of the day.

What about International Computer Systems? Yes, I was a non-computer person. But I did not need to sell what was true. I had been a small business owner for ten years and knew what the problems were. I spoke the language. I had a burning desire to be effective in the businesses and lives of the ICS customers. I could do it. I was already successful. All I needed to do now was to play it out.

In Tampa, Henry had told me that the ICS sales manager's name was Johnny. I was now writing on a Sunday; Monday was Memorial Day. I would go see Johnny on Tuesday and enroll him in my joining ICS. I would tell him that what the company was doing absolutely inspired me and say that I wanted to be a part of it. I would work for no salary, only a commission as a rookie salesperson starting at the bottom. I would do whatever it took to learn the business and succeed. My intention was to help customers by encouraging them to introduce a computer into their businesses. I was totally convinced of its power and that we had only begun to use it. I learned fast, and far as I was concerned, I was already a successful ICS salesperson.

That Memorial Day a professional acrobat, dressed in a Spider Man costume, climbed the entire outside of the hundred-and-ten-story Sears Tower in Chicago using suction cups on the windows. If he could do that, I could be extroverted enough to succeed with Johnny.

o

FIRST THING THAT Tuesday morning, I drove down to Ponce de Leon Boulevard in Coral Gables and walked into ICS cold, brimming with pure intention. I asked for Johnny, and when he walked into the showroom, he did not look anything like the technical expert I had expected to find.

Johnny was a thin, fortyish old hippie. He had shoulder-length blond hair, tinted glasses, and an open-collar silk shirt more proper for barhopping than for business. Bell bottom pants and brown boots completed the California image, except that when he opened his mouth, out came pure Brooklynese.

Kindly and attentive, Johnny listened to my pitch. I told him I was his most successful salesperson, and it just had to manifest. As I spoke, I demonstrated a big part of the est Training—verbally declaring a framework and then stepping inside it.

It worked! Johnny hired me on the spot and had me start the next day. To my surprise, the job included a small salary of $150 a week, and commissions were a generous 10% of retail. In those days, an Apple II with a pitiful four kilobytes of random-access memory, two five-and-a-quarter-inch floppy disk drives that stored only a hundred and sixty kilobytes of data, a boxy black-and-white monitor and a huge dot matrix printer would set you back about $10,000. And at that price, they were flying off the shelves.

We shook on the deal. "Come into the back with me, Ben," he said as he started walking.

"This is the order machine," he said as he swept his hand over some equipment pushed up against a side wall. "It is configured exactly as you will be selling it."

A blinking dot sat in the top left corner of a black and white monitor.

"What's that?" I asked, pointing to the dot. "I realize how dumb that question is."

He laughed. "That's the cursor. It is where you start typing. Watch."

He showed me how to key in anything I sold. It was mindlessly simple. He entered a four-digit product code, and the system automatically priced it and asked if he wanted to print an invoice.

I loved his cheerful outlook. The next day, he put me on the floor to talk with walk-ins and volunteered to help me close any sales. I was so enthusiastic about what the Apple II could do and was so quick to learn how to demonstrate its power, that I was able to answer everything but the customers' technical questions. Johnny kindly did that for me.

The following day, and with only a minor assist from Johnny, I sold my first hardware and software package. It came to over $11,000, which put a commission check for $1,100 into my hands the following week. It is hard to overstate the positive impact that check had on my self-esteem and on my eagerness to do more of this work.

o

SELLING AS A profession was alien to me, so for security I quickly built a process. Sales was a numbers game. For every hundred phone calls to local small businesses, a certain percentage would make an appointment to come in. Only some of those would show up for a demonstration, and of those who did, a certain number would buy. It was just a matter of getting the percentages right at each level.

This was known as the sales funnel. I constantly had to get in touch with the est distinctions to be outgoing enough to guide customers through each stage to a sale. But the sales funnel reduced the anxiety around doing that. I could get by with less extroversion by just focusing on the funnel and the numbers.

Coming out of the est Training, I had guessed my compulsion for processes might lessen or go away. But now that I was selling computers, I was again relying on a process, now more strongly than ever.

This brought out something the trainer had said about winning formulas that, at the time, did not register with me: they never go away. No matter how much you are aware of them, no matter how much you see through them, they tend to stay with you for a lifetime. Yes, you can mitigate them and lessen their hold over you. But they are always there as a default when things get tough.

o

IN SERVICE OF the sales funnel, I worked the phones relentlessly. I tracked the fractions at each level, compiled the data, and reliably produced sales at such a rate that within one month I was the top floor salesperson in the store. It helped that we had a hot, unique product, and that nobody else on the sales staff was milking it the way I was. They could not match my levels of determination or production.

After a few months, I graduated from cold-calling businesses out of the phone book to managing a stable of large clients, some of whom were my customers and others that the store had turned over to me. The store called my area the Business Analysis Group, so inevitably I became known as the B.A.G. man. The repeat business was lucrative, the work fairly easy. It was enough to live on and pay some small debts.

How I was able to create that out of nothing was no mystery. In the est Training, I had learned that in life, you do not get what you want; you get what you intend. And if you want to know what you have intended until now, look around at your life.

I also learned that creating intention was not complicated. All it took was for me to make repeated proclamations about what I intended, backed up by an unwavering commitment to make it happen. In time, that would offset whatever unconscious, default intention I had created.

A deliberately driven intention was the product of passion. And a great way to kindle it was to ask how I could contribute to others in some way. As soon as I did that, a vision of the Apple II appeared in my head, and I was on my way. It was completely "unreasonable," and it worked, helping to restore my confidence in the training. Plus, it added some much-needed, long-sought security to my life.

All that was wonderful. But it was not effective enough for me to keep my children.

# Chapter 17
# Acceptance

JULY 1981. MIAMI SHORES, FLORIDA. I now had success in sales and a few new friends at work, but by Fourth of July weekend, I was lonely. Hannah and Conor were up north with Ida's family and would be there for weeks. I missed them desperately.

On Saturday, I went to the beach at Key Biscayne by myself and spent almost ten hours there. When I arrived, I looked out to sea. Even after years in Florida, I could not get used to how calm the Atlantic surf was compared to the crashing waves in California. But the salt air blowing in smelled just the same, and it was bracing.

In the three months since the divorce, I had not intended to find another partner. I was too broke and too preoccupied with trying to make a living. Now that I had some success in selling computers, I began to think of reaching out. I was more alone than I could ever remember being and longed for the feeling of safety that a loving relationship could provide.

But lonely as I was, I was no longer looking for someone to take care of me. As I discovered with Ida, that did not work. More importantly, after the est Training I now was committed to being fully responsible in any new relationship, coming at it from a position of accountability rather than one of need.

My mind had a full set of criteria worked out. She would be as busy as I was. She would have her own life but also be looking for a relationship after someone had burned her. That part was key, so she would not be willing to settle for the first guy she found. She would be available to me in exact proportion to my availability to her. We would have only a limited time to be together. We would make love passionately during brief intervals, then after charging our batteries would retreat to our respective lives.

I expected that the appearance of a woman in my life would closely parallel the appearance of money. Not because money made women possible, but because both women and money were a function of intention. Until I created intention, I did not have a job. And so it would be with a new partner. If I put myself out there, was willing to make mistakes, and had a high level of intention about a relationship, it would appear.

What did putting it out there look like? There were a lot of beautiful and interesting women in my post-est Training seminars. But I always felt so transparent. And gawky. And uncool. The wonderful thing about est was that you got to be however you were. Putting it out there would be going up to someone and sharing that I wanted to meet her but could not think of anything to say, so there I was. In est, somehow that worked.

I soon found myself checking out the ring finger of every attractive woman I saw in the est seminar to see if she was available. I had already spotted three or four I would like to talk with.

Yet I was torn. I knew that seeking love did not work. What did work was to encompass a new woman in the exuberance and spontaneity of my own life. If a new activity had as its main purpose the expansion of my inner self, then it would work.

o

A FIRST STEP was to practice sharing myself with people in general. Fortunately, my positive experience in doing that during the est Training eased my anxiety about reaching out. And that Monday, July 5, a brilliantly sunny day, I had the opportunity to practice.

I went back to Key Biscayne and this time took my skim board. It was the same circular, laminated piece of plywood Ida and I had used in Laguna before I went to Vietnam. I looked up and down the coast to find a flat part of the beach and started using it to ride the slush of sand as water retreated back into the ocean. It gave me a chance to talk and share with a lot of people, even though every one of them was a stranger.

First was a guy with a crew cut named Joe who was coming in from swimming and stared at me with wide eyes as I skimmed over the sand. I asked him if he wanted to use it, and did he ever. It reminded him of when he did the same kind of thing as a kid in Miami streets after a big rainfall. He called it "womping" instead of skimming. His girlfriend tried it and fell down a few times, getting her long red hair full of sand; we all three had great laughs when she tumbled into the surf with a splat.

Then there were two kids the ages of Hannah and Conor, except that the blond boy, Todd, was the oldest.

Katrina had a great smile and followed Todd around like a puppy. At first, they were scared to ask, but then they got brave. I threw the board for them a few times so they could learn to jump on it and stay on. Pretty soon their super-fit father, Craig, came over and tried it. He owned two clothing stores, one in Coconut Grove and one in South Miami. I even got in a pitch for an Apple computer. I gave him the specifications on the skim board, and he said he would make one with Todd.

After a while, two little black-haired Colombian kids, Maria and Tomasito, began to use the board. He threw it on the slush and promptly fell.

"¡Ay Tomasito, qué pena!" (What a pity!) Maria said, laughing.

The second time he threw it, he got a good ride. They were not surprised that I could speak Spanish, because this was Miami, and people everywhere could speak it.

"Ahora me toca a mí," (Now it's my turn) she said, with authority. Same result: a fall on the first try but a decent ride on the second.

They used it for a long time, running with it, hopping on it, and sitting down. I went into the deeper water, and they followed me in with the board, which I knew would be dangerous if a wave caught it.

"Ya niños, regresemos a la playa,"—"OK kids," I said, "let's go back to the beach."

Tomasito then put the board in a shallow pool, and a one-year-old kid, a gringo with blond hair, seemed quite delighted with himself just to sit naked on it. His young mother, Nicole, was with him. We sat and talked for a while with the Colombian kids looking on. She was from Buffalo and had been in Miami for less than a year.

I was not sure if she was married (no ring) but after a while, the conversation became distant, so I moved on.

The world was such a rich and varied place. I got a lot of satisfaction by reaching out from love and acceptance. Doing that was so unfamiliar to me. But it gave me a sense of safety, and of connection, to everyone I spoke with.

Unfortunately, it did not last. Within a day, the ache of loneliness returned.

o

MY RELATIONSHIP WITH Ida was evolving; I was finding ways to be helpful to her. I noticed that I wanted to do things so she would acknowledge me for them, but she did not. I then wondered why I bothered to help her at all.

Her situation was getting desperate. She had no job, needed to move soon, and was pressuring me to take off from work to help move her up north as last year I had said I would. I was not keeping my agreement with her on this, and I needed to clean it up. I could do so by giving her money, but I was finding all sorts of excuses as to why I could not do that. I did not have any spare cash, and why should I help her take the kids away from me? Plus, it would probably not matter; with or without my help, she most likely would leave. I was not earning enough by selling computers to help her financially to the point where she might consider staying.

I recalled that I had played "take care of me" not only with my father and Bruce, but also with Ida. One night in Brooklyn in 1965, I had come up from my Army post in Baltimore to see her at my Aunt Rae's brownstone. Outside, it was freezing. We were alone on the couch in the downstairs living room. I had my head in Ida's lap, something we had never done before. She stroked my head, she kissed me, she took care of me. That was it. She overwhelmed me with love. I had found what I wanted. I did not have to be alone anymore. She was the first woman I had ever met who did not scare me in some way, and I married her.

We got married to take care of one another. To not call each other on our crap. To be mutual crutches. I wanted someone who would hold my head in her lap and always be there for me to lean on. She wanted the same thing, and I could not provide it. I pushed her away. I could not bear taking care of her, because I thought I deserved for her to take care of me. I became bitter and aloof, condescending and cold. She became the same way, and we got a divorce.

Nowhere was there an intention to have an experience of Ida as Ida, to accept her magnificence exactly as it was. I tried to remake her, and in the last year of our marriage, I got the same treatment back. We were like two mirrors reflecting each other. Now she was alone, frightened, and wondering if she could possibly cope with everything. I had the same feelings, but after the est Training was beginning to crawl out of my hole.

The most painful memory of the divorce, which usually occurred first thing in the morning while I was getting dressed, was that I did not have Ida's familiar presence to take care of me anymore. To iron my shirt, fix me breakfast, be there all day so I could relate to her and make excuses for not wanting to relate to anyone else, be there when I got home to fix dinner and support me in thousands of ways. For twelve years, I played that game, and she wearied of it. So did I, not realizing it brought diminishing returns. Now I had no one to take care of me, but there was progress; I was slowly increasing my level of satisfaction on my own.

I had always seen women as filling a gap in my life, performing a personal and social function, rather than a complementation of who we both were. It was as if I was hiring her for a job rather than making a difference in her life with the expectation of nothing in return.

That seemed to be what Prince Charles was doing late that July when he married Diana Spencer. She would look great at royal receptions.

When I walked into International Computer Systems after Memorial Day, I created a job out of pure intention. I was not up to doing that yet with a relationship. Instead, I was creating loneliness so I could have *that* experience first and clear it up.

o

DESPITE MY REFUSAL to seek another new relationship, I tried to fight the feelings of loneliness that threatened to overwhelm me

I filled the hours with work. When it got too bad, I went to my room, held a picture of the kids in my lap, and cried for a while. I loved them so. I experienced being with them, of holding them close to me, of feeling their little arms around my neck. That was the only form of skin contact I had with another human being, and now it was virtual. I held them to me and told them how much I loved them, smoothed their clothes, and played with their hair, then squeezed their hands and sent them off again, satisfied with having had an experience of their love.

At work, Johnny occasionally brought in his daughter Abby, who was eleven. Happy and alert, she said one day that I was beautiful. She was so fresh and sincere that I believed it. I never expected anyone would say something like that to me. She penetrated right to the core of who she thought I was. She let me see that all there was in life was love, and we were all here to experience that.

A few days later, I was working a chiropractor's convention in a high-ceilinged room in a Miami Beach hotel overflowing with tourists and the smell of suntan lotion. Abby came in with Johnny and a little cousin and told me they were playing Cinderella. The hotel was the palace, and I was the prince because I was so beautiful. It made me cry to think of that. There was so much depth to life, and little children were in touch with something special that we, as adults, had forgotten.

Ida's brother Leo Junior would arrive in a few days with a rental truck to move her to New Jersey. She would live with her parents until she found a job and an apartment, so the kids could start school there. Her sister, Naomi, had just gotten married and lived in the neighborhood with her new husband and son Thomas, who was Hannah's age; the two of them and Conor had always gotten along well. Ida's brother and other sister lived only a few hours away, so Ida would have plenty of family support to draw on.

As Ida's departure date approached, she softened her stance towards me. She wanted to talk, so we met one night in the parking lot of a Publix supermarket on South Dixie Highway. We sat on the shabby front seat of my aging AMC Hornet two-door for our first face-to-face conversation in months. She looked drawn and exhausted.

"Ben," she began, "I want you to know that I'm moving out of necessity. It promises more growth for me. I hope you're not taking this as some kind of retaliation."

That surprised me. "Thanks for that, Ida. I appreciate it. I have accepted the move. I'll miss the kids more than I can possibly say, but I don't have any ill will towards you."

The loud grind of an eighteen-wheeler's engine passed on the highway just yards from us. While we waited for it to be quiet enough to talk again, I saw that she had started to choke up. "The kids deeply need you as their father, Ben. I will do whatever I can to make it easier for you to fly up to see them. I'll pay part of the air fare if I can."

That touched me, because financially, she was even worse off than I was.

o

WHAT I DID not say was that in the past few months, I had bound myself to the children more deeply than before. The est Training woke me up to how precious they were to me, and our twice-weekly visits were things I looked forward to as if each time were Christmas. Ida's impending move with the children was so dark that I felt acute sadness.

A few weeks after they left, I plunged into deep grief. True to form, the only advice my recipe provided was to change the subject by telling me to throw myself into the sales funnel process at work. I tried that, but soon found it to be useless.

When the anguish became intolerable, I resolved to do something about it. During the est Training we had done an exercise designed to help us get complete with someone who had died. It was brutal, but I knew if I could get through it, the grief would not run me anymore.

One night I sat in a chair in my room, unplugged the phone and turned out all the lights. I put a box of Kleenex nearby.

I then visualized bringing my children to me. I imagined little Conor stepping out of an elevator in front of me, running to me, and jumping in my arms. I held him and wept, knowing this was the last time I would ever see him. Then the elevator doors opened again, and Hannah came out, scampering to me and sitting on one knee while I held Conor on the other one. They were so beautiful, so smart, so very dear. I cried and cried, rocking back and forth with them in my lap until I thought I had no more tears left.

When I knew it was time for them to go, I gently set them on the floor. They stood in front of me, each one reaching out to touch my face and give me a kiss, then throw their arms around my neck to tell me they would always love me. I set them down again, and they slowly started to back away from me, blowing kisses and waving. The elevator doors opened, they stepped inside, blew another kiss to me, and disappeared.

I sobbed for an hour, lost in loneliness and despair. Exhausted, I turned on the lights and gulped down a glass of water to replenish the fluid I had cast off as tears.

I was numb. I went into the bathroom. It smelled faintly of the Ajax I had used to clean the sink that morning. Standing there, I recalled a time in the first rental house when the children were so small I could bathe both in the tub at the same time. Once, when I was washing them, I had the thought that even though the house Ida and I tried to build had been taken away, I would never have to give up the two toddlers in front of me. Back then they had looked up at me with wet and smiling faces, comforting me more than they could know.

Now they were gone. Ida would likely remarry, and another man would raise them. When that thought hit me, I had to steady myself against the sink.

> "Ida's impending move with the children was so dark that I felt acute sadness."

Days passed. The ache inside slowly unwound itself, and I was able to concentrate on my selling. My mind returned often to Hannah and Conor, but after a week, I noticed that the charge was far less; I missed them terribly but no longer felt incapacitated by uncontrollable depression.

One day, it did return. That night, I did a repeat of the death exercise and from then on, my longing to be with them hardened into a tiny marble within my chest, one I could massage and placate by recalling happy times. Doing that transformed my experience of the loss, taking the charge out of it and allowing me to include the children in my thoughts with love instead of desperate sorrow.

Psychologists say that grief occurs in stages, starting with denial and ending in acceptance. Accepting death does not mean liking what happened, but coming to terms with the reality of it. The experience I put myself through sped all of that up so much that I got to acceptance swiftly, in just an hour of intense pain rather than weeks or months of gradually decreasing agony.

That was a severe solution. But it worked in an area of life where my winning recipe had been useless.

o

MY ROOM WAS such a sad place.

In there, my severe depression over Memorial Day weekend had been close to dangerous. After a happy Fourth of July, I went back inside those four walls and slipped into loneliness. And now I had sat in the room twice and consciously imagined saying good-bye to my two little children forever.

What I did not know was that soon this room would be the setting for some of the happiest moments I would ever have.

# Chapter 18
# The Girl From Saga Bay

OCTOBER 1981. CORAL GABLES, FLORIDA. At the ICS store in Coral Gables, I worked with intelligent people in their twenties who loved to have fun. Just being around them helped me to pull my attention away from myself and onto other people.

John Travolta's *Urban Cowboy* continued to be ragingly popular, spawning several new country and western bars in South Florida that some of the other salespeople went to regularly. One time, they invited me to go with them. Unlike at Harvard, where I shunned all after-hours contact with peers, here in my post-training mindset, I thought the idea was great. I bought a pair of boots, a western shirt, and a cowboy hat, and went with two young women and two young men to a place called Club Dallas in Fort Lauderdale.

I had a blast. I didn't know the Texas two-step or any line dances such as the Cotton Eyed Joe, but I watched the others and more or less caught on. I ended up dancing with a gorgeous Colombian girl who had only been in the country for a few months and loved the whole cowboy scene. When the DJ played Conway

Twitty's "Tight Fittin' Jeans," I figured he must have been looking at her. She drifted off and danced with half a dozen other guys, but I was happy just to be out there doing something new and strange and fun.

It also helped that I was still doing weekly post-est Training seminars. I was enrolled in one called "The Experience of Integrity," where we explored insights such as: integrity is more than just telling the truth; it is also about keeping your agreements, even the tiniest ones, and cleaning up the mess if you fail to do what you promise.

At one point, a young woman stood up in front of over a hundred people and took the microphone from a runner. As her eyes scanned the audience, she looked like she was scared to death.

"My husband Nathan and I own a small business," she said. "I hired a woman named Vicki to be our new receptionist, and Nathan and she are now openly having an affair."

A murmur spread across the room.

"I have two small children and no other source of income. Nathan wants both of us, and until tonight, I believed it was *his* integrity that was out."

She paused to collect herself.

"But what I have to say is that sitting here in my chair, I just got that it is *my* integrity that is out for allowing this shit to continue!"

The room exploded in applause.

"I am done!" she said over the applause. "I am finished with him!"

o

ONE EVENING A few weeks later, during a break in the integrity seminar, I looked across three rows of chairs to the front of the room and noticed a woman standing there. She turned around and looked at me. It was the one who had spoken to the group so powerfully a few weeks before.

"Didn't I see you at Club Dallas?" she said, smiling.

The night she had spoken to the group, I was so impressed with her words that I had not really looked at her, and now I was stunned at how graceful and pretty she was.

Before I could answer her, the seminar leader called everyone back to their seats. I stuffed my introversion down and rushed around the end of my row to sit in an empty chair right next to her. I was improvising and felt excited to be doing it.

I noticed how put together she was. She was wearing a satin turquoise blouse, tan slacks, and four-inch tan heels, complemented by beautiful nails, a professional brown hairdo, and subdued makeup.

Women never approached me, ever. Now this lovely young woman was smiling to the point where her eyes glistened and invited me to talk to her.

"You sure did see me there," I said. "I went for the first time with some friends. How about you?"

"I went with a girlfriend. It was my first time too." She looked right at me and gave me a gentle smile.

Before we could say anything more, the group went back into session. It was just before the evening was scheduled to end, and as it did, the seminar leader asked everyone to turn to the person next to them and exchange phone numbers. We were to be phone buddies for the coming week to discuss the homework he had given us.

I was thrilled. Est homework was deep. It asked the

participants to share openly about their insights, foibles, and triumphs. It was common for people who did not know each other but were est graduates to share the most intimate details of their lives with the hundred strangers in the group. These were things they might not tell their own families. In that environment, I knew we would get to know each other with lightning speed.

And we did, talking the next night for four hours. Amid an evening downpour that drove noisy raindrops against my sliding glass door, I learned her name was Sandy. She was thirty-three and recently separated. She lived in a development called Saga Bay just north of Cutler Ridge in southern Dade County. She had a six-year-old named Rachel, a four-year-old named Rosie, and two Siamese cats: Charlie and Chou (pronounced "Joe").

The homework must have had something to do with sex because the topic came up quickly. Sandy pointed out that people needed communication in sex—to start it and during it. She then asked if a woman had ever asked *me* to have sex.

I almost fell off my chair. Not only had no woman ever asked me that, but also no such idea had ever even occurred to me. Nor had I ever thought to ask a *woman* to have sex. That idea was so unfamiliar as to be scary. The rejection could be brutal. But in that moment, I saw that any future rejection would likely be no worse than my present frustration at having no sex at all.

The more we talked, the more I had an incredible desire to hold Sandy and make love to her. I heard how gentle and sensitive she was, and how horny she was. She said that as a result of our talk, she realized that she wanted a lover, a divorce, and a job.

After we hung up, my mind worked tirelessly. My concerns about her flew out the window. She smoked, she had domestic priorities the way Ida did, and she had small children. But I no longer cared. All my defenses were down. The communication was two-way, with each of us listening intently and speaking from the heart. I experienced a gentle flowing, a parallel movement that was devoid of threats. I felt safe and warm.

Yet, what we talked about was painful for both of us. She spoke of her dead brother whom she loved so dearly. She asked how long it had been since I had had sex, and when I told her eighteen months, she could not believe it. It had been only six months since the divorce, but Ida and I had stopped having sex over a year earlier than that. For her, it had been only six weeks, and she was having a hard time with it.

o

AT THE NEXT seminar meeting, I asked her if she would like to go to the beach the following Saturday, and she accepted.

To avoid the crowds, we went in the afternoon as the sun was dropping low over the Atlantic; a cool November breeze blew over us, but the sun kept us warm. Sandy took off her beach robe, revealing the two-piece bathing suit below, and all I could think of was how remarkable she looked and how happy I was to be there with her.

We waded into the warm surf and watched the horizon to see a ship pass slowly by; we did not swim but went back to our towels. After revealing so much of ourselves that night on the phone, we were curiously quiet, as if the words might destroy the pleasure of just being near each other.

I wanted to touch her but did not know how to start, so I asked if I could give her a foot rub. She grinned and reclined on the towel, extending her gorgeous legs for me. I looked down and noticed that the trim and polish on her toenails were immaculate.

I cupped one hand on the top of her left foot and pressed on the ball of the foot with my other hand. I worked my fingers along the underside of each toe pad and along the seam that ran across the base of them.

I had no idea that the seam could produce such emotion. She closed her eyes, dropping her mouth slowly open as if she could hardly drink in so much pleasure. I later learned she had never been touched like that in her entire life and felt like she wanted more of it to make up for what she had missed.

I switched to the other foot, and she started to moan. I saw how powerful a simple foot rub could be for a woman who longed for touch.

Soon, the wind became too chilly to stay on the beach, so we gathered up our towels. She put the robe back on her beautiful body, and I drove her home.

The next weekend, I asked if she would go dancing with me at Club Dallas. She loved the idea and dressed up as the cutest cowgirl I ever saw: a western hat, country blouse, jeans, and soft boots with tassels hanging down the sides. I showed her the two-step; since I was such a novice myself, I got it wrong, but it didn't matter. We danced for two hours and just loved holding each other tight, especially during the slow songs.

Since she lived so far south, and the house where I lived in Miami Shores was on the way north to Fort Lauderdale where the club was, she drove her 1972 Mercedes 240D to my place and parked it there. We went on to Club Dallas in my beat-up Hornet, feeling safer parking that piece of junk at the bar instead of her spotless Mercedes. Afterwards, we drove back to the 240D and stood in the driveway to say good night.

This lovely woman utterly captivated me. She only wanted the gentleness that she had never known. I could not help but start planting light kisses on her forehead, her cheeks, and finally her lips; she embraced me, and we kissed for a long time. I told her I wanted to make love to her, then continued putting my lips very lightly all over her face with small little kisses. She asked where, and I said in my room in the house.

I was thirty-eight years old and had never asked a woman to accept me in that way. I was prepared for her to say no because this was only our second date, but we knew more about each other than if we had been dating for months. She hesitated for so long that I was sure she was going to decline; I was fine if she did because I loved just holding her and kissing her.

"Let's go," she said, with a nod towards the house.

o

SANDY TOLD ME later that if my room had been a mess, she would have walked out. But it was tidy, and the bathroom was sparkling clean. I had not expected to bring her back that night; it was just the way I liked to keep things.

Before our first time, she told me I did not need to use a condom because she had her tubes tied after her second daughter was born. This was well before the AIDS epidemic became widespread—the first cases had appeared only a few months earlier in June—and she figured I was safe because I had been celibate for so long.

At that point, I was aware of other sexually transmitted diseases, but not of AIDS.

Neither of us had had much experience beyond our exes, so we both were nervous. But we enjoyed each other so intensely that over the next few months we returned to that room again and again, transforming it from a place of sadness into a site of joy. She craved a slow and gentle touch; I craved a woman as passionate as she was and soon fell in love with her. Her twelve-year marriage had been hard on her, so she was cautious, but I was patient. Within six weeks, we both realized we had something special that went beyond sex and declared our love for one another.

The more I came to know Sandy, the more I adored her. She was impeccable in keeping her time and other agreements. She communicated fully and easily. She was highly organized, as much of a planner as I was. She said things that were funny as hell. She was fully present when we were together. She was gentle and could go long periods without saying anything but was no introvert. And she was a grownup, taking responsibility for her life and children with no excuses. She lived the distinctions of est as a normal and natural part of her life, as I was coming to do as well, so we had a solid relationship based on trust and safety. After the est Training, I was just as clear about personal responsibility in life as she was, and consequently had absolutely none of the desire to be taken care of that I'd had with Ida.

The ICS computer sales showroom was across the street from the Southern Bell building on Ponce de Leon Boulevard. They had a bank of free phones at a sit-down counter for the public to use. So, in an age long before

*Fig. 8 Sandy. Miami Shores, FL, 1981.*

smartphones, I crossed the busy traffic on Ponce every day to call her. She spoke often about how anguished she was over her marriage.

One day, I could tell she was shaking when I called her. "Ben," she said, "I've decided to stop seeing you."

I let that sink in. I could not speak.

Nathan had called her a few hours earlier to say he wanted to get back together. He had hurt her so badly. But he was her husband, and she knew how much their little girls needed him.

Relieved that the nightmare was over, she had gone to the Publix supermarket on Allapattah to pick up the makings for lasagna, his favorite dinner. She had just gotten back.

"I want to be with the father of my children," she said, "regardless of how hard it might be on me."

"You were so sure about leaving him. . ."

"I have to give it another try," she said, almost in tears.

My heart broke. I assumed that was what I got for fooling around with a married woman.

I went to the vacant lot next to ICS and lay on the grass in the shade of the building. It felt cool and comforting on my back, but there was nothing I could do. She was the dearest treasure I had ever found, and now she was gone. It was late in the day, so I finished up in the showroom and went to my car.

The trip home on I-95 was the saddest, most morose drive I ever made. I had come so close to happiness. This loss was searing, grievous, and it would take months or even years to heal.

When I walked into my room the phone was ringing. It was Sandy.

"Ben," she said, "Nathan called again. He is not coming. He said he just cannot leave Vicki. I feel so foolish...I am so terribly sorry for putting you through all of this." She choked up and took a few moments to collect herself.

Then she said, "Would you be willing to see me again?"

I almost crawled up the phone wire. Of course I would! I loved her more than anything in the world, and I could not wait to hold her again. We set another date, and after we hung up, I wept.

He never again tried to come back.

In est, they suggested that men either *married* women like their mothers or did *not* marry women like their mothers. With Ida, I had definitely not married my mother, whose drinking and consequently loud behavior I hated. She was extremely talkative, and I ran away from that. In Sandy, I had someone much closer to my mother—minus the drinking and excessive chatter—

happy, willing to speak her mind, and hilarious to listen to at times. Getting complete with my mother in est had allowed me to be open to a woman like Sandy and to be massively attentive to her.

Years later, I asked her what she saw in a geeky guy who lived in a single room and drove a piece of crap car.

"You were so *into* me," she said. "It was all the foot rubs and back scratching when we snuggled in bed. You were always so good to me and allowed me to be who I was and who I was not."

"But I was so broke," I replied.

"Well, when I peeked into the closet in your room one day, I saw your Harvard MBA diploma on the wall. I figured there might be some potential there."

After her breakthrough sharing in "The Experience of Integrity," Sandy had sought a divorce, and in the spring of 1982, it became final.

o

IN THE SEMINAR I was taking with Sandy, I had learned that whatever people resisted in life tended to persist. As counterintuitive as it seemed, the best approach to something you could do nothing about was to surrender to it. I had imbibed that insight deeply. Even though I was devastated when she said she decided to stop seeing me, I had not argued with her, nor had I resisted what was happening. I did not know how I would ever find another woman I could love with such passion. But I still drove home in a mood of complete capitulation to the event.

Years later, Sandy told me that if I had resisted her terrible news I could well have made the situation worse. It would have pissed her off. After her ex backed out, she might have then decided she did not want to be with a man who had opposed her over something as important as her decision to take Nathan back. I had not tried to stop her, and that made it easier for her to return to me.

I had not been able to control what she and her ex would or would not do. But I had been able to control myself by surrendering to the news that had brought me such grief.

o

THINGS HAD NOT worked out for Ida up north. To my immense joy and relief, she moved back to Miami with the kids in the early summer of 1982.

When she found out I was seeing someone, she insisted on meeting the woman before she would allow Hannah and Conor to be around her. So, Sandy invited Ida down to her modest house in Saga Bay for tea and pastries. She was only a recent smoker and had stopped months earlier, so the house smelled fresh. The visit could potentially be awkward, and I was nervous.

When Ida and the children appeared at the door, Sandy was there with her two adorable girls. Rachel had dark hair and appeared in a frilly white dress and patent leather shoes. She had a perpetually mischievous look on her face. Rosie was blonde, an innocent cutie pie who was not old enough yet to care about how she looked, although her simple dress was pretty.

Sandy was utterly taken with Hannah and Conor, allowing Ida to see right away that this lady was a caring mother just like her. As everyone walked into the living room, I felt relieved to see both women smiling. During a delightful visit, the four kids sized each other up and played together. Sandy's warmth and loving nature made

Hannah and Conor feel accepted. From that moment on, I never detected that they had any concerns about me dating someone new. And Ida never again had a doubt about the quality and kindness of the woman I was with.

In July 1982, I traveled to upstate New York for the est Six-Day Course. It was an intensive, eighteen-hour-a-day program designed to dig even deeper into all the "stuff" people still carried around after the training. The one hundred men and women slept separately, in bungalows that housed groups of four people. Each day, we were loudly awakened at 6:00 a.m. to run uphill for fifteen minutes, wolf down breakfast, and pack ourselves into a training room for lectures, sharing, and "processes" that lasted until midnight.

> *"I had learned that whatever people resisted in life tended to persist."*

The course challenged people to face their fears in an elemental way. Inside the seminar, people often fell asleep when confronting things that made them anxious. To counteract that, the seminar leader had dozens of two-foot, rough-hewn logs placed on the floor around the edges of the room. When people started to go unconscious, they were required to get up out of their chairs, go to the back or sides of the room, pick up a log, and hold it over their heads until they were awake enough to be present. Like many others, I spent a lot of time stiff-arming heavy logs above my head.

o

WHEN I GOT back from the course, I realized even more what a treasure Sandy was, and knew I wanted to spend the rest of my life with her. I also realized my future in selling computers had limits. There now was more competition; the work had become so repetitive that its novelty had worn off; and I had to be "up" emotionally all the time at a level of extroversion that was not natural to me. I went to work each day amid increasing anxiety.

I knew I had to create something more secure. I observed from talking to my customers that service stations were a market opportunity; there was no specific program for that industry. So, I decided to design one: a software accounting package for gas stations. I met a talented young programmer named Gerome Davies and formed a fifty-fifty partnership with him called Southeast Technology. He wrote the program based on my specifications, and soon I started selling systems around Miami. Meanwhile, I kept my day job at ICS.

A benefit of the shift into the software business I did not realize at the time, was that it freed me from being so obsessed with the sales funnel. It still applied to selling software, but not to design or customer support. As my attention fell from the funnel, I filled the void with a focus on Sandy. My reduced attention to a process was allowing me to appreciate that the love of my life was right in front of me.

In early 1983, I quit ICS and went full-time into designing enhancements for our software, selling systems, and supplying customer support while Gerome oversaw the technical end. Meanwhile it had become too taxing for both Sandy and me to be located thirty miles apart, so I answered a "roommate wanted" ad and moved into another guy's apartment in Cutler Ridge, just minutes from her house. This allowed us to spend time together each weekend when our four kids were with our exes. When I told her my roommate was a slob, and I was looking for another apartment, Sandy invited me to move in with her. And I did.

In July 1983, Sandy did the Six-Day Training herself, and I went with her to assist as a volunteer in the kitchen with a dozen other graduates. The work was hot, messy, exhausting, and frustrating to no end, because as we prepared the food, we had an agreement not to nibble on any of it. Most of the other kitchen staff were women; they complained about their feet hurting, so on breaks I started giving regular foot rubs to anybody who wanted one. I received many marriage proposals but had to tell them I was already taken.

One day on a break, Sandy and I met in the outdoor pavilion for brown bag sandwiches of cheddar cheese, cucumbers, and mustard on whole grain bread. Between bites she told me that in the previous hour she had just realized her integrity was out.

"Because of the girls, I don't want to be living together without being married."

A lightning flash of insight pierced through me. I saw it would never, ever be better than this, that I would never be able to find a more perfect life partner than Sandy.

"Well, let's get married, then!" I said, before I even had time to think.

She had not tried to provoke that reaction from me, nor even expected it. When she realized what I was saying, she got a big grin on her face and leaned over the table to kiss me. We were engaged!

Part of my volunteer assisting duties were in the course room, running microphones to people who wanted to share, and doing errands for the seminar leader. So, nobody thought anything of it when I snuck into the back of Sandy's next course hour.

As he often did, the seminar leader asked if anybody had something to share, since breaks were fertile times for people to realize things about their lives. Sandy raised her hand and said she had something to say from the front of the room. Once there she pointed to me and asked me to come up and stand next to her. I put my arm around her, and as soon as she said we were engaged to be married, the room erupted with cheers and applause. We kissed and got even more applause.

o

SANDY'S SISTER LEAH and her husband Adam kindly made their beautiful home in Hollywood, Florida available for the wedding. It took place in their living room on October 9, 1983. We had a big crowd, mostly Sandy's parents and relatives.

Our four children were there, and at ages six through eleven, thought the whole thing was hilarious, laughing and stifling giggles even as we said our vows. Sandy dressed the three girls in color-coordinated outfits, and I put a white shirt and bow tie on Conor. All four looked adorable.

It heartened me that Hannah and Conor had accepted Sandy so quickly and wholeheartedly. She was always sweet to them, and they could see how happy I was to be with her. Sandy's youngest daughter Rosie readily accepted me, but Rachel, the older girl, held back a bit and in later years would much prefer to spend time with her father and Vicki, who was now his wife.

My marriage to Sandy turned out to be magnificent for my relationship with the kids. It provided a loving space, stability, and a partner in dealing with life.

Sandy was thirty-five, and I was forty. We were in love more deeply than either of us had ever been in our lives. Rather than dwell on our past histories of one failed marriage apiece, we chose to reinvent marriage as a possibility and face the future together. That gave me the greatest peace of mind I had ever known.

o

AS WITH THE fear and danger I had experienced over the years, my winning recipe had been a complete bust in dealing with vulnerability.

My anguish over the loss of Ida and my partner Bruce got resolved after the est Training when I went outside the recipe and took responsibility for both situations. In the depths of my Memorial Day depression, it was not a step-by-step process, but the discovery of intention that brought me back from the brink.

When the grief over the loss of my children was at its nadir, I did engage in a methodical approach, the death process. But that was far more powerful than the sales funnel my recipe reflexively wanted me run as a distraction. And the non-resistance I adopted when Sandy said she was taking Nathan back was the opposite of the "let's talk this through" approach that my recipe likely would have urged.

All these experiences were escapes from the formula. But they were one-offs, individual wins that did nothing to undermine the staying power of my obsession.

Now that I had Sandy in my life, my winning recipe stayed away from the domain of relationships. It never again would call me to look for security in that area, because I already had more of it than I could ever want.

But the domain of business was different. My search for financial security would endure for more than another quarter century, a long period during which the recipe would be tireless in creating successive calamities, or inserting itself into them. Safety would stay well out of reach.

Part 5

# The Satisfied Introvert

# Chapter 19
# End of the Line

## 1983-1992: Ruin

FOR THREE YEARS after the wedding, I sold computers to gas stations. By 1986, however, the business had fizzled out due to increased competition. So, I launched two new projects and worked them simultaneously, counting on at least one of them to come through.

The first was MicroSomnia, a sleep reduction program for busy businesspeople. Using health principles known as *sleep hygiene*, I convinced over a hundred entrepreneurs and professionals that they could gain valuable work time by safely cutting back on sleep for up to three hours a night. Despite successfully using the method myself and working the sales funnel for years, I eventually had to give it up. My relentless focus on the sleep and sales processes themselves prevented me from seeing the small size of the market.

Good thing, because if I had succeeded, I would probably be in jail right now. Researchers discovered in the 2010s that the body pumped spinal fluid through the brain during sleep. This meant that getting less than seven hours a night was a recipe for contracting Alzheimer's and other forms of dementia. Sustained sleep reduction was madness.

The other project was Documentation by Mail, a manual-writing service for small software developers. I used a three-draft process to produce bite-sized modules that explained the customers' programs using step-by-step instructions, something my winning recipe uniquely qualified me to produce. At the beginning, I had a lot of business. But again, my obsession with a process—this time the one for creating the small modules—kept me from seeing how small and poorly funded the market was.

Our cash flow was so uncertain from these businesses that it caused both of us, especially Sandy, a great deal of distress. Each year, we had the choice of saving for taxes or buying groceries, and eventually it caught up with us. To prevent the IRS from seizing our house, we had to file for bankruptcy in May 1992. Some twenty-three years after graduating from the Harvard Business School, I was now forty-nine and broke.

We did not think things could get any worse, but we were wrong. On August 24, just three months after we went bust, a Category 5 hurricane named Andrew slammed into Miami and destroyed our home. Sandy and I lost almost everything. My winning recipe always called me to be methodical, and when we stood in the muck trying to decide what to do first, it demanded that I prioritize everything before taking any action. In this situation, such advice was paralyzing, but Sandy quickly got me out of my head. She said it didn't matter what we did first, and that got us both into action.

## 1992-2001: Numbness

DAYS AFTER THE storm, we drove three hundred and twenty miles north to Gainesville, Florida to look for work. In time, we both found jobs there at a small medical practice management software company.

Throughout the 1990s the firm prospered, as did Sandy and I. She served as the executive assistant to the CEO, while I built and ran a twenty-writer documentation department. These roles gave us a decade-long run of security during which we repaired our finances. The firm went public in 1997, and three years later WebMD acquired the company.

In those years we both did the Landmark Forum, the successor program to the est Training of the 1980s. The Forum and its subsequent evening seminars helped us to deal with the challenges of our new roles in Gainesville.

I refined the documentation process into a high art, overlaying a standard format across more than ten thousand pages of manuals covering every company software product from managed care to prescriptions. My winning recipe loved it, because for the first time it could operate inside of a solid company. But after a few years, I became numb, which illustrates what usually happens with every recipe: it gave me a job I knew how to do and was good at, but it did not produce satisfaction. I was finally safe, but I was uninspired. Year after year, even as it produced stability and good income, it left me feeling anesthetized and wanting more out of life.

## 2001-2006: The Boot

IN 2001, I finally tired of the monotony of the documentation process. So, I requested a transfer to a team within the company called Network Services. I knew nothing about it, but they had a serious process problem I thought I could solve, namely, how to increase the glacial speed with which we enrolled doctors in submitting their claims electronically. I struggled for two years but made no progress in streamlining the enrollment process.

On September 3, 2003, the FBI and the IRS mounted massive raids on our Gainesville and Tampa sites, and on WebMD headquarters in New Jersey. A former employee had alleged that some of the executives had engaged in stock fraud, but it took until 2010 for a court to declare there was absolutely no evidence to support the claim. Due to stress, Sandy left the company in 2003. I did so at the end of 2004, knowing that for my non-performance in Network Services I was about to be fired.

Now age sixty-one, I was on the street. I could not trade on my Harvard MBA because in the past decade, I had done nothing to indicate I was top management material. Convinced I had failed at WebMD because I had tried to execute a process without being an expert in it, I got certified in a statistical discipline that was in high demand, called Six Sigma.

Blue Cross Blue Shield of Minnesota promptly hired me as their Six Sigma Deployment Manager. Sandy and I moved to Minneapolis in early 2006, but I lasted only eight weeks before getting fired. I had paid so much attention to the statistical process itself and so little to promoting my team and Six Sigma across the company, that my manager lost all confidence in me. It was July 2006, and this time I was out of work at age sixty-three.

## 2006: Desperation

MY RECIPE OBSESSION had led me to declare bankruptcy, suffer near-paralysis during the Hurricane Andrew cleanup, attempt to reinvent a process at WebMD in an area where I had no expertise, and prioritize a statistical process instead of the people I was hired to manage at Blue Cross.

Yet, incredibly, I was no closer to seeing that the recipe itself was the root cause of why I had failed to find safety in these four cases.

By the summer of 2006, all this had again put Sandy and me in a bind. I was well-past the age when many employers considered someone to be too old to hire. Worse, my strategy of running a process where I was an expert, Six Sigma, had failed miserably. I was clear that I did not have the people skills to be a deployment leader. That made my costly investment in the discipline close to worthless.

This was a terrifying realization. In the past, my process work had always helped me to compensate for my lack of extroversion. But now, even though I had a new type of expertise, it had not been enough for me to be successful.

My lifelong approach using formulas and systems had finally reached its limit. In my forties, it had led me into bankruptcy, in my fifties into numbness in a safe but boring job, and now in my sixties into two job losses in a row. My recipe had run its course, and now—at last—I was clear about the futility of it.

Our situation was desperate. We had nowhere near enough savings to start retirement, and because of my age, I had no prospects for ever getting us to that point.

But I had survived a hurricane. And a bankruptcy. And a divorce. And a war. Now I just had to find a job.

I picked myself up and got to work.

# Chapter 20
# The King
# of All Processes

JUNE 2006. MINNEAPOLIS, MINNESOTA. Just three and a half weeks after Blue Cross threw me out, I landed on my feet. I was now working across town at UnitedHealthcare, looking around like a cat that had just jumped off a wall.

o

THE SIX SIGMA outlay in time and money had not been a waste after all. On June 10, I found a Director of Process Improvement opening at United that did require leading a Six Sigma team, but not from a promotional perspective—a competent deployment leader was already in place. United simply wanted someone who could get results.

I applied and on June 28 got a call from Julia Kowalski, the hiring manager herself, a senior vice president. From that one phone call, I could tell how different the culture in a for-profit enterprise like United was from Blue Cross. If Julia stood for the quality of the people there, it would be like going back to Harvard or Stanford, a place where the people around me were brilliant and stimulating. The thought scared me. But if they asked me to join them, I thought, it could be one of the most rewarding experiences of my life.

At the end of the call, she invited me in for an interview. The next day, I drove to United on a dazzlingly sunny day that reminded me of Florida, except that at forty-five degrees north latitude, the June air in Minneapolis was crisp and dry.

I was wary. This time, I would listen extremely carefully during the interview process to make sure this was not a promotional job in disguise, the way it had been at Blue Cross. If the Black Belts were competent, I knew I could be an introvert and still do the job.

When I walked into United's building in Edina, I saw it was old and chopped up, an extensive facility that seemed to wander over acres on various levels built at different times. Yet it was clean and had character. It felt as lived in as an old shoe, quite a contrast from the sterile modernity of Blue Cross. United was a place of vibrancy and life; I expected that here people would not condemn me for walking too fast, something my team had said about me at Blue Cross.

o

MY FIRST MEETING was with Julia. Tall, thin, and fortyish, she not only had a Master's in Healthcare Administration but was also a Registered Nurse and a Six Sigma Black Belt. She was highly professional, spoke to the point, and had a great sense of humor. I liked her instantly.

We met one-on-one for fifteen minutes. She did most of the talking and then brought in Ralph Jenner, a twenty-something director-level recent hire from a major consulting company. Don Little also came in; he was a five-year Black Belt with thinning hair and appeared to be in his late thirties. During the ensuing twenty minutes, Don was silent, and Ralph asked most of the questions. I could tell by his reaction, and Julia's, that they were happy with my answers.

When the two of them left, Don and I went to the cafeteria. The hallway was half a story higher than the floor of the restaurant, giving us a view of scores of people in eager conversation, or working on laptops, or just eating and staring into space. We walked down, passed up the food and got a table.

Don began by describing United's culture and the team of four Black Belts. During a pause I said, "I just came from Blue Cross, where seven Black Belts have been working for over a year. They have not produced a dime in savings. How many Black Belts are on our team?"

"Four."

"What kind of savings have they produced?"

"Over $14 million in only six months. And every month we generate more."

That was astonishing. I could tell Don was several cuts above any of the Black Belts at Blue Cross, and I guessed that to produce those kinds of numbers, the others had to be as well.

I then met with Orin Williams, the Chief Medical Officer of United. A tall, gaunt, bearded, prematurely gray, and lawyer-like guy in his late forties, Orin conducted one of the most intense and unusual interviews I had ever been in. He wanted me to trace my entire background starting at Stanford and took notes as I went. He interrupted to ask pointed questions, such as why I chose a particular path and what I learned from it.

At the end, he asked, "What question did I *not* ask that I should have to really find out what makes you tick?"

I thought for a moment and said, "Why aren't you further along in life? You're a Harvard MBA who has had many years of experience. Why aren't you the CEO of a company somewhere?"

I could tell the bluntness and honesty of the question took him aback. He himself had an MBA from Stanford in addition to being an MD, so perhaps he was thinking the same thing. He asked me to tell him what the answer was.

"I never did any career planning," I replied. "I spent years in the wilderness of being an entrepreneur. I always jumped into what was in front of me, executing it with passion."

Entrepreneurship was the most visible reason why I had not gotten very far. It had provided an arena where I could freely design processes to my heart's content. But the root cause for my slow career was my obsession with the underlying processes. I planned to get into that if he continued probing, but he did not.

Instead, he asked, "Do you have any regrets?"

"At one level I do," I said. "I have not been able to give my children everything I might have if I had been a CEO. But my kids are wonderful. My daughter Hannah is a speech pathologist, and my son Conor is an MIT and Harvard-educated architect. My stepdaughter Rachel is a successful communications executive in New York, and my other stepdaughter Rosie is a rising star in a property insurance company in Tampa. So, on balance, no, I have no regrets. I've had a wonderful, exciting life, and I would not change it."

The answer seemed to hit home with him.

During each interview, I listened with acute interest. I concluded that this job did not require me to be extroverted—all I had to do was help my team to stay focused on getting results.

The next day, Julia called to say they wanted me to join the company. HR would be making me an offer within the next day and a half. It turned out to be almost 20% more than I had earned at Blue Cross.

I had walked into this opportunity with two strikes against me, being let go at WebMD and at Blue Cross. I intended to make sure there would not be a third.

o

I GOT THE new job partly because I was a Six Sigma Black Belt. But that formula had just failed me, and I did not want to tie myself to it again too strongly. I would do the work, of course. But my passion for the method, and my ability in it, were only a veneer.

As I got the lay of the land at United, a spark went off inside me about a completely different process I had tried back in Gainesville, before WebMD appeared. Called the balanced scorecard, it consisted of a powerful graphic that drew a picture of a company's strategy on a single piece of paper. A list of measurements supplemented the map by clearly telling the company how it was doing in meeting its strategic goals.

In January 2004, I had taken a two-day balanced scorecard seminar and returned as an evangelist, but nobody was interested. At United, the situation was different. My new boss, Orin Williams, was curious. In September 2006, I built a strategy map for his department, and he not only valued it but publicly acknowledged me for the work.

Encouraged, I started making the rounds. The Chief Human Capital Officer wanted a map for his department. So did the Chief Financial Officer. Because these were C-suite executives in a $35-billion company, they really got my blood pumping. I saw that the balanced scorecard was the biggest, most effective, most salable process I had ever found in my life. I dove in deep.

Orin, ever the supporter, suggested that I approach the Chief Operating Officer of UnitedHealthcare, Kevin Ruth. When I sent Kevin a PowerPoint presentation on how the thing worked, I thought he was going to lose his mind. In a phone meeting, he said this went so far beyond what he had been trying to do on the back of an envelope that he wanted to meet with me right away. A blizzard raged outside our building, but in my chest, I felt an expanding warmth.

Kevin was a muscular man who stood over six feet tall. Forty-seven years old, he had a receding hairline, sleepy eyes and a compassionate face that hid the determination that had driven him up the hard way from a boyhood in rural Pennsylvania. He put himself through Temple University in Philadelphia, became a CPA, and from a start at the bottom in healthcare moving laundry in a hospital, he had become the CEO of a whole region of health plans at UnitedHealthcare. And now he was the Chief Operating Officer. Plain spoken, articulate, and gentle, he was afraid of nothing. Just by being himself, Kevin elicited enthusiastic loyalty from the people around him.

"You know what I like the most about this?" he asked. "We can use it to kill useless projects by comparing them against the strategy map."

"That's right," I agreed. "If there is no fit, we now have a good reason to stop the work in its tracks."

He grinned. "And nobody can argue with it."

By February 2007, six major departments had told me they wanted to pursue the balanced scorecard. In addition to Human Capital, Finance, Operations, and Orin Williams in Clinical Advancement, I was also talking with UnitedHealth Networks and ACME, our back-office processing department.

As I met with each executive, I never tired of looking out their corner office windows to see the snowplows and salt trucks hard at work outside. I also noticed that all the leaders carried a BlackBerry phone. Its tiny keyboard seemed so hard to use. A few weeks earlier, Steve Jobs had launched something called the "iPhone," and I wondered if it would get any traction among these leaders.

o

KEVIN'S MIND BECAME infected with the balanced scorecard, particularly with a strategy map I had prepared for United at the corporate level. I guessed I might be working for him soon.

He got into gear. He invited me to a meeting of the six Regional CEOs in the impressive UHC board room to make a presentation. I sat in a chair at the back of the room next to a fragrant tray of coffee pots and pastries. But he stood up and invited me to take his seat at the huge table, an unbelievably strong endorsement for someone as new to the company as I was.

He lobbied to put me on his team and soon succeeded. He spoke to the CEO of United, Miles Bramovich, who stopped me in the hall one day and asked me to be sure to collaborate with his whole team. I was already talking to six of them and could not believe this was happening.

I forgot I was an introvert. Unlike with the est Training and the Forum, which required weekly attendance at seminars to keep me stoked, the balanced scorecard elicited a passion from within me that was so strong I just threw myself into situations I normally would have recoiled from. This was a sea change, the first process that I genuinely cared about. It was no longer about the mechanics of driving a formula; it was about discharging the strange fervor that welled up from inside me. Caring was something that had been missing from my processes all along.

Why was I so taken with this? For one thing, it drew on every ounce of my analytical ability. For another, it allowed me to dig beneath the surface like a detective to produce "AHA!" moments in leader after leader. In addition, it addressed the single biggest problem any company faced, especially ours: how to turn the pages of high-sounding rhetoric in our planning documents into a strategy that people from customer support reps to top executives could execute. But most importantly, it was the first process since college that truly made me feel secure. It allowed me to hide my introversion and still produce guaranteed results.

Offsite, I attended two more Kaplan and Norton seminars on the balanced scorecard and learned that building a strategy map for a department or a company took twenty hours. Four were for a preparation session with the senior leader and all his direct reports, and sixteen hours over two days were to coach the group to hammer out the map itself.

I soon found myself in the front of rooms leading most of those meetings, driven by the excitement of seeing, as I looked from face to face, that I was making a huge difference for each group. I led the finance sessions in June 2007 and supported a friend in leading the ones for Marketing in June and July. I also facilitated Dental and Vision, Product, and Human Capital. The United Leadership Academy approached me to do a two-and-a-half-hour training on strategy maps, and when I emailed David Norton, co-founder of the concept, he said he was open to speaking at it. There seemed to be no end to where United would go with this.

o

YET THERE WAS an end, and it came overnight. In May 2008, Miles Bramovich, the United CEO who so strongly supported Kevin and me, was out.

Laura Schmidt replaced him. She had a promoting behavioral style, tending to focus on the big picture and not get into details. Without support from the top, the balanced scorecard could not advance. By February 2009, United had announced at least three different, non-integrated strategies; the following month the senior team was back to doing business as usual.

Ironically, around that time, I completed all my Kaplan and Norton studies, passed the certification exam, and became one of only nine hundred Balanced Scorecard Practitioners in the United States.

Consequently, I was despondent. With Kevin's relentless support, I had come so close to getting the balanced scorecard implemented that I could taste it. I was planning to set up and run an Office of Strategy Management, and now the opportunity was gone. Laura assigned Kevin to head the alignment of our clinical organization, and it looked like I would follow him there. We would build a map and compare initiatives to it, but that was it: there would be no companywide implementation.

I sat in my office and looked at the light sparkling on the small crystal alligator I had brought with me from Florida, reflecting on how different things were from my expectations. Except for the modest wins and respect I now enjoyed at UnitedHealthcare, since the day I got my MBA, I had never achieved significant business success. Now at age sixty-six, I still had only a small nest egg and no ability for Sandy and me to retire.

At the same time, I saw that, with Sandy, I had the most fabulous relationship a man could ever ask for. I had a twenty-seven-year history with a woman I adored who was a partner in every aspect of life. She was sexy, funny, enlightened, organized, committed, and strong—someone who had made the past three decades a joy despite all we had gone through and who promised to make the next three the best of our lives. Who knew what kind of person I would have been by now without her; how Hannah and Conor, Rachel and Rosie would have turned out; and whether I would be anywhere near as healthy and happy as I now was. At United, I saw up close in others that financial success in business often came at a terrible personal price. I never had had to pay it, and my life was much the better for it.

Early one morning while swishing a spearmint mouthwash, I looked in the mirror and had an insight. I saw that while we could say nature's purpose for humanity was reproduction, my purpose as a post-reproductive human being was longevity. It meant I needed to do things that supported and prolonged my mental, emotional, and physical health. And in turn, *that* meant I needed to give up the stress of trying to be more outgoing than I actually was. I had to start living openly as an introvert.

Seen through that filter, setting up and running an Office of Strategy Management could well have been a bad idea. Much as I loved the work, it would have required me to engage in a great deal of long-term, highly extroverted behavior that over the years might have worn thin. But staying where I was at United might under-challenge me, so the goal was to find a middle ground: a way to be a valuable contributor without killing myself in the process.

I had been chastising myself for not progressing further in my career. I still did not have the financial security that for decades I had been pursuing through my winning recipe. But at this point, it was not about progression. It was about contribution. And I now saw I could do that best as a straight-up introvert, offering the back-of-the-room skills that came most naturally to me. For me, this was a new context. For the first time ever, I made the choice to go through life with no outer shell of a recipe around me.

But rather than stressing me out, that choice made me feel safer than I had in a long time. Being able to just be myself avoided the anxiety involved in trying to use a recipe to cover up who I really was.

Over several days, I re-established my equilibrium and gradually let go of the balanced scorecard. It was the most powerful process I had ever found. But I quietly detached myself from it.

For two full weeks I lived in peace.

o

THEN ON JULY 2, 2009, a company called Cancer Therapy Professionals posed a job description online. It came into my home inbox via an automatic feed I had not yet turned off.

I saw it and gasped.

# Chapter 21
# The Recipe Strikes Back

JULY 2009. MINNEAPOLIS, MINNESOTA. Cancer Therapy Professionals (CTP) was looking for a Strategy Management Director. The job involved building a strategy map and balanced scorecard for the corporation, then setting up and running an Office of Strategy Management.

This was the epitome of the balanced scorecard—the ability to start from nothing in a company with top-down CEO support and engage the entire management team. After my acute disappointment at UnitedHealthcare, I was salivating.

CTP was a growing chain of specialty hospitals that focused on treating cancer. Based in the Pittsburgh area, they were a private company and had a highly unusual business model for healthcare. They competed based on excellence at the medical condition level, instead of by specialty like everybody else. They used multi-disciplinary teams to treat patients while most other clinics did not bother to coordinate care. And they had already started reporting outcomes, something few health systems in the industry were doing yet.

This was next-generation stuff. Such a model, plus the company's spectacularly all-embracing focus on the balanced scorecard, quickly seduced me into abandoning my detachment from the method. I once again fell under its spell, and with it, that of my winning recipe.

I could not get CTP out of my mind, so in late August I decided to apply. My mindset was different from when I first saw the ad. Passion no longer blurred my vision. Instead, I was taking a sober look at the possibility that a future at CTP might or might not be more satisfying than one at United.

Within a week, I had a phone interview with CTP's Chief Strategy Officer, Evan Patel. He was a serious, thoughtful guy who reported directly to the CEO, and was in lockstep with him about the need to implement the balanced scorecard in the company. The CEO and leadership team had already met with Robert Kaplan, one of the scorecard's founders, over the phone for ninety minutes. The whole team was convinced they needed to do this.

On the call with Evan, I was so enthusiastic that I found myself standing up and gesturing as I spoke. He likely was not prepared for such depth of feeling. We talked for over an hour, and at the end, he invited me down to meet the CEO and the executive team. When I hung up the phone, I said, "Yes!!" I looked out the glass panel of my office to the sea of cubicles outside it and imagined myself flying above all of them and out the window on the far side of the building all the way to Pittsburgh.

Before going, I did some checking. The company was extremely successful, enjoying its ninth straight year of growth. It seemed to have plenty of cash, but not so much as to make it a lucrative takeover target. This was a live opportunity. But my eyes were still open to any sign of risk that might emerge.

o

ON SEPTEMBER 5, I went to Pittsburgh and nailed the interviews. Any lingering doubts I had about the company and its people all but vanished.

The firm had sent a driver and white stretch limousine to pick me up. A brilliant late summer sun shone down on the freeway, reflecting sunlight off the chrome on the cars around us. As I looked through the tinted glass of the salon where I sat, those bright spots appeared blue. I extended my legs and lowered a window a crack to breathe in the fresh summer air, not believing that any of this was happening.

Compared to United, CTP was a tiny company, and its Pittsburgh facility reflected it, making even the old Edina building at United seem more dignified. Fake wood paneling, pleather chairs and inexpensive rugs gave the CTP headquarters the feel of a lawyer's office in a strip mall.

As soon as I walked in, I recalled what one doctor at United had told me about CTP that I had promptly repressed: they were on the fringes of the medical establishment.

"Look at their consumer advertising," he had said. "Rather than a reputation for medical excellence, they rely on ads to gain patients."

"Interesting," I replied. "They also include acupuncture, meditation, and chiropractic in their treatments."

He nodded. "Valuable in some settings, but unproven for cancer. And the patients they attract tend to have few comorbidities. Their success ratios are skewed in favor of the those who are most likely to survive."

At the time, I discounted all that as sour grapes. CTP was succeeding in a market where United was struggling, so leaders in our company might have a bias against the company. Since I was not there to evaluate the furnishings, I chose to ignore the kitsch, and the doubts, and get on with the interviews.

The first was with Evan Patel, the fortyish, pensive Chief Strategy Officer I had spoken with on the phone. He was an academic, a Ph.D. candidate in epidemiology and biostatistics. Every time I pulled out some of the generic strategy map examples I had brought, he was amazed at the simplicity and clarity of the method.

Next, Evan and I met with Kirby Stone, the CEO. Kirby was a silver-haired, dapper, and kindly gentleman in his late 60s with a sharp analytical mind, a way with words about the company, an appetite for detail, and a strong commitment to managing strategy in the way described by Kaplan and Norton.

During the last hour of our ninety-minute meeting, I went over half a dozen sheets of examples with him. I showed him sanitized strategy maps, balanced scorecards, and grids detailing how to end non-strategic initiatives. He had the same reaction as Evan: incredulity at the simplicity, concreteness, and plain good sense of it all. Once again, the innate power of this methodology had brought me out of myself.

I met with three other leaders and after the visit was over, called Sandy on the way to the airport to report all of this with breathless enthusiasm. Yet after we hung up, I sipped from a cold bottle of Nestle water and noticed that something was starting to bother me. As the CTP limo wound its way through freeway traffic, I recalled that the CEO wanted me to report to Evan. Yet he was quite junior to me in strategy execution, maturity, and experience. He seemed to have far more passion for research than for strategy.

It was time for me to talk to Kevin. We had shared our mutual unhappiness with the direction that strategy was going at United, so it was no surprise when I called him on my return to let him know I might be leaving. I shared that this opportunity had all the ingredients of success: enthusiastic support by the CEO, a management team that knew they needed a system for managing their strategy, and a business model that was truly distinctive and driving 20% annual growth.

"Ben, I support you one million percent," he said. "You are at the time in life where you need to be doing what you want, and I would never do anything to hold you back."

"At the same time," he said, "I don't want you to take my calm demeanor as a sign that I want you to leave. I very much do not. I hope the deal falls through, and if it does, I have a thousand things for you to do. I will miss talking to you and will continue interacting with you normally until you tell me you are definitely leaving."

He went on. "I will be waiting for you to call me any day to break my heart. If so, it will not be good-bye; we will remain friends, and I will be calling you after you leave." He laughed. "At that point, I won't be writing your reviews, so I'll be able to speak more openly than I can now!"

An outpouring of emotion washed over me.

"Kevin, you mean more to me than I could ever express. After having such an unstable career, I had come to doubt my own competence. But in just two years you have helped me to heal." For years I had shared myself in est and Forum seminars with that kind of heartfelt wording, and it expressed exactly how I felt.

o

I FACED A stark choice. On one hand, I had stumbled on the process of a lifetime—the balanced scorecard—and a company that was ready to hire me to drive it across their entire business.

On the other hand, at United I had built a close relationship with an inspiring boss, one whom I trusted and who made me feel better about myself every time I interacted with him. He actively drew on my strengths as a quiet person by assigning me a steady flow of research and writing projects, thereby providing me with secure work as an introvert. Around him, I felt peace, satisfaction, and relief.

Ever since I was ten years old, I had been running stepwise processes to get predictable results without having to engage other people all that much. Was I now going to abandon that approach just for a professional relationship? Give up what could not only be the pinnacle of my career, but also let go of a system so sophisticated and powerful that it could propel me to more success and security than I had ever known? My gut reaction was that to do so was unthinkable.

At United, I had seen that my highest loyalty was to a magnificent process I cared about deeply. But during my weeks of disengagement from it, I discovered something I cared about even more: my own longevity. It would come from having less stress, specifically by living and contributing openly as an introvert. And now I was unearthing something I had come to care about even more than that, because it made being a straight-up introvert possible: working with Kevin Ruth.

Formulas had attracted me for a lifetime, and now something was happening I never would have expected. A relationship, the very thing I had sought to minimize my whole life, was now more important to me than the best process I had ever found.

Prioritizing Kevin added a valued individual to my very small circle of close people. However, doing that did not tempt me to expand that circle any further.

My winning recipe was fine with that. But giving up the balanced scorecard was something it did not like. It had already struck back once, and I could feel it gearing up to do so again.

# Chapter 22
# Baronial Splendor

SEPTEMBER 2009. MINNEAPOLIS, MINNESOTA. After due consideration, I told my recipe to stuff it. On September 18, I formally withdrew my application from CTP.

A few days later, Kevin wrote me a note saying he was so glad to have me back in the game. What an incredible guy—most bosses would have been upset that I even looked at another company. Kevin was not only happy I stayed but also willing to say so openly.

I got to work improving the strategy map for his new Enterprise Clinical (EC) group. This was my fourth attempt. A few slides into the presentation I asked him how he was doing, and he laughed. He said, "You had me at hello. This is very cool and very timely. People have been asking me to explain the EC strategy, and they will love this."

I still valued the balanced scorecard and would continue to promote it at United as much as I could. But I had gotten some distance from it. I was not willing to upend my career and personal life to pursue it.

THAT WAS THE best business decision I ever made.

Over the next decade, CTP opened no new hospitals, laid off hundreds of employees, and took flak for its heavy consumer advertising and questionable use of alternative medicine in cancer care. In contrast, United had ten straight years of growth and provided me with fascinating work and steadily increasing income.

For the first time ever, I intentionally started working without a guiding process. I became a pinch hitter for Kevin, doing detailed research and building PowerPoint presentations for him to circulate among senior management. He considered himself to be a rabble rouser and often took positions contrary to the conventional wisdom in the company. We did not always get agreement with what we proposed, but we got enough wins to make the effort worthwhile.

When my recipe struck back, I stopped it in its tracks by choosing to stay with him instead of going elsewhere to implement the balanced scorecard. But doing so was not a larger move into relationships. I still honored my childhood choice to avoid overstimulation by minimizing contact with others.

Staying with Kevin brought me closer to the one person who could permit me to contribute at work by using my full range of quiet person capabilities. That made it much easier for me to back away from my winning recipe. I had built it to use processes to get results and in turn, seem more outgoing. But now that I was directly getting results as an introvert, my recipe no longer had a job to do.

In 2013, Susan Cain's *Quiet: The Power of Introverts in a World that Can't Stop Talking* appeared and had an immediate effect on me. Not being okay with who I was had led to my first step-by-step approach in the 1950s and had been behind my serial creation of other processes for decades. The book removed the last vestiges of any desire to live by processes because it convinced me that being an introvert was okay: *I had no defect to compensate for.* My level of sociability was just fine.

Now that the flaw was gone, I was not only reconciled to my introversion, but proud of it. Good thing, because an event soon after I read the book indicated that after four years of having me work backstage, Kevin was now asking me take on a more public role.

He was leading an all-day conference called Reversing Trend, during which we planned to highlight the ways in which United could overturn the inexorable rise in the US medical cost. In front of a team of leaders he had assembled, he asked if I would facilitate one of the sessions for thirty to forty people.

## *"The book convinced me that I had no defect to compensate for."*

I declined with a smile, politely and confidently, and he instantly got it. He never again asked me to get in front of a room. From then on, he consistently played to my strengths as a back-of-the-room guy.

o

TO MY GREAT surprise, doing that year after year brought me even more satisfaction than working with the balanced scorecard had. I dealt with few people and was free of any concerns about trying to be more extroverted.

For more than a decade, Kevin and I met every Friday morning at 8:00 a.m. He overflowed with ideas about how to streamline operations, improve customer service, make our insurance more affordable, and otherwise better serve our customers. Frequently, however, his ideas were half-baked, and he knew it. So often, after sharing one of his new notions, he would say, "Could you Ben Plumb this for me?"

What he meant was for me to research his concept down to the bare metal, then deliver the results to him verbally at our next meeting via a PowerPoint presentation. I loved doing that work more than anything I had ever engaged in before. It was pure-play research and writing, something far more rewarding to me than any of the processes I had implemented.

The reason was simple: I was *not* doing the work to cover up some supposed defect. All my previous processes, even the balanced scorecard, had been efforts to appear to be more extroverted than I really was. In contrast, Ben Plumbing things allowed me to lean straight into my strengths as an introvert: deep thought, unusual focus, and joy in detecting patterns. Expressing those qualities allowed me to be my full, authentic self.

Moreover, I was now a totally out introvert who had no requirement ever to speak in public, or to interact with more than the small team around Kevin. If the Harvard Business School had been introvert hell, this was introvert paradise.

o

UNFORTUNATELY, WHEN STEPHEN Hemsley stepped down as the longtime CEO of UnitedHealth Group in 2017, Kevin lost his main champion. By late

2019 his team, including me, was on the street. Kevin's own departure followed in early 2020.

We had no regrets. We had given our all every year and felt good about what we had done, even though the new regime was undoing some of it. Kevin and I remain personal friends and still talk on the phone every two weeks.

He is a good man. His coaching of me and his receptivity to my coaching of him—as seventeen years his senior—has always made for a productive two-way relationship that enriches us both.

The most unexpected outcome was that when I was laid off, I discovered Sandy and I could retire right then, when I was seventy-six, rather than having to wait as planned until I was eighty. We had more assets than we realized.

My former partner Bruce Fraser had coined the phrase "baronial splendor" back in the 1970s when he, our Chilean partner, Max, and I were eking out a living building houses in Latin America. I never formed a mental picture of what such splendor would look like beyond physical prosperity. But now I knew, almost fifty years later, that whatever it might be, the most important part of it was not material wealth.

In each other, Sandy and I have the love of our lives. Even during the long lockdowns of the COVID-19 pandemic, we kept busy, had fun, and enjoyed hanging out with the one person who had meant the most to us for almost forty years. Our love seemed to get deeper every week. We adored each other, acknowledging and holding one another close every day. We were happy beyond words just to share the same space. And except for minor aches and pains, and a case of asthma that

Sandy developed, our health was good. If all of this was not baronial splendor, then we did not know what was.

o

WE REJOICE IN the success of our children.

Hannah, 49, earned a master's degree in speech-language pathology at Florida State University and is a senior speech pathologist working with children at a nationally acclaimed health system in Tampa. Her husband is a partner in his own law firm.

Conor, 46, received a bachelor's degree in architecture from MIT, then completed his master's at Harvard. He and his wife, also a Harvard-educated architect, operate their own design and construction firm in Cambridge, Massachusetts, in which they focus on building sustainable housing.

Rachel, 46, earned an English degree from Syracuse University and is a highly successful communications consultant in the pharmaceutical industry in the New York metropolitan area. Her husband is a talented advertising director in New York.

Rosie, 43, graduated from the University of Florida in political science and is a respected manager in one of the largest property insurance firms in Tampa. Her partner is an attorney engaged in drafting judicial decisions for judges across Hillsborough County.

Between the four children we have ten grandchildren—five in the North and five locally.

All parents doubt their child-rearing abilities, and Sandy and I were no exception. But how our four children turned out made us realize that despite everything, we had provided the emotional support and guidance they needed. All four were now raising their own families using the compassion and good sense we had always hoped to provide as parents ourselves. Since nobody was in jail, or on drugs, or living with us—and neither were their kids!—we figured that we, along with Ida, and Sandy's ex-husband, Nathan, must all have done our jobs.

Sandy bought me a cup that said, "Introvert: Social Distancing Expert" as a joke, but it accurately reflected where I was in my relationships, other than a few close friends and family members. Because of the pandemic and serious concern over the impact the COVID-19 virus could have on Sandy's asthma, we stayed in touch with family almost exclusively via FaceTime for over a year and a half. That was harder on Sandy than it was on me, hence the cup.

o

IDA NEVER REMARRIED. Some years after the divorce, she earned a master's degree in art therapy and began consulting regularly in elementary schools. Unfortunately, she had to give that up when she suffered a series of falls in 2018, after which she was diagnosed with Parkinson's disease. She now lives in an assisted living facility not far from Hannah. Ida's mother Kate died in 2013 and her father Leo in 2020.

My mother died in 1995 and my father in 2000. I had never repaired my relationship with him over the money I had borrowed in the 1970s. I was not able to finish paying it off until just before he died, and he was not lucid enough at the end to understand I had finally squared the debt. To this day, I regard borrowing those funds as one of the greatest mistakes I ever made.

I flew to Los Angeles for my father's memorial and

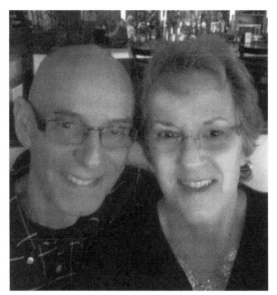

*Fig. 9 Sandy and Myself. Odessa, FL, 2018.*

afterwards visited the cemetery where my parents' ashes lay. I had not grieved for either one of them until that moment. At the graveside, I silently thanked them for always making my sisters and me feel good about ourselves. They used words as a salve to reward us for behavior they knew would build character. They never once belittled us.

When it was time to go, I knelt and kissed the grass. I stayed there for a long moment with the flat of my hand on the graves, thanking them again for the magnificent humanity they had shown to me and my sisters and for the wondrous love they shared between themselves and with us. It was a gift to the whole world, and through their great-grandchildren, that love would endure.

I HAD BELIEVED a process of some kind would get me to this place in life, but it did not. Such devices did insulate me from people for decades and did create some predictable outcomes based on formulas. But I always felt dependent, and they often produced disastrous results.

When it came down to it, I realized that as an introvert, I had no flaw to compensate for and could best gain the security and satisfaction I sought by proudly and openly emphasizing my quiet person strengths.

I still admired powerful processes. But for the last ten years of my career, none of that ran me any longer. I was free to be me.

# Epilogue

AS INTROVERTS, WE attempt—as children—to cope with an extroverted world by adopting some kind of winning recipe. We try to be inclusive, or precise, or driven, or dependable, or any other way we think will make us feel safe in the world.

In this story, I offer the warning that while such mechanisms may produce good results every once in a while, they almost always generate unintended consequences, put distance between us and other people, and ultimately do not provide security or satisfaction. My own winning recipe, an obsession with processes, had those results in ways I shared throughout my story.

The worst problem with this approach, was that it was an attempt to offset who I was. I could not embrace being an introvert, so instead I embraced one external process after another in a fruitless search for security. Eventually that turned out to be a ruinous way to live.

The root cause was the paradox that emerged when I tried to use my recipe as a general approach to life: it promised safety, but most often was the very thing that prevented me from attaining it. For decades, this kept me stuck in recurring anxiety and dissatisfaction.

Only at the very end was I able to distance myself from the need to compensate for being an introvert. In so doing, I barely escaped making yet one more mistake by changing companies. I chose to give up one of the greatest processes in the world for a professional relationship, and once I did so, had ten of the best years of my life.

The ray of hope in this story is that as introverts we are all okay. We can be proud of our ability to listen closer and think more deeply than many of the people around us. We can take satisfaction in our skill at expressing things in writing more than in conversation. We can celebrate our avoidance of conflict and small talk. And we can rejoice in our capacity for deep concentration, a slow work pace, and a laser-like focus on whatever we are doing.

o

IT TOOK ME over six decades to learn all this. In the end, I detached from my recipe by bringing three tools to bear:

*A New Context.* In Chapter 20, I showed that in 2009, I stepped inside a new framework: that henceforth my life would be about longevity, instead of the stress of trying to be more outgoing through a winning recipe. It was the first thing that ever put some daylight between me and my recipe. It made me feel safe, perhaps because it was the recipe itself that had been causing problems all along. However, on its own, the context was not enough. It only lasted for two weeks before the recipe struck back. That threw me off balance, and I almost left the great job and boss that I had. But I soon mounted a counterattack from an unexpected direction.

*A Prized Relationship.* In Chapter 21, I chose my manager—my most valued business relationship—over my recipe. That did not reverse the choice I had made as a child to distance myself from other people to cut down on noise. But it did draw me closer to the one individual at work who could most actively help me live openly as an introvert. He allowed me to feel secure about contributing as a quiet person, and that kept my recipe at bay for another four years.

*No Defect To Fix.* In Chapter 22, I related that by 2013, my manager was moving towards having me take a more active public role. That year, after reading *Quiet*, I saw that as an introvert, I was okay exactly the way I was. I could best contribute by *leaning into my strengths as an introvert*: deep focus, single-minded concentration, and thoughtful analysis. Based on that realization, when he asked me to facilitate a large meeting, I felt safe enough to decline. From then on, he accepted my role as being exclusively in the back room. What resulted were the financial security I had always sought and more emotional satisfaction from just being a straight-up introvert than I ever thought possible.

o

I AM STILL drawn to using processes to improve my diet, exercise, and sleep routines. They help me to stay healthy by rotating the foods in my vegan diet, by alternating between cardio and weight-bearing exercise, and by supplementing seven hours of nighttime sleep with a regular schedule of short naps. But my winning recipe no longer runs me. I am free to be the introvert I had always tried to hide.

Hopefully, my story will inspire you to learn all this more quickly than I did.

As an introvert you are at your best when you accept and enjoy who you are. You need make no apologies for being quieter than others. Your introvert traits make you an asset to everyone you know.

*Before You Go:* Please take a moment to rate this book by going to the product detail page on Amazon. Scroll down to "Review this product" at the bottom of the left-hand column, and click "Write a customer review." Then click the number of stars you want to assign to this book. If you have time, a review would also be greatly appreciated. Thank you for your honest opinion!

For coaching on how to identify and detach from your winning recipe, please visit www.thesatisfiedintrovert.com.

*Fig. 10 Image from Post #1 on thesatisfiedintrovert.com. 2022.*

You can follow Ben on www.facebook.com/ thesatisfiedintrovert

# Acknowledgments

MANY HEARTFELT THANKS to all of the following people, every one of whom provided vital and inspiring help during the creation of this book:

Chantel Hamilton, who always provided wise counsel, expertly assembled a first-rate team of editors, and was the first literary professional to believe in this book.

Ariel Curry, who helped me turn the manuscript into a readable and compelling story, and consistently delivered outstanding insights that markedly improved the content and flow of the book.

Lauren Terrell, whose sharp copyediting eye tightened up the text, and saved me from making many embarrassing gaffes.

Sandy Kreps, whose technical wizardry and impeccable accuracy in inserting my hundreds of proof edits made the publishing process a true pleasure.

Kevin Ruth, who as my manager at United-Healthcare made it possible for me to live and work openly as an introvert for the first time ever.

And a special thank you to my wife, Sandy Plumb, who not only shared with me many of the adventures in this book for almost forty years, but also read the manuscript countless times, helping me to evolve it from raw journal entries into a worthy representation of my life.

# About the Author

BENJAMIN PLUMB was born and raised in Los Angeles as the only introvert in a family of five.

Like all introvert children, he sought to feel safe in an extroverted world by adopting a "winning recipe." At age ten, he decided he would be methodical in everything he did—one of the thousands of possible recipes that quiet people choose.

This formula brought him honors at Stanford and an MBA from Harvard, but it enticed him into unsatisfying careers as an entrepreneur and an executive. Those roles led ultimately to a divorce in his thirties, a bankruptcy in his forties, and two job losses in a row in his sixties.

At last he saw that what all these failures had in common was the recipe. He taught himself to detach from it, openly embraced his introversion, and thereafter worked quietly as a writer and researcher. In so doing, he finally attained the success and safety that he was never able to achieve through a winning recipe.

Ben and his wife Sandy of nearly forty years live in the Tampa Bay area. They have four children and ten grandchildren.

Printed in Great Britain
by Amazon